T0304262

Handbook
of Product Placement
in the Mass Media:
New Strategies
in Marketing Theory,
Practice, Trends, and Ethics

Handbook of Product Placement in the Mass Media: New Strategies in Marketing Theory, Practice, Trends, and Ethics has been co-published simultaneously as *Journal of Promotion Management,* Volume 10, Numbers 1/2 2004.

The *Journal of Promotion Management* Monographic "Separates"

Below is a list of "separates," which in serials librarianship means a special issue simultaneously published as a special journal issue or double-issue *and* as a "separate" hardbound monograph. (This is a format which we also call a "DocuSerial.")

"Separates" are published because specialized libraries or professionals may wish to purchase a specific thematic issue by itself in a format which can be separately cataloged and shelved, as opposed to purchasing the journal on an on-going basis. Faculty members may also more easily consider a "separate" for classroom adoption.

"Separates" are carefully classified separately with the major book jobbers so that the journal tie-in can be noted on new book order slips to avoid duplicate purchasing.

You may wish to visit Haworth's Website at . . .

http://www.HaworthPress.com

. . . to search our online catalog for complete tables of contents of these separates and related publications.

You may also call 1-800-HAWORTH (outside US/Canada: 607-722-5857), or Fax 1-800-895-0582 (outside US/Canada: 607-771-0012), or e-mail at:

docdelivery@haworthpress.com

Handbook of Product Placement in the Mass Media: New Strategies in Marketing Theory, Practice, Trends, and Ethics, edited by Mary-Lou Galician, EdD (Vol. 10, No. 1/2, 2004). *"COMPREHENSIVE. . . . A fascinating handbook for practitioners and students. . . . The content and presentation are superb." (Dr. Ronald A. Nykiel, CHA, CHE, Conrad N. Hilton Distinguished Chair, University of Houston)*

Handbook of Product Placement in the Mass Media: New Strategies in Marketing Theory, Practice, Trends, and Ethics

Mary-Lou Galician, EdD
Editor

Handbook of Product Placement in the Mass Media: New Strategies in Marketing Theory, Practice, Trends, and Ethics has been co-published simultaneously as *Journal of Promotion Management,* Volume 10, Numbers 1/2 2004.

Routledge
Taylor & Francis Group

NEW YORK AND LONDON

First Published by

Best Business Books®, 10 Alice Street, Binghamton, NY 13904-1580 USA

Best Business Books® is an imprint of The Haworth Press, Inc., 10 Alice Street, Binghamton, NY 13904-1580 USA.

Transferred to Digital Printing 2010 by Routledge
270 Madison Ave, New York NY 10016
2 Park Square, Milton Park, Abingdon, Oxon, OX14 4RN

Handbook of Product Placement in the Mass Media: New Strategies in Marketing Theory, Practice, Trends, and Ethics has been co-published simultaneously as *Journal of Promotion Management,* Volume 10, Numbers 1/2 2004.

The development, preparation, and publication of this work has been undertaken with great care. However, the publisher, employees, editors, and agents of The Haworth Press and all imprints of The Haworth Press, Inc., including The Haworth Medical Press® and Pharmaceutical Products Press®, are not responsible for any errors contained herein or for consequences that may ensue from use of materials or information contained in this work. Opinions expressed by the author(s) are not necessarily those of The Haworth Press, Inc.

Cover design by Jennifer M. Gaska

Library of Congress Cataloging-in-Publication Data

Handbook of product placement in the mass media : new strategies in marketing theory, practice, trends, and ethics / Mary-Lou Galician, editor.
       p. cm.
       Published simultaneously as Journal of promotion management, Volume 10, Numbers 1/2 2004.
       Includes bibliographical references and index.
       ISBN 0-7890-2534-5 (hard cover : alk. paper) – ISBN 0-7890-2535-3 (soft cover : alk. paper)
       1. Product placement in mass media. 2. Subliminal advertising–United States. 3. Advertising–Moral and ethical aspects. I. Galician, Mary-Lou. II. Journal of promotion management. II. Title.

HF6146.P78H36 2004
659.1–dc22

                                                                                    2003027329

Publisher's Note
The publisher has gone to great lengths to ensure the quality of this reprint
but points out that some imperfections in the original may be apparent.

Indexing, Abstracting & Website/Internet Coverage

This section provides you with a list of major indexing & abstracting services. That is to say, each service began covering this periodical during the year noted in the right column. Most Websites which are listed below have indicated that they will either post, disseminate, compile, archive, cite or alert their own Website users with research-based content from this work. (This list is as current as the copyright date of this publication.)

Abstracting, Website/Indexing Coverage . . . . Year When Coverage Began

- *ABI/INFORM. Contents of this publication are indexed and abstracted in the ABI/INFORM database, available on ProQuest Information & Learning @http://www.proquest.com* 2002

- *CNPIEC Reference Guide: Chinese National Directory of Foreign Periodicals* 1996

- *Communication Mass Media Index (CMMI); EBSCO Publishing* . . 2003

- *Educational Resources Information Center (ERIC)* . . . . *

- *Foods Adlibra* 1991

- *Human Resources Abstracts (HRA)* 1991

- *IBZ International Bibliography of Periodical Literature <http://www.saur.de>* 1996

- *Management & Marketing Abstracts <http://www.pira.co.uk/>* . . 1991

- *Operations Research/Management Science* 1991

  *Exact start date to come.

(continued)

- *ProQuest 5000. Contents of this publication are indexed and abstracted in the ProQuest 5000 database (includes only abstracts . . . not full-text), available on ProQuest Information & Learning @http://www.proquest.com* **1993**

- *ProQuest Banking Information Source. Contents of this publication are indexed and abstracted in the ProQuest Banking Information Source database (includes only abstracts . . . not full-text), available on ProQuest Information & Learning @http://www.proquest.com* **1993**

- *Referativnyi Zhurnal (Abstracts Journal of the All-Russian Institute of Scientific and Technical Information–in Russian)* **1991**

- *In addition,* **Journal of Promotion Management** *is recognized in* **Cabell's Directory of Publishing Opportunities in Marketing** *and at the* **KnowThis.com Marketing Virtual Library** *site with "links to leading academic journals in marketing fields"* *<http://www.knowthis.com/publication/online/journalsonline.htm>*

Special Bibliographic Notes related to special journal issues (separates) and indexing/abstracting:

- indexing/abstracting services in this list will also cover material in any "separate" that is co-published simultaneously with Haworth's special thematic journal issue or DocuSerial. Indexing/abstracting usually covers material at the article/chapter level.
- monographic co-editions are intended for either non-subscribers or libraries which intend to purchase a second copy for their circulating collections.
- monographic co-editions are reported to all jobbers/wholesalers/approval plans. The source journal is listed as the "series" to assist the prevention of duplicate purchasing in the same manner utilized for books-in-series.
- to facilitate user/access services all indexing/abstracting services are encouraged to utilize the co-indexing entry note indicated at the bottom of the first page of each article/chapter/contribution.
- this is intended to assist a library user of any reference tool (whether print, electronic, online, or CD-ROM) to locate the monographic version if the library has purchased this version but not a subscription to the source journal.
- individual articles/chapters in any Haworth publication are also available through The Haworth Document Delivery Service (HDDS).

Handbook of Product Placement in the Mass Media: New Strategies in Marketing Theory, Practice, Trends, and Ethics

CONTENTS

RESOURCE GUIDE

ABOUT THE EDITOR

Mary-Lou Galician, EdD, is Head of Media Analysis & Criticism in the Walter Cronkite School of Journalism & Mass Communication at Arizona State University in Tempe. She has conducted and published research and led national seminars about product placement in the mass media. She is a media literacy advocate.

Known nationwide as "The *Original* Dr. FUN," she is the creator and presenter of *FUN-dynamics!®–The FUN-damentals of DYNAMIC Living*, a musical motivational program that helps people get "F-U-N," her acronym for "Fired Up Now!" An award-winning researcher, educator, and performer with more than 25 years of professional experience in print journalism, television, public relations, advertising, and marketing, she joined the faculty of ASU's Cronkite School in 1983. She has taught a variety of courses related to her professional background and academic research, and she also directed the Cronkite School's Public Relations Internship Program for nine years.

She has served as National Vice President/Director of FarWest Region and National Board of Directors Member of Women in Communications, Inc. (WICI) and as founding Vice Head and Program Chair of the Entertainment Studies Interest Group (ESIG) of the Association for Education in Journalism & Mass Communication (AEJMC). Her research has been published in *Journalism Quarterly, Journal of Mass Media Ethics, IABD Business Research Yearbook, Journalism History, Southwestern Mass Communication Journal, Popular Music and Society,* and *Journalism Educator.* Her commentaries appear in the professional and popular media, where she has also been interviewed and cited as an expert more than 100 times. She conducts workshops to help academics and professionals "translate" their scholarship and expertise for the public and the media.

Based on her research of what she calls "The Romanticization of Love in the Mass Media," she created *Dr. FUN's Mass Media Love Quiz©,* which she has shared via national network television, radio, newspapers, and magazines as well as at national scholarly conferences and on her websites (*www.asu.edu/cronkite/faculty/galician/drfun/*) and (*www.*

RealisticRomance.com). Her *Quiz* and her *Dr. Galician's Prescriptions™ for Getting Real About Romance* form the core of her textbook *Sex, Love, & Romance in the Mass Media: Analysis & Criticism of Unrealistic Portrayals & Their Impact*. She is happily married to Dr. David Natharius, a Professor of Communication, Humanities, and Visuality. Together they conduct "Realistic Romance"™ workshops, seminars, and presentations.

Handbook
of Product Placement
in the Mass Media:
New Strategies
in Marketing Theory,
Practice, Trends, and Ethics

Handbook of Product Placement in the Mass Media: New Strategies in Marketing Theory, Practice, Trends, and Ethics has been co-published simultaneously as *Journal of Promotion Management,* Volume 10, Numbers 1/2 2004.

Introduction:
Product Placements in the Mass Media:
Unholy Marketing Marriages
or Realistic Story-Telling Portrayals,
Unethical Advertising Messages
or Useful Communication Practices?

Mary-Lou Galician

The work presented here by many leading experts represents an exciting compilation of research and commentary addressing the theory and practice of product placement in the mass media–a promotion management subject that is both important and engaging.

Product placement is a $1.5 billion practice in movies and television and now even novels that partners marketers (who value it for cost-effectively creating consumer awareness) and mass media producers (who rely on it for reducing production and advertising costs). Approximately 1,000 brand marketers utilize it in their advertising mix. Because of the subtlety of product placement embedding and other related promotional techniques, audience members are often completely unaware and, therefore, highly susceptible. The purported influence is so great that product placement's detractors have sought federal regulation of the practice.

[Haworth co-indexing entry note]: "Introduction: Product Placements in the Mass Media: Unholy Marketing Marriages or Realistic Story-Telling Portrayals, Unethical Advertising Messages or Useful Communication Practices?" Galician, Mary-Lou. Co-published simultaneously in *Journal of Promotion Management* (Best Business Books, an imprint of The Haworth Press, Inc.) Vol. 10, No. 1/2, 2004, pp. 1-8; and: *Handbook of Product Placement in the Mass Media: New Strategies in Marketing Theory, Practice, Trends, and Ethics* (ed: Mary-Lou Galician) Best Business Books, an imprint of The Haworth Press, Inc., 2004, pp. 1-8. Single or multiple copies of this article are available for a fee from The Haworth Document Delivery Service [1-800-HAWORTH, 9:00 a.m. - 5:00 p.m. (EST). E-mail address: docdelivery@haworthpress.com].

Digital Object Identifier: 10.1300/J057v10n01_01

This volume examines the wider contexts and varied texts of product placement and related mass media marketing strategies. The contributors listed in the Table of Contents represent a rich variety of methodological approaches and viewpoints, which should stimulate readers to think about this complex issue in an appropriately multifaceted fashion and to triangulate their own study.

THE ORIGINS OF THE RESEARCH
AND COMMENTARY PRESENTED HERE

My own interest in product placement goes back to the 1970s, when I was an advertising executive in the national headquarters of the Maybelline company, which topped the list of television's cosmetics spenders and advertised in more than 100 women's beauty/fashion and service magazines. I confess to having been pleased when many of those magazine editors gratuitously identified their models' makeup as Maybelline.

Mark Crispin Miller's brilliant critique of product placement–"Hollywood the Ad"–in the April 1990 issue of *The Nation* revived my earlier interest. (Dr. Miller is the subject of a personal interview in this volume.) By then, I was a tenured professor, and I began including a module about the subject in my Mass Media & Society classes. My students always expressed great interest in this controversial issue. In fact, one of my former graduate students–Peter Bourdeau–is responsible for extending my interest to the on-going study that resulted in this volume. I directed his master's degree research of this subject, and we have since collaborated on related publications and presentations that ultimately brought together the experts who are the contributors here.

A great deal of information about product placement and related media marketing strategies is proprietary. However, two unpublished seminal documents served as the foundation of our own work: (1) Samuel Turcotte's excellent 1995 master's thesis, "Gimme a Bud! The feature film product placement industry," proved "a blueprint for conducting the business of product placement, whereby the interests of both the filmmakers and the corporate marketers are maximized" (based on his in-depth interviews with industry professionals and corporate marketers), and (2) a well-constructed content analysis of product placement in the 25 top-grossing films of 1991 that was presented by Barry Sapolsky and Lance Kinney at the 1994 Conference of the Academy of Advertising. Because Coca-Cola was the "uber-placer" in our own research of product placement in top-grossing Hollywood films, Peter entitled the study *Cue the Soda Can*–paying homage to Sam's earlier work. (Mr. Turcotte has since produced his own film with a dozen product placements, and this collection also includes a personal interview with him.)

The respected authors of the research and commentary in this volume came together as a result of the first national presentation of the *Cue the Soda Can* study at Media Forum at the 2000 National Communication Association (NCA) Annual National Convention. Because of the great number of diverse concurrent sessions at this annual meeting of the world's largest communication organization, individual programs often have audiences of only 10-20 people. However, the Media Forum on product placement drew more than 70 educators and professionals who were highly interested in this topic. In addition to sharing the findings (including Peter's many film captures), I also screened a not-quite-completed version of an exceptionally well-conceived and well-produced educational video–*Behind the Screens: Hollywood Goes Hypercommercial*– at the special request of its Media Education Foundation producers. (A review is included here.)

The significantly above-average attendance validated the broad-based interest in and importance of this subject. Attendees expressed a desire to extend the examination and discussion to a longer timeframe that would also accommodate wider contexts of product placements and other related mass media marketing strategies as well as the related economic and ethical considerations.

And so, the following year at the 2001 NCA convention, we gathered to share our research and our viewpoints in a lively day-long seminar entitled *Video Presentations and Discussions of Product Placements in the Mass Media: Unholy Marketing Marriage, Realistic Portrayals, or Unethical Advertising?* The planners and/or presenters–all represented in the current volume–were Peter Bourdeau, Ted Friedman, Mary-Lou Galician, Susan Kretchmer, Charles A. Lubbers, David Natharius, Richard Alan Nelson, Scott R. Olson, Paul Siegel, Christopher R. Turner, and Kathleen J. Turner. This, too, sparked much interest resulting in additional such panels at NCA, the Association for Education in Journalism and Mass Communication (AEJMC), and other major forums.

RAISING THE QUESTIONS THAT WE CONTINUE TO ASK

This group asked and began to answer some of the following questions:

- What are the wider forms and contexts of "product placement" and related mass media marketing strategies (tie-ins, co-ventures and co-promotions, web-based marketing, licensing, merchandising, "theming," environmental simulacra, etc.)?
- Does product placement enhance realism, as users claim, or is it merely a marketing ploy?
- How does the introduction of pastiche and irony into product placement (e.g., *Wayne's World*) change its effectiveness and viability? What is the effect of "self-referential product placement"?
- How widespread is the general practice of "synergy" (using multiple media platforms to sell a single product)?
- What are the ramifications of "environmental simulacra"–the advertising of movies or television shows through the creation of theme-park rides (*Star Wars, Jurassic Park,* etc.) or locations (*Cheers* bars in airports), which then themselves sell the movie or show and are, in turn, sold by them?
- What are economic and ethical repercussions of such marketing practices?
- Can these marketing practices ever be ethical?
- Should these marketing practices be regulated?
- Advertising succeeds by getting a message through cluttered information channels to overwhelmed consumers. Product placement provides a new channel. What happens when the glut of placements becomes itself overwhelming–and postmodern audiences tire or become disengaged from the practice?
- What do media and consumer critics say about these practices, and what is the role of critics?
- What can/should media consumers do?

We worked hard and learned a lot from each other. I've never collaborated with a more congenial and generous group. At the end of our intensive day, we realized we had only scratched the surface, and we knew we had to join forces to share our pooled knowledge and continue this crucial line of inquiry–both in subsequent interpersonal forums and in a single publication that would bring together a diversity of foci and approaches all centered around product placements. You now hold the published outcome in this special issue of *Journal of Promotion Management*, co-published as a book. My 17 colleagues who contributed their research and commentary to this publication and the four additional authorities who are the subject of the interviews that appear at the end of this volume are all nationally respected authorities. I'm delighted and honored to present their ideas to you. Of course, we'd be pleased to hear from you as well.

OVERVIEW OF THE RESEARCH AND COMMENTARY IN THIS COLLECTION

The Practice of Product Placement

First, *The Practice of Product Placement* provides a general context, beginning with media and rhetorical historian Kathleen J. Turner's essay, "Insinuating the Product into the Message: An Historical Context for Product Placement," which sketches the background of the early development of product placement in single-sponsored programs in radio and early television, the introduction of the magazine concept of advertising placement in the 1950s, and the effects of the quiz show scandals.

In "The Evolution of Product Placements in Hollywood Cinema: Embedding High-Involvement 'Heroic' Brand Images," Peter G. Bourdeau and I present key findings of our *Cue the Soda Can* content analyses that document and describe the increasingly dominant role product placements have come to play in the narratives of blockbuster movies since 1977.

Cultural critic Susan B. Kretchmer explores a similar evolution in television and internet entertainment vehicles created solely to spotlight specific advertiser–from the popular Taster's Choice couple ("Sharon" and "Tony")–to online advergames– in her essay, "Advertainment: The Evolution of Product Placement as a Mass Media Marketing Strategy."

Then media scholars and practitioners Charles A. Lubbers and William J. Adams shed light on two under-examined multi-billion-dollar revenue producers in the current movie promotion mix–merchandising and promotional/partner ties-ins, two major elements–in their essay, "Merchandising in the Major Motion Picture Industry: Creating Brand Synergy and Revenue Streams."

This foundational section concludes with "The Extensions of Synergy: Product Placement Through Theming and Environmental Simulacra," an examination of a larger part of the focus wherein the normal distinctions between the cinematic world and the real world are obscured, by Scott Robert Olson (whose most recent book, *Hollywood Planet: Global Media and the Competitive Advantage of Narrative Transparency*, contains a critical analysis of product placement as part of global corporate strategy).

Controls on Product Placement

The second section–*Controls on Product Placement*–provides a closer look at the complex legal and ethical issues surrounding the theory and practice of this controversial industry. As is appropriate for this kind of assessment, some cogent arguments are made and some new questions are raised by mass media law scholar Paul Siegel in "Product Placement and the Law," an argument against locating product placement within the Supreme Court's commercial speech doctrine. Lawrence A. Wenner's "On the Ethics of Product Placement in Media Entertainment" presents a thorough analysis of the ethical challenges and controversies surrounding the practice. Dean Kruckeberg and Kenneth Starck, who are public relations practitioners as well as mass media ethicists, in their "The Role and Ethics of Community Building for Consumer Products and Services," offer a review of consumer communities that urges the adoption of a public relations approach rather than a marketing viewpoint.

Case Studies of Product Placement

Several intriguing case studies are delineated in the third section. Beng Soo Ong, an academic who has also worked as a brand placement consultant, in "A Comparison of Product Placements in Movies and Television Programs: An Online Research Study" found that although three-fourths of the sample were aware of the practice in both movies and TV shows, respondents appeared to have less exposure to embedded brands in television than in films.

In "Product Placement of Medical Products: Issues and Concerns," Christopher R. Turner–who holds an MD degree in addition to a PhD and an MBA–extends the legal-ethical discussion in his examination of direct-to-consumer pharmaceutical marketing and focuses on an episode of television's *Chicago Hope* touting the use of a medical device that had not earned FDA approval.

Cultural critic Ted Friedman's essay "*Cast Away* and the Contradictions of Product Placement" argues that Tom Hanks' 2000 film serves as a valuable case study because of the conflict between its relentless product placement and its dark vision of contemporary global capitalism, four aspects of which are investigated.

In "Brand Placement Recognition: The Influence of Presentation Mode and Brand Familiarity," Ian Brennan and Laurie A. Babin present an empirical study that demonstrated audio cues are a significant factor in the success of movie product placements.

Journal of Promotion Management Editor Richard Alan Nelson examines an intriguing new form of paid product placement–in novels–in his essay, "*The Bulgari Connection*: A Novel Form of Product Placement."

Commentary, Interviews, and Roundtable

The final sections include a variety of more personal reflections. David Natharius' whimsical commentary "When Product Placement Is NOT Product Placement: Reflections of a Movie Junkie" interrogates the distracting contra-placement practice of introducing fake, generic, or disguised products into films–including a "Suny" VCR box.

Four experts granted me personal interviews especially for this volume. To preserve the full flavor of their comments, the interviews are presented in Q&A style. First, cultural critic and author Mark Crispin Miller, whose 1990 *Atlantic Monthly* article inspired my teaching and research interest in product placement, reiterates and updates his arguments against the practice. As counterpoint, we next offer the favorable comments of Samuel A. Turcotte, whose master's thesis stimulated Peter and me in our studies and who has completed an independent film with 12 major product placements that he unflinchingly defends as realistic in terms of the drama and the economics of his movie about wrestling. In the early 1990s, Michael F. Jacobson, Executive Director of the Washington, DC-based Center for Science in the Public Interest (and its Center for the Study of Commercialism), petitioned the FTC to ban product placements or to require movies to list all their placements in their opening credits. More recently, his group launched *www.saveharry. com* to urge consumer protest of Coca-Cola's reported $150 million payment to Warner Bros. for exclusive global marketing rights to *Harry Potter and the Sorcerer's Stone*. And Pulitzer Prize-winning *Los Angeles Times* media critic Howard Rosenberg offers his always spot-on candid insights about the insidious use of television newscasters in all manner of promotions and tie-ins, which he considers unethical.

Interviews with several leading cultural critics (including Mark Crispin Miller) are also included with illustrative clips of popular recent movies and promotions in the Media Education Foundation's 2000 video *Behind the Screens: Hollywood Goes Hypercommercial*. **My review** of the documentary lauds this entertaining pedagogical tool that captivates audiences and also teaches important lessons.

Because this collection of research and commentary about product placement was conceived by the majority of the authors who came together from all parts of the country to share their diverse work and viewpoints at national seminars, it is fitting that we end by coming together (albeit it electronically, via the Internet) to offer answers to five key questions and make predictions about the future of product placement. The expertise and energy of this group is apparent in their thoughtful and dynamic *Product Placement in the 21st Century* **roundtable** comments, and I trust that the synergy of my esteemed collaborators' individual responses will stimulate you–as they did me–to begin thinking about a variety of new trends we should watch and studies we should conduct.

The *Product Placement Resource Guide* of recommended articles, books, and websites prepared by Richard Alan Nelson provides a wealth of starting points for this ongoing work.

THE PRACTICE
OF PRODUCT PLACEMENT

Insinuating the Product into the Message:
An Historical Context
for Product Placement

Kathleen J. Turner

SUMMARY. The cozy arrangement of marketers embedding their products in mediated messages has its antecedents in radio and television, when sponsors often controlled the entirety of programs, from writing to casting to pitches for the products within the program. This essay sketches the rise and fall of this system as it paved the way for contemporary product placement. *[Article copies available for a fee from The Haworth Document Delivery Service: 1-800-HAWORTH. E-mail address: <docdelivery@haworthpress. com> Website: <http://www.HaworthPress.com> © 2004 by The Haworth Press, Inc. All rights reserved.]*

Kathleen J. Turner (PhD, Purdue University) is the Knight-Crane Professor of Communication and Chair, Department of Communication, Queens University of Charlotte, 1900 Selwyn Avenue, Charlotte, NC 28274 (E-mail: kjturner3@juno.com).

[Haworth co-indexing entry note]: "Insinuating the Product into the Message: An Historical Context for Product Placement." Turner, Kathleen J. Co-published simultaneously in *Journal of Promotion Management* (Best Business Books, an imprint of The Haworth Press, Inc.) Vol. 10, No. 1/2, 2004, pp. 9-14; and: *Handbook of Product Placement in the Mass Media: New Strategies in Marketing Theory, Practice, Trends, and Ethics* (ed: Mary-Lou Galician) Best Business Books, an imprint of The Haworth Press, Inc., 2004, pp. 9-14. Single or multiple copies of this article are available for a fee from The Haworth Document Delivery Service [1-800-HAWORTH, 9:00 a.m. - 5:00 p.m. (EST). E-mail address: docdelivery@haworthpress.com].

http://www.haworthpress.com/web/JPM
© 2004 by The Haworth Press, Inc. All rights reserved.
Digital Object Identifier: 10.1300/J057v10n01_02

9

KEYWORDS. History, product placement, quiz shows, radio, television

INTRODUCTION

Most of the articles gathered here examine the placement of products into contemporary mediated messages. The collaboration between producers of goods and producers of media, however, has a long history. This essay traces the antecedents of product placement in the broadcast media. My purpose is to offer a historical sketch that will serve as a background for the assessments that follow, rather than a fully developed portrait.

RADIO BECOMES A PROMOTIONAL MEDIUM

In the eyes of most of those who invented and developed radio–from Guglielmo Marconi to Lee De Forest to Edwin Armstrong–the new medium had a nobler role than to carry advertising. Yet, this disdain was not universal. Key to the difference was a reconceptualization of radio. Originally, Marconi envisioned radio as a wireless version of the telegraph, serving as a means of business communication between one point and another. The fact that others could eavesdrop on the wireless transmissions constituted a problem in this framework. Yet, some innovators saw that "leakage" as an opportunity rather than a problem. Frank Conrad's experimental broadcasts in his garage in 1920 convinced Westinghouse engineers that radio could be marketed as a broadcasting medium that could inform and entertain hundreds at a time–and in the process, drive the demand for radio sets so that the broadcasts could be received. AT&T, one of the corporate pioneers in broadcasting, took this notion a step further when it wanted to make more money from its radio investments. It turned WEAF into a "toll broadcasting" station, like long-distance lines: you could pay to get your message to your audience. Thus, the first radio ad aired in 1922, a ten-minute spiel for apartments in Jackson Heights (Barnouw, 1996, p. 110).

The idea of advertising as a means of funding the young medium soon caught on among radio executives. Soon, shows and sponsors developed an integral relationship. The A&P Gypsies and the Ipana Troubadours warbled the virtues of their namesakes, while the Shadow hawked Goodyear tires in between solving the latest mysteries. In "McGee's Magic Act" (1948), *Fibber McGee and Molly* worked an ad right into the storyline. About halfway into the program, a knock on the McGees' much-visited door yields Mr. Wilcox, who responds to Fibber's query about an interest in "legerdemain" by saying that he sells magic–in the form of Johnson's Self-Polishing Glo-Coat wax. During the two-minute exchange, straight product-benefit pitches are mixed with jokes. When Molly observes that she's surprised Mr. Wilcox stopped talking about Johnson's Glo-Coat long enough to propose to his wife, he notes that he just asked her to close her eyes and tied a string around her finger– to remind her to pick up more Glo-Coat. Her eyes filled with tears at his thoughtfulness, he reports–as the studio audience chortles. Fibber's role is to gently deprecate the advertising function, as when he asks Mr. Wilcox whether it's possible to have a conversation without bringing in a commercial (the pitch man considers briefly, but concludes it is not). Repeated references to Johnson's Glo-Coat permeate the conversation that is embedded right into the program, so that listeners would continue paying attention.

TELEVISION EMULATES RADIO

By 1929, fully 55% of the programs on radio were not only paid for by advertisers, but created by advertisers and ad agencies (MacDonald, 1979, p. 32). When television emerged as the new mass medium in the late 1940s and early 1950s, it drew wholesale from radio, including programs, stars, and means of revenue: advertising. By 1957, more than a third of television programs were created and controlled by advertisers and their agencies (Head and Sterling, 1982, p. 194; Sterling and Kittross, 1990, p. 398). For example, Camel cigarettes sponsored *Man Against Crime* (1949), starring Ralph Bellamy. The company issued strict instructions to the writers, directors, and actors (Barnouw, 1970, pp. 22-23): "Do not have the heavy or any disreputable person smoking a cigarette. Do not associate the smoking of cigarettes with undesirable scenes or situations plot-wise." Cigarettes were to be smoked gracefully, not puffed nervously–and the creators should never, ever suggest that a character have a smoke to "calm nerves," which might suggest a narcotic effect. No one on the program could cough, and doctors were to be shown only in "the most commendable light." The tobacco company's directions permeated the production.

And Milton Berle, who had been so-so on radio, became a major audience and advertising draw on television. In the early fifties, he headed the *Texaco Star Theatre*, which started each week with a chorus of Texaco'd guys singing,

> Oh, we're the men of Texaco, we work from Maine to Mexico.
> There's nothing like this Texaco of ours.
> Our show tonight is powerful.
> We'll wow you with an hour full
> of howls from a shower full of stars. (Simon, 2001)

Later, Berle's services appeared to the viewing audience courtesy of an automobile manufacturer, as the Buick/Berle show opened with a full minute's worth of title sequence linking star and car both visually and verbally (Berle, 1953). The announcer booms, "It's the Buick Show! It's the Berle Show! It's the Buick/Berle Show!!" as the names are flashed in neon lights. A mixed chorus then croons a ditty about "how I love to drive my Buick" as "Mr. Television" and three comely young lasses cruise down the street in a Buick convertible. Special guests are announced via billboard and voiceover before the choir returns to a reprise on the virtues of the car. Pitches for the carmaker also appeared during and at the end of the program.

Advertising control affected not only entertainment shows but also news programs. A classic example is *Camel News Caravan* (1950) with John Cameron Swayze–yes, brought to you by the same makers of smokes as *Man Against Crime*. The broadcast opened: "The makers of Camel cigarettes bring the world's latest news events right into your living room. Sit back, light up a Camel, and be a witness to the happenings that made history in the last 24 hours. Produced for Camel cigarettes by NBC." Not only did two Camel ads punctuate the newscast, including a vocalist trilling "so mild, so mild!", but a lit cigarette stayed on Swayze's desk throughout the show. The broadcast ends with "John Cameron Swayze saying good night for Camel cigarettes" as the camera zooms in on a cigarette burning in the ashtray.

Cigarette makers did not hold a monopoly on sponsorship. A very young Mike Wallace, for example, delivered the CBS mid-morning newscast, and then walked over to a backdrop to pitch Bond suits, with not one but two sets of trousers!

But networks didn't really like this system: it put them at the mercy of advertisers, who could dictate not only scripts and actors but entire series, and could pull out with a few weeks' notice if they didn't like how a show was going. So Pat Weaver (Sigourney's father) took on this issue once he was appointed president of NBC by David Sarnoff in

1953 (Barnouw, 1970, pp. 59-60). First, he increased program length from fifteen minutes, the standard for radio shows, to thirty and sixty minutes, which made cost of owning an entire show prohibitive for many advertisers. Then, he pushed the magazine concept of advertising placement: rather than a single sponsor owning the entire show, advertisers bought insertions into a program created and controlled by the network. Using these concepts, Weaver created the *Today* and *Tonight* shows–although he had to overcome a taboo for the former, because "like sex and alcohol, television was deemed proper only after sundown" (Metz, as cited by Head and Sterling, 1982, p. 194). These longer shows, created and controlled by NBC, allowed advertisers only to buy insertions rather than the whole kit and caboodle.

The kicker came with the quiz show scandals. Adapted from radio, quiz shows made it big on TV. One example: the audio version of *The $64 Question* became the vastly richer video version of *The $64,000 Question*, and thrived. Revlon plastered its name all over the set, from the elaborate entryway through which all entered to the "isolation booth" in which contestants were cloistered for their grilling. As a result, in January of 1956, the chair of the board of Hazel Bishop had to explain ruefully to his stockholders that the surprising loss of revenue in 1955 was "due to circumstances beyond our control" (note the use of television language!), because during the preceding six months "a new television program sponsored by your company's principal competitor captured the imagination of the public" (Barnouw, 1970, pp. 57-58). By the 1957-58 season, almost two dozen quiz shows aired on network television.

SCANDALS CHANGE SOME BUSINESS PRACTICES

Yet, this silver lining had a cloud. As Robert Redford's docudrama *Quiz Show* relates, rumors started circulating in late 1958, and broke wide open less than a year later. Charles Van Doren, whose success on *Twenty-One* led to such popularity that he'd gotten a permanent gig on the *Today* show, confessed that he'd lied: he'd been fed the questions and answers by the producers, and had stumbled and paused intentionally on occasion to help build the suspense. At this point, the producers revealed that Revlon had often instructed them as to which contestants should continue, and which should be helped off the air. A few, they admitted, had confounded them: for example, Dr. Joyce Brothers was considered dull as dirt and therefore designated for elimination, but she kept answering the questions designed to cut her out correctly (Barnouw, 1970, pp. 122-125; Metz, 1976, pp. 204-215).

What ensued was a national scandal. Our innocence about television was shattered, and it drove the last nail in the coffin of the single-sponsored program. By 1968, fewer than 3% of network programs were created by advertisers, and those few endured increasing control and scrutiny by the networks (Head and Sterling, 1982, p. 194). Nowadays, we see an occasional *Hallmark Hall of Fame*, or a clearly labeled "infomercial"–but the sponsors' explicit and direct control of television content exited, stage left. Enter, stage right, the contemporary context for advertising–and for advertisers to sneak the product back into the program in a variety of clever ways. The essays that follow delineate some of the many ways in which this sleight of hand has been performed, and explore the ramifications.

REFERENCES

Barnouw, E. (1970). *The Image Empire.* New York: Oxford University Press.

Barnouw, E. (1966). *A Tower in Babel.* New York: Oxford University Press.

Camel News Caravan (1950). Videotape of television program. New York: Museum of Radio and Television.

Milton Berle Show (1953). Videotape of television program. Oklahoma City, OK: Concord Video.

Fibber McGee and Molly: McGee's Magic Act (1948). Audiotape of radio program. Houston: Pastime Products.

Head, S. W., and Sterling, C. H. (1982). *Broadcasting in America.* Boston: Houghton Mifflin.

MacDonald, J. F. (1979). *Don't Touch that Dial.* Chicago: Nelson-Hall.

Metz, R. (1976). *Reflections in a Bloodshot Eye.* New York: New American Library.

Simon, S. (2001, May 17). *Product Placement.* News report on *All Things Considered.* Washington, DC: National Public Radio.

$64,000 Question (1957). Videotape of television program. Sandy Hook, CT: Video Yesteryear.

Sterling, C. H., and Kittross, J. M. (1990). *Stay Tuned.* Belmont, CA: Wadsworth.

The Evolution of Product Placements in Hollywood Cinema: Embedding High-Involvement "Heroic" Brand Images

Mary-Lou Galician
Peter G. Bourdeau

SUMMARY. This content analysis of the 15 top-grossing motion pictures of 1977, 1987, and 1997 uncovered 546 product placements present in fully one quarter (24%) of the total running time of the 45 movies. Product leaders were automobiles (21% of all placements), beer (14%), and soda (11%), with Coca-Cola the overall brand leader. Full-display appearances remained dominant throughout. Most appearances were brief; however, "key" placements–lengthier showcases featuring brands in central heroic roles and in idealized images resembling TV commercials–increased over the 20-year period. Other related notable changes were increases in high-involvement placements (89%), implied endorse-

Mary-Lou Galician (EdD, Memphis State University) is Associate Professor and Head of the Media Analysis and Criticism Concentration in the Walter Cronkite School of Journalism and Mass Communication, Arizona State University, Tempe, AZ 85287-1305 (E-mail: DrFUN@asu.edu). Peter G. Bourdeau (MMC, Arizona State University) earned his degree in 1999. He is a technology consultant.

A summary of an earlier version of this research was presented at the National Communication Association Annual National Convention (Seattle) in November 2000.

[Haworth co-indexing entry note]: "The Evolution of Product Placements in Hollywood Cinema: Embedding High-Involvement 'Heroic' Brand Images." Galician, Mary-Lou, and Peter G. Bourdeau. Co-published simultaneously in *Journal of Promotion Management* (Best Business Books, an imprint of The Haworth Press, Inc.) Vol. 10, No. 1/2, 2004, pp. 15-36; and: *Handbook of Product Placement in the Mass Media: New Strategies in Marketing Theory, Practice, Trends, and Ethics* (ed: Mary-Lou Galician) Best Business Books, an imprint of The Haworth Press, Inc., 2004, pp. 15-36. Single or multiple copies of this article are available for a fee from The Haworth Document Delivery Service [1-800-HAWORTH, 9:00 a.m. - 5:00 p.m. (EST). E-mail address: docdelivery@haworthpress.com].

ment placements (83%) (coupled with a 9% rise in "verbal/hands mentions," the most valued placement), and "mentioned" placements (75%) (similarly coupled with a 9% rise in "used" placements), and the number of brands placed (32%) along with decreases in liquor placements (60%), association with minor characters (40%) and non-stars (36%), and both "signage" (24%) and "clutter" (20%) placements, the least valued. *[Article copies available for a fee from The Haworth Document Delivery Service: 1-800-HAWORTH. E-mail address: <docdelivery@haworthpress.com> Website: <http://www.HaworthPress.com> © 2004 by The Haworth Press, Inc. All rights reserved.]*

KEYWORDS. Brand names, brand placement, cinema, Hollywood, marketing, motion pictures, movie production, product placement, promotion

INTRODUCTION

The History of Product Placement in Movies

The history of Hollywood is a tale of the collision of art and commerce (Puttnam and Watson, 1998). Weisberg (1985) suggested that product placement–the practice of purposely placing brand-name products in the context of feature films–is Hollywood's latest and sometimes stormiest marriage between these competing cinematic interests.

Motion picture studios have been using marketers' products and advertisements as props in their films for decades (Magiera, 1990b; Turcotte, 1995). Rothenberg (1991) offered evidence that motion picture studios used product placement before the First World War. However, the practice intensified during the 1930s, when studios slowly advanced the idea of promoting products in movies by sending marketers shot-by-shot breakdowns of scripts with promotional opportunities clearly indicated to marketers.

When undershirt sales plummeted nationwide after matinee idol Clark Gable took off a dress shirt and exposed his bare hairy chest on screen in *It Happened One Night* (1934), corporate America took notice (Baird, 1997; Caro, 1996). By 1939, Metro-Goldwyn-Mayer had become the first studio in history to open a placement office (Rothenberg, 1991), and Walt Disney Studios began selling plates and glassware depicting images from its popular films ("Tie-in Advertising," 1951). In the first documented instance of a movie star's plugging a brand-name product in a Hollywood film, movie audiences watched Joan Crawford slug Jack Daniels liquor in the Warner Brothers drama, *Mildred Pierce* (1945) (Nebenzahl and Secunda, 1993).

Product placement expanded slowly until the late-1960s, when a few movie directors began emphasizing reality-based themes in their films and, accordingly, infusing them with actual brand label products and advertising images (Weisberg, 1985). Driven by their own economic considerations, movie executives latched onto this directorial trend. While studio bosses had long recognized product placement as a means of subsidizing the enormous production and advertising costs incurred when making and marketing their movies, the studios' acute financial struggles in the early 1970s led to an increased emphasis on the device as a revenue source. Faced with diminishing ticket sales and skyrocketing film budgets, movie executives came to rely on product placement as a means of support for their beleaguered budgets (Magiera, 1990a).

But it was not until E.T. gobbled up Reeses Pieces in Steven Spielberg's 1982 movie–a placement credited with causing sales of the candy to leap 65% in three months–that marketers, now fully understanding product placements' commercial impact, began actively seeking their own product placements (Caro, 1996). Likewise, emboldened by this obvious proof of product placements' effectiveness at generating sales, Hollywood began courting movie placement deals with this waiting line of corporate marketer suitors.

The Evolution and Influence of the Practice

As the interdependence between studio executives seeking cost and advertising support and corporate marketers desiring product exposure has increased, the practice of product placement has evolved. What was once a Hollywood-based cottage industry has become a multi-million dollar enterprise (Caro, 1996). In 1998, the North American theater audience for Hollywood movies was almost 1.5 billion filmgoers; the international audience was twice that (Marshall, 1998; "Primetime," 1999). This massive, worldwide audience makes Hollywood an excellent communication medium and a very powerful consumer influence. Marshall (1998) estimated that approximately 1,000 brand marketers utilized product placement as part of their overall advertising mix.

Acknowledging the vast influence of movies on audiences, movie critics and consumer advocates alike have warned of the insidious nature of product placement (Miller, 1990) (see interview with Mark Crispin

Miller in this volume). In fact, opponents of product placements have gone so far as to ask for federal regulation of the practice (Magiera and Colford, 1991) (see interview with Michael Jacobson in this volume).

The practices and underlying beliefs of professionals working with brand placements have only been reported in a limited fashion by both the trade and popular press (Karrh, 1994). Because most of the information regarding marketers' use of product placement remains proprietary. In their content analysis of the 25 top-grossing films of 1991, Sapolsky and Kinney (1994) documented the amounts and kinds of nationally recognized brands embedded in motion pictures. Partially replicating the work of Sapolsky and Kinney (1994), the current study tracked the evolution of brand placement in Hollywood motion pictures from 1977 to 1997.

STATEMENT OF THE PROBLEM

The research reported here asked the question: *How has product placement in the 15 top-grossing motion pictures of the year evolved from 1977 to 1987 to 1997?*

Eleven sub-questions focused the study:

1. Has the number of appearances of product placements changed from 1977 to 1997?
2. Has the length of appearance of product placements changed from 1977 to 1997?
3. Has the dominant type of product appearing in a product placement changed from 1977 to 1997?
4. Has the number of brands changed from 1977 to 1997?
5. Has the level of plot involvement (high or low) of product placements changed from 1977 to 1997?
6. Has the primary association with character (major character[s], minor character[s], or equal) of product placements changed from 1977 to 1997?
7. Has the primary association with star (star[s], non-star[s], or equal) of product placement changed from 1977 to 1997?
8. Has the theatrical context (positive, negative, mixed, or neutral) of scenes containing product placements changed from 1977 to 1997?
9. Has the level of display (full or partial) of product placements changed from 1977 to 1997?

10. Has the type (seen, mentioned, or used) of product placements changed from 1977 to 1997?
11. Has the level of value (clutter, signage, implied endorsement, or verbal or hands mention) of product placements changed from 1977 to 1997?

METHODOLOGY

For this trend study, the 15 top-grossing Hollywood-produced motion pictures with nationwide domestic release dates of 1977, 1987, and 1997 (i.e., 45 movies) were selected using the annual wrap-up of the "Weekend Box Office Report" in the motion picture industry trade publication *Variety*. (Four motion pictures released in the last few weeks of 1976 (*A Star is Born*, *King Kong*, *Rocky*, and *Silver Streak*) were included as 1977 motion pictures because their total box office grosses were based primarily on 1977 attendance. For a listing of all 45 motion pictures analyzed for the three years, see Table 1.) All 45 movies were rented and viewed multiple times by the researchers.

The unit of analysis was the individual appearance of a brand (product or service) whether seen, mentioned, or used. Because it was not possible to distinguish intentionality from random inclusion, all brands observed were coded as product placements. An "appearance" was a contiguous product placement with limited interruption throughout a single scene. A product placement might have multiple appearances in a movie.

FINDINGS

The answers to the 11 research sub-questions are presented first, followed by the answer to the overall research question.

#1. Has the Number of Appearances of Product Placements Changed from 1977 to 1997?

The number of appearances remained fairly constant from year to year: 182 in 1977, 170 in 1987, 194 in 1997 (see Table 2). (Note: These totals reflect every single separate appearance by any brand; therefore, several individual brands might have multiple appearances.)

TABLE 1. The 15 Top-Grossing Motion Pictures of 1977, 1987, and 1997*

1.	Star Wars (1977)	$461.0 million
2.	Close Encounters of the Third Kind (1977)	$128.3 million
3.	Smokey and the Bandit (1977)	$126.7 million
4.	Rocky (1976)**	$117.2 million
5.	Saturday Night Fever (1977)	$94.2 million
6.	The Spy Who Loved Me (1977)	$46.8 million
7.	In Search of Noah's Ark (1977)	$55.7 million
8.	Annie Hall (1977)	$39.2 million
9.	Across the Great Divide (1977)	$18.8 million
10.	For the Love of Benji (1977)	$17.7 million
11.	Kingdom of the Spiders (1977)	$17.0 million
12.	Looking For Mr. Goodbar (1977)	$16.9 million
13.	Silver Streak (1976)**	$89.2 million
14.	A Star is Born (1976)**	$104.6 million
15.	King Kong (1976)**	$89.7 million
1.	Three Men and a Baby (1987)	$167.8 million
2.	Fatal Attraction (1987)	$156.6 million
3.	Beverly Hills Cop II (1987)	$153.7 million
4.	Good Morning Vietnam (1987)	$123.9 million
5.	Moonstruck (1987)	$80.6 million
6.	The Untouchables (1987)	$76.3 million
7.	The Secret of My Success (1987)	$67.0 million
8.	Stakeout (1987)	$65.7 million
9.	Lethal Weapon (1987)	$65.2 million
10.	Dirty Dancing (1987)	$63.9 million
11.	The Witches of Eastwick (1987)	$63.8 million
12.	Predator (1987)	$59.7 million
13.	Throw Mama from the Train (1987)	$57.9 million
14.	Dragnet (1987)	$57.4 million
15.	The Living Daylights (1987)	$51.2 million
1.	Titanic (1997)	$600.8 million
2.	Men in Black (1997)	$250.1 million
3.	The Lost World: Jurassic Park (1997)	$229.1 million
4.	Liar Liar (1997)	$181.4 million
5.	Air Force One (1997)	$172.7 million
6.	As Good as it Gets (1997)	$147.7 million
7.	Good Will Hunting (1997)	$138.4 million
8.	My Best Friend's Wedding (1997)	$126.8 million
9.	Tomorrow Never Dies (1997)	$125.3 million
10.	Face/Off (1997)	$112.3 million
11.	Batman and Robin (1997)	$107.3 million
12.	George of the Jungle (1997)	$105.3 million
13.	Scream 2 (1997)	$101.4 million
14.	Con Air (1997)	$101.1 million
15.	Contact (1997)	$100.9 million

*according to *Variety*'s *Weekend Box Office Report*
**released in the last few weeks of 1976 but included as 1977 motion pictures because their total box office grosses were based primarily on 1977 attendance

TABLE 2. Product Placement Appearances in the 15 Top-Grossing Motion Pictures of 1977, 1987, and 1997

Year	Appearances
1977	182
1987	170
1997	194
TOTAL	546
MEAN	182

#2. Has the Length of Appearance of Product Placements Changed from 1977 to 1997?

The average total length of appearance per movie diminished slightly from 1977 (28.7 minutes) to 1997 (26.8 minutes) (see Table 3). Although accurate, these averages ultimately fail to effectively reflect how the length of product appearances has changed over time due to the influence of longer product appearances in the analysis. For example, during the climax of the movie *Face/Off* (1997), Nicholas Cage and John Travolta each commanded a Seacraft speedboat in a water chase scene lasting 13.3 minutes, skewing the average appearance length for *Face/Off*, whose other 17 appearances averaged only 5 seconds each. The Seacraft plug was emblematic of the failure of the means method to render a reliable average for appearance length over time.

Proportional analysis. For this reason, a proportional analysis of on-screen appearances to movie length was conducted, yielding the following: 25% in 1977, 25% in 1987, 22% in 1997; thus, for all three years, on-screen placements accounted for approximately one quarter of the length of all movies. That the percentage of on-screen time of appearances to movie length was constant is significant because the average movie length increased (1977 [116 minutes], 1987 [110 minutes], and 1997 [124 minutes]) while the number of appearances remained steady during that same period (1977 [182], 1987 [170], and 1997 [194]). On average, the top 15 movies of 1997 were 14 minutes longer than in 1987, and 8 minutes longer than in 1977. With the number of appearances approximately equal, this comparison indicates an increase in length of appearance from 1977 to 1997. Overall, the range for length of appearances was .04 (minutes) to 17.9 (minutes). In 1977 the range was .01 (minutes) to 18.6 (minutes), in 1987 .06 (minutes) to 12.9 (minutes), and in 1997 .06 (minutes) to 22.1 (minutes).

TABLE 3. Length of Appearance of Product Placements in the 15 Top-Grossing Motion Pictures of 1977, 1987, and 1997

	1977	1987	1997	Mean
Average length of movie (minutes)	116	110	124	117
Average length of appearance per movie (minutes)	28.7	27.9	26.8	27.8
Appearance/movie length	25%	25%	22%	24%
Length of appearance (range in minutes)	.01-18.6	.06-12.9	.06-22.1	.04-17.9
Number of Appearances (N)	182	170	194	182

"Key" placements. Although many of the appearances analyzed by the study remained brief throughout the 20-year period, the study identified a trend towards numerous "key" placements with an increasing length that have more in common with television commercials than traditional cinematic narratives. These key placements–some of them lasting as long as 10 minutes or more–often entailed an extended series of shots that featured the brand in an idealized display frequently characterized by rapid shifts in perspective and lightning-quick editing. Notable among them was a scene in *Tomorrow Never Dies* (1997), in which Pierce Brosnan, as Agent 007, escapes from thugs with the help of a BMW motorcycle.

#3. Has the Dominant Type of Product Changed from 1977 to 1997?

Automobiles were the most dominant type of product appearing during each year studied (see Table 4). Of the 546 product appearances observed, 21% (104) featured automobiles, 14% (73) featured beer, and 11% (60) featured soda. Combined, these three categories alone accounted for 49% (182) of all product appearances in 1977, 44% (170) in 1987, and 38% (194) in 1997. Liquor appearances, the fourth most frequently observed type of product overall (7%), decreased from 8% (15) of all product appearances in 1977 and 10% (17) in 1987 to just 3% (6) in 1997.

Automobiles as heroes. Automobile appearances represented the most egregious examples of overused commercial film techniques–perhaps related to the extensive reliance on auto placements by many studios because of the expense of the vehicles. This study found it common for a filmmaker to zoom in on the auto's brand-name, thereby connoting an auto placement deal. In 1977's *For the Love of Benji*, a low-budget movie that relied heavily on placements, director Joe Camp used this

TABLE 4. Ten Most Dominant Product Types Appearing in the 15 Top-Grossing Motion Pictures of 1977, 1987, and 1997

1977	n	%	1987	n	%	1997	n	%
Auto	30	16%	Auto	39	23%	Auto	35	18%
Beer	30	16%	Soda	19	11%	Beer	26	13%
Soda	29	15%	Beer	17	10%	Soda	12	6%
Liquor	15	8%	Liquor	17	10%	Cable Co.	9	5%
Truck	7	4%	Cigarettes	6	4%	Television	7	4%
Airline	6	3%	Detergent	6	4%	Sunglasses	6	3%
Magazine	6	3%	Diapers	5	3%	Cigarettes	6	3%
Gas Co.	5	3%	Champagne	5	3%	Liquor	6	3%
Restaurant	5	3%	Television	3	2%	Cellphone	5	3%
Aspirin	4	2%	Motorcycle	3	2%	SUV	5	3%
TOTAL	137	75%	TOTAL	120	71%	TOTAL	117	60%
	(N = 182)			(N = 170)			(N = 194)	

commonly observed technique to make sure audiences knew which auto maker provided the car for his film. *Smokey and the Bandit* (1977) also had extensive product placements, but what is interesting to note about that paean to Coors beer and long-haul trucking is that although Burt Reynold's Trans Am was integral to the narrative and featured throughout the movie, this placement did not engender the sense of intrusiveness observed in later movies like *Jurassic Park, The Lost World* (1997), whose Mercedes-Benz SUV placement exudes a sense of slick commercialism: The camera lingers so lovingly on a pair of Benz SUVs that it is clear this movie is being used as a showcase for the autos. In one scene, the newly developed Mercedes SUVs are filmed as if they were movie star heroes, riding out of the jungle and across the verdant plain of a fictional tropic isle. In another scene, the Benz SUV, along with its state-of-the-art push-button four-wheel-drive capability, saves Jeff Goldblum and Julianne Moore from plunging over a 500-foot cliff. In fact, Daimler Benz had mounted a much-publicized multi-million dollar co-promotional ad campaign prior to the movie's release, supporting the Spielberg dino-epic and hailing the German carmaker's entry into the lucrative SUV market (Jensen, 1997).

Alcohol's disappearance. The product types featured in the 15 top-grossing movies from 1977 to 1997 also provided a reliable reflection of changing societal conventions of their eras–for example, the major decrease in the number of liquor placements from 1977 (15) to 1997 (6).

In 1977's *A Star is Born*, Kris Kristofferson's randy fondness for liquor was fully portrayed; however, 20 years later, that kind of blatant alcoholic consumption did not appear in any of the 15 top movies of the year. Nevertheless, beer placements were the second most frequent product type from 1977 to 1997.

#4. Has the Number of Brands Changed from 1977 to 1997?

As expected, the study found an increase in the number of individual brands embedded in Hollywood's 15 most popular films during 1977, 1987, and 1997 (see Table 5). The use of individual brands increased 12% from 1977 (117) to 1987 (131), and 18% from 1987 (131) to 1997 (154), with an overall increase of 32% in the number of individual brands from 1977 (117) to 1997 (154).

Coke is it. Coca-Cola was by far the most frequently observed brand-name overall with 44 appearances in a total of 20 motion pictures over the 20-year time span (see Table 6). Coca-Cola (Coke and Diet Coke) was the most frequently observed brand in 1977 (25 appearances in 8 movies) and 1987 (15 appearances in 8 movies) but was ranked only eighth in 1997 (4 appearances in 3 movies), when several other brands garnered more screen time: Mercedes-Benz (9 appearances in 4 movies), CNN (9 appearances in 4 movies), Pepsi-Cola (8 appearances in 2 movies), Chevrolet (7 appearances in 6 movies), BMW (6 appearances in 3 movies), and Marlboro (5 appearances in 3 movies).

The second most frequently observed brand overall was Mercedes-Benz with 18 appearances in 9 motion pictures.

#5. Has the Level of Plot Involvement (High or Low) of Product Placements Changed from 1977 to 1997?

In both 1977 and 1987, the ratio of placements with low-level to high-level plot involvement was approximately 4:1 (see Table 7). How-

TABLE 5. Brand Appearances in the 15 Top-Grossing Motion Pictures of 1977, 1987, and 1997

Year	Brands
1977	117
1987	131
1997	154
MEAN	134

TABLE 6. Ten Most Dominant Brands Appearing in the 15 Top-Grossing Motion Pictures of 1977, 1987, and 1997

Brand	Number of Appearances	Number of Movies
Coke	44	20
Mercedes	18	9
Miller	17	8
Chevy	15	10
Pepsi-Cola	13	5
Schlitz	12	3
BMW	10	7
Jack Daniels	10	4
Cadillac	9	5
CNN	9	4

ever, this proportion changed dramatically in 1997 to 2:1, when the amount of high-involvement placements increased to 70 (36%), effectively doubling those of 1977 (37, or 20%) and 1987 (36, or 21%), whereas the number of low-involvement placements decreased to 124 (64%), compared with 1977's 145 (80%) and 1987's 134 (79%). This recent trend toward placements with more high-involvement with plot also caused the overall low-to-high ratio to drop to 3:1 (74%:26%).

James Bond never dies. The exemplar for this new trend was the 1997 James Bond film, *Tomorrow Never Dies,* a movie with more than 22 minutes' worth of on-screen product appearances. In addition to the sheer number of multi- million dollar placements in this film, its producers also included numerous scenes in which Pierce Brosnan's 007 must save the day with the help of several brand-name products, including an Ericcson cellular phone used as a remote control for a car and a thumb-print imager, an Omega watch used to foil a rocket launch, a BMW 750 used by Bond to escape his enemies by catapulting off a five-story parking garage, and a BMW motorcycle used by 007 to literally ride over the whirling blades of a chasing helicopter. For good measure the producers also included plugs for Avis, Heineken, Smirnoff, and Range Rover.

#6. Has the Primary Association with Character (Major Character[s], Minor Character[s], or Equal) of Product Placements Changed from 1977 to 1997?

A large majority of product placements were associated with major character(s) (more than 50% association with character integral to plot)

TABLE 7. Level of Plot Involvement of Product Placements in the 15 Top-Grossing Motion Pictures of 1977, 1987, and 1997

	1977		1987		1997		Total	
	N	%	N	%	N	%	N	%
High	37	20%	36	21%	70	36%	143	26%
Low	145	80%	134	79%	124	64%	403	74%
TOTAL	182		170		194		546	

compared to other associations in all three years: 1977 (98, or 54%), 1987 (110, or 65%), and 1997 (97, or 50%) (see Table 8). While individual placements associated equally with major and minor characters increased over the 20-year period, association with minor character(s) clearly decreased.

#7. Has the Primary Association with Star (Star[s], Non-Star[s], or Equal) of Product Placements Changed from 1977 to 1997?

Product placements primarily associated with "star(s)" (more than 50% association with an actor named in the film's opening credits as having a starring role) were a clear majority of those found in 1977 (84, or 46%) and 1987 (95, or 56%); however, this trend changed in 1997 when placements with "equal" association with star(s)/non-star(s) (83, or 43%) gained a slight edge over scenes with "star(s)" only (79, or 41%) (see Table 9). Most tellingly, scenes with placements associated only with "non-star(s)" decreased greatly from 1977 (50, or 27%) to 1987 (30, or 18%) and 1997 (32, or 16%).

The study uncovered a veritable *Who's Who* listing of Hollywood actors who appeared in movies plugging products. Even "auteur" Woody Allen and soon-to-be Oscar-winner Diane Keaton appeared wielding Dunlop tennis racquets in several scenes in the 1977 movie *Annie Hall*.

#8. Has the Theatrical Context (Positive, Negative, Mixed, or Neutral) of Scenes Containing Product Placements Changed from 1977 to 1997?

Surprisingly, product placements appeared not only in scenes with a "positive" theatrical context but also in "negative," "mixed," or "neu-

TABLE 8. Association with Character of Product Placements in the 15 Top-Grossing Motion Pictures of 1977, 1987, and 1997

	1977		1987		1997		Total	
	N	%	N	%	N	%	N	%
Major	98	54%	110	65%	97	50%	305	56%
Equal	42	23%	40	23%	72	37%	154	28%
Minor	42	23%	20	12%	25	13%	87	16%
TOTAL	182		170		194		546	

TABLE 9. Association with Star Status of Product Placements in the 15 Top-Grossing Motion Pictures of 1977, 1987, and 1997

	1977		1987		1997		Total	
	N	%	N	%	N	%	N	%
Star	84	46%	95	56%	79	41%	258	46%
Equal	48	26%	45	26%	83	43%	176	32%
Non-Star	50	27%	30	18%	32	16%	112	21%
TOTAL	182		170		194		546	

tral" contexts (see Table 10). The study found an increase in "mixed" context placements from 1977 (42, or 23%) to 1987 (50, or 29%) and even more to 1997 (63, or 33%). In fact, scenes with "negative" contexts were the most frequent type in 1977 (50, or 27%) and second in both 1987 (46, or 27%) and 1997 (60, or 31%). "Neutral" context placements experienced a major decrease in 1997 (20, or 10%) compared to 1987 (30, or 18%) and 1977 (43, or 24%).

Negative placements. One of the most telling examples of marketers' indifference to the nature of a scene context is 1997's *Scream 2*, a film about a pair of psychotics busy murdering nearly a dozen small-town college students. This slasher film contained many prominent placements that were snappily interwoven with extremely violent and gory scenes of murder and mayhem. The Pepsi-Cola company evidently had few qualms about having its brands in *Scream 2*, a movie literally awash in Pepsi and Diet Pepsi images, including one scene in a cafeteria with dozens of Pepsi-Cola cans on every table.

Director John Woo's 1997 action thriller, *Face/Off*, is another movie with numerous product placements spread among its many negative and

TABLE 10. Theatrical Context of Product Placements in the 15 Top-Grossing Motion Pictures of 1977, 1987, and 1997

	1977		1987		1997		Total	
	N	%	N	%	N	%	N	%
Positive	47	26%	44	26%	51	26%	142	26%
Negative	50	27%	46	27%	60	31%	156	28%
Mixed	42	23%	50	29%	63	33%	155	28%
Neutral	43	24%	30	18%	20	10%	93	18%
TOTAL	182		170		194		546	

disturbing scenes, including depictions of a vicious prison beating and mass murder. Nevertheless, the movie attracted several marketers with prominent product placement appearances, including Chiclet's chewing gum as bad-guy Cage's gum of choice.

#9. Has the Level of Display (Full or Partial) of Product Placements Changed from 1977 to 1997?

In all three years, "full" level of display was used in approximately 60% of the 546 product placements in the 45 movies, as compared with 40% for "partial" placements (see Table 11).

Techniques. Even more important, significant qualitative changes occurred in the way these placements were filmed. Over time, an increased use of film techniques that emphasize the product to the detriment of the other movie elements can be observed. Among the most extreme examples of this phenomenon is a coffee placement in the movie, *George of the Jungle* (1997). The director simply pasted an actual television commercial as part of the film's narrative–filling the movie screen with the brand's image accompanied by a rousing corporate jingle. This technique occurred in several other motion pictures with the same effect.

Many of the motion pictures analyzed also contained product appearances in which their directors' blatant use of extreme close-ups to emphasize the product's brand label was obtrusive. Similarly, panning shots–with camera lenses trained on the brand–lingered ever so briefly before cutting away to other action, as in the Tag Heuer watch placement in *Scream 2* (1997).

Yet another method, also obviously borrowed from television commercials, framed a brand's image to the exclusion of all other shot ele-

TABLE 11. Level of Display of Product Placements in the 15 Top-Grossing Motion Pictures of 1977, 1987, and 1997

	1977		1987		1997		Total	
	N	%	N	%	N	%	N	%
Full	108	59%	97	57%	118	61%	323	59%
Partial	74	41%	73	43%	76	39%	223	41%
TOTAL	182		170		194		546	

ments, ensuring that the placement received the full attention of the movie audience, such as a scene from 1977's *Close Encounters of the Third Kind* that featured McDonald's golden arches or the one from *Dragnet* (1987) that featured a beer truck that filled the entire movie screen with the Miller Genuine Draft brand.

#10. Has the Type (Seen, Mentioned, or Used) of Product Placements Changed from 1977 to 1997?

The most frequently observed type of product placement in all three years was the so-called "seen" placement, which accounted for 50% (273) of all appearances (see Table 12). However, placements in this category decreased slightly (6%) with time, whereas "used" placements (204, or 37%), which ranked second, increased 9% over the 20-year period, and "mentioned" placements (69, or 13%)–the least frequently used overall–increased the most dramatically: 75%. Per Turcotte (1995): "Used" is any touching or interaction of a brand by a character; "Mentioned" is any appearance of a brand, including off-screen narration; and "Seen" is any visual appearance of a brand. For the current study, if a brand placement met more than one condition, it was coded according to the highest level (i.e., most valuable) of an accepted hierarchy of value established by the placement industry: A usage placement is more valuable than a mentioned placement, which is more valuable than a seen placement ("Let Us Put," 1996).

"Mentioned." A scene in *Throw Mama from the Train* (1987) provides an example of just how gratuitous a "mentioned" product placement can be. Toward the end of the film, Billy Crystal asks Danny DeVito if there is anything he wants. From out of nowhere, the obvious plug is visited on the audience when the diminutive DeVito utters, "Get me a Chunky."

TABLE 12. Type of Product Placements in the 15 Top-Grossing Motion Pictures During 1977, 1987, and 1997

	1977		1987		1997		Total	
	N	%	N	%	N	%	N	%
Seen	98	54%	83	49%	92	47%	273	50%
Mentioned	16	9%	25	15%	28	14%	69	13%
Used	68	37%	62	36%	74	38%	204	37%
TOTAL	182		170		194		546	

"Used." While the prevalence of placements that are "used" by the actors remained constant from 1977 to 1997, there was also a change in the manner in which they were constructed. When an actor interacted with a brand-name product in a 1997 movie, the director would leave nothing to chance. Rarely would a 1997 appearance with an actor holding a product entail only a wide-angle shot, possibly producing an ambiguous placement that might leave the audience unaware of the brand-name or of the character's use of it. More often than not, a 1997 "used" appearance would include a tight-angle shot, focusing not on an actor holding the product but on the product being held in an actor's hand.

#11. Has the Level of Value (Verbal or Hands Mention, Implied Endorsement, Signage, or Clutter) of Product Placements Changed from 1977 to 1997?

Of the placements observed, the majority were valued as "verbal/hands mentions" (the highest level of value, per CES): 1977 (70, or 38%), 1987 (58, or 34%), and 1997 (76, or 39%) (see Table 13)–representing an increase of 9% over the 20-year period (and 31% from 1987 to 1997). Product placements valued only as "clutter" were the second most frequently used overall though they dropped 20% over the 20-year period, to third place by 1997. "Implied endorsements," third most frequently used overall, increased a whopping 83% from 1977 (29, or 16%) to 1987 (40, or 24%) and again to 1997 (53, or 27%), taking a clear second place. "Signage" dropped 24% (to lowest place overall) over the studied period. This was analyzed per the method of rating brand placements as described by Creative Entertainment Service (CES), the recognized authority on post-production product placement analysis ("Let Us Put," 1996). CES ranks product placements hierarchically from highest to lowest: "Verbal or Hand Mention" is an oral mention or phys-

TABLE 13. Level of Value of Product Placements in the 15 Top-Grossing Motion Pictures of 1977, 1987, and 1997

	1977		1987		1997		Total	
	N	%	N	%	N	%	N	%
Verb./Hands	70	38%	58	34%	76	39%	204	37%
Imp. Endorse.	29	16%	40	24%	53	27%	122	23%
Signage	33	18%	25	15%	25	13%	83	15%
Clutter	50	27%	47	28%	40	21%	137	25%
TOTAL	182		170		194		546	

ical contact of a brand by an actor or narrator; "Implied Endorsement" is an unseen or unspoken suggestion that a brand that is shown on-screen in close proximity to a character(s) has been or will be used by that character(s); "Signage" is a prominent display of a brand-name in the background of a scene, and "Clutter" is a non-prominent display of a brand in a scene.

Overall Research Question: How Has Product Placement Advertising in the 15 Top-Grossing Motion Pictures of the Year Evolved from 1977 to 1997?

This content analysis of the 15 top-grossing motion pictures of 1977, 1987, and 1997 uncovered 546 product placements present in fully one quarter (24%) of the total running time of the 45 movies. Although the actual number of product placement appearances as well as the average length of each (about 28 seconds per appearance) remained fairly constant, the number of individual brands increased dramatically (32%). While the majority of the 546 appearances lasted only 5 seconds or less, many so-called "key" placements actually increased in length over time, so that by 1997 some individual product appearances ("key" placements) lasted more than 10 minutes and one was longer than 20 minutes.

Product leaders in all three years were automobiles (21% of the 546 appearances observed), beer (14%), and soda (11%). Coca-Cola was the most frequently observed brand with 44 appearances in 20 motion pictures. Surprisingly, placements were no more likely to appear in positive contexts than negative contexts.

In addition to the increase in the number of brands, other notable changes from 1977 to 1997 were major increases in high-involvement placements (89%), implied endorsement placements (83%) (coupled with a

9% rise in "verbal/hands mentions," the most valued placement), and "mentioned" placements (75%) (similarly coupled with a 9% rise in "used" placements), along with decreases in liquor placements (60%) and association with minor characters (40%) and non-stars (36%). "Signage" and "clutter" placements, the least valued, decreased 24% and 20%, respectively. Full-display appearances remained dominant at around 60% in each of the three years.

Even more telling than mere quantitative findings are the related qualitative changes: Brands in longer "key" placements typically were showcased in heroic roles crucial to the plot. Further, these placements were presented in idealized images resembling television commercials, often enjoying use or endorsement by major characters who were also usually the stars of the movies. In some cases, these key placements, which usually filled the screen with purposive zoom-ins and close-ups of the brand, were gratuitous and obtrusive.

CONCLUDING OBSERVATIONS

Implications

In the three years studied, an astounding one-quarter of the running time in top-grossing Hollywood movies contained some kind of brand message. The startling increase in products other than the three dominant categories (i.e., autos, beer, and soda) may indicate a growing interest among marketers to add product placement advertising into their advertising mixes. (The decrease in the number of liquor placements in 1997, after being the fourth most frequent product type in 1977 and 1987, might be a reflection of the diminishing tolerance for liquor consumption.) This dramatic increase in the number of placed products and brands suggests that the practice of product placement has indeed gained acceptance among brand marketers over this 20-year period. Assuming this is indeed the case, what needs to be determined are the reasons for this growth and whether it can be sustained.

Underlining this acceptance of the practice is one of the study's surprising findings. The literature suggested that most brand managers would hesitate to affiliate their brand with a negative film message and thus would be less willing to have their product appear in a film with an unsettling or violent storyline or alongside an unsavoury character. (Some product placement deals actually stipulate positive context placements.) However, this study found a prevalence of brand-name products placed in such gory and violent movies as *Face/Off* (1997) and *Scream 2* (1997). Surprisingly, product placements in negative contexts were slightly more prevalent than those in positive contexts, suggesting that what marketer's value most from product placement is the exposure it affords their brands, regardless of the tone. Beginning in the 1980s, when marketers began seeking placements based strictly on a film's likelihood of becoming a box office smash, the storyline has been considered secondary. Aiming to have their brands seen by the millions of teen fans expected to flock to *Scream 2* (1997), brand managers did not seem to mind being associated with a film containing scenes of murderous mayhem. Today's marketers may be operating under the maxim that there is no such thing as "bad publicity."

Regardless of the context, the new role of placed products appears to be set well within measurable parameters. What is most important regarding the evolution of product placement is the increasing number of high-involvement placements found during the 20-year period of the study. These high-involvement appearances nearly doubled from 1977 to 1997, further indicating that product placement has become an integral aspect of making Hollywood movies. A closely related trend–that the majority of all product appearances were associated with major characters and stars, while there was a major decrease in the number of placements associated only with minor characters and non-stars–further documents the full-scale foregrounding of these products. It might be that marketers are insisting on placements associated with a star, even if that star is not alone in the movie frame.

This figurative foregrounding of placed products is literally underscored by the consistent 3:2 ratio of full-to-partial display. Clearly, filmmakers take care to create placements in which their marketing clients' brand labels are not obscured. Again, it is worth noting that the qualitative nature of a so-called full placement has changed from 1977 to 1997. What is noticeable about many full placements is their singular on-screen presence in certain movies. The study found numerous examples of a camera zooming in on a brand label to the point that the entire screen contains the brand image. Viewed on a standard-sized movie theater screen, that image was a 10-foot tall can of soda or beer.

While "seen" placements accounted for half of all the placements in each of the three years, "used" placements were observed in more than one third of all placements during each year, and "mentioned" placements increased 75% over the studied period. Viewed in the context of a movie, "mentioned" placements are singularly obtrusive and distracting. Filmmakers must recognize that inserting a named brand into the narrative runs the risk of distracting movie audiences. This is not to say that a "mentioned" placement cannot be inventive or entertaining; to the contrary, they can be quite humorous when used by a thoughtful, subtle director. However, most such plugs display neither of these directorial attributes, and, in most cases, having an actor use a brand-name as part of the dialogue provides a lackluster or perhaps even annoying product plug. Moreover, although "seen" placements are, for the most part, subtler than "mentioned" placements, they became increasingly intrusive over the 20-year period of the study. For the most part, the product appearances in 1977 were far more likely to be embedded quickly, without any undue intrusiveness. Conversely, the placement appearances in 1997 were more intrusive and seemingly designed with the sole intent of directing audience attention to the branded products. Likewise, in terms of the CES-rated value of the placements to their marketers, the majority of product placements in this study were the highest-rated "verbal or hands mention." "Implied endorsements" appearances (ranked second in value by CES) increased greatly, while the lower ranked placements–"signage" and "clutter" appearances–diminished greatly.

A disturbing trend is that film directors have shifted toward using narrative and cinematic techniques that actively and often blatantly highlight the brands featured in their movies. The unmistakable impression after observing the 546 placements in the 45 movies analyzed for this study is that many of the scenes contained in Hollywood's most popular movies have come to resemble standard television commercials rather than traditional cinematic fare. (The only difference is that the movie versions of these commercials are much longer and the audience is "captive.") Placed products are now central to the plot (usually as heroes), idealized in visual presentation, and endorsed by the stars who portray the major characters. The dominant type of high-involvement "key" product placement–automobiles–is a prime example of this evolution. The influence of advertising techniques, such as zooming-in or lingering on a brand label to highlight the brands when filming these "key" placements, is obvious and intrusive, particularly when the screen is filled gratuitously with close-ups of them to the exclusion of anything or anyone else. Similarly, the increase in "used" and "mentioned" placement appearances displays a reliance on advertising film techniques by moviemakers. If this phenomenon continues, placement critics might be validated in their long-held argument that the practice has led to an over-commercialization of the cinematic art.

Of course, the increasing symbiotic economic benefits of product placement for brands and studios signal an ongoing demand for more product placement opportunities. Expecting this to change in the immediate future seems unrealistic. It appears that the Hollywood motion picture industry will continue to expand its use and dependence on product placement advertising as well as on the tie-ins and cross-promotions that are part of this profitable practice. This study revealed that product placement practitioners have evolved specific styles and techniques when embedding brand images into motion pictures, which might lead to their overexposure–resulting in Hollywood motion pictures over-saturated with brand-name images that are all presented in the same manner. The parody presented in *The Truman Show* might become the norm.

Limitations of the Study

This analysis of product placement advertising in 1977, 1987, and 1997 could be used as a benchmark to predict future trends in the placement industry and their effect on the motion picture industry. This study examined product placements only in movies that ranked among the 15 top-grossing movies of the studied years. Because only one year was used to represent each of the three decades (i.e., a total of three years), the findings must be interpreted cautiously, and no confirmed "trends" can be established. Further research is needed to ascertain whether these three "snapshot" years at 10-year intervals are representative of their entire decade and, therefore, generalizable. Also, because of the proprietary nature of the product placement industry, it is not possible to confirm whether all observed product placements are intentional. Although precise operational definitions guided the coding of most of the categories, a few categories remained nevertheless somewhat subjective; thus, analysis by a different coder might yield different results. At any rate, it must be emphasized that content analysis does not allow the drawing of conclusions about audience impact or resulting consumer behavior.

Recommendations for Future Research

Further study in this area should be conducted to examine whether and how product placements in Hollywood motion pictures have changed since 1997. Also, the attitudes of movie audiences towards product placement advertising in motion pictures need to be re-examined using movies released since 1997. Likewise, the effectiveness of product placement advertising regarding audiences' recall of brand-name products in motion pictures and brand awareness should be re-examined using motion pictures released since 1997.

REFERENCES

Baird, R. (1997, March 14). Patent place. *Marketing Week, 19*, 46-49.

Caro, M. (1996, August 20). Of all the Jim Beam joints. *Chicago Tribune*, E17.

Jensen, J. (1997, April 14). High hopes for *Men in Black* and for Ray Bans. *Advertising Age, 68*, 1, 52.

Karrh, J.A. (1994). Effects of brand placements in motion pictures. Paper presented at the 1994 Conference of the Academy of Advertising, Athens, GA.

Let us put you in movies. (1996, September 16). *Brandweek, 37*, 2-10.

Magiera, M. (1990b, October 15). Disney plugs up new film. *Advertising Age, 61*, 43.

Magiera, M. (1990c, November 8). Madison Avenue hits Hollywood. *Advertising Age, 61*, 24, 26.

Magiera, M., and Colford, S. (1991, June 10). Products in movies: How big a deal? *Advertising Age, 55*, 4.

Marshall, N. (1998, February 9). Product placement worth more than its weight. *Brandweek, 39*, 16-17.

Miller, M.C. (1990, April). Hollywood the ad. *Atlantic Monthly, 63*, 41-68.

Nebenzahl, I.D., and Secunda, E. (1993). Consumers' attitudes toward product placement in movies. *International Journal of Advertising, 12*(2), 1-11.

Primetime at the box office. (1999, March 10). *USA Today*, E1.

Puttnam, D., and Watson, N. (1998). *One Picture was Worth a Million Bucks*. New York: Knopf.

Rothenberg, R. (1991, May 31). Critics seek F.T.C. action on product as movie stars. *New York Times*, D1.

Sapolsky, B., and Kinney, L. (1994). You ought to be in pictures: Product placements in the top-grossing films of 1991. Paper presented at the 1994 Conference of the Academy of Advertising, Athens, GA.

Tie-in advertising. (1951, January). *Consumer Reports, 23*, 43-44.

Turcotte, S. (1995). Gimme a Bud! The feature film product placement industry. Unpublished masters thesis, University of Texas, Austin.

Weisberg, L. (1985, December 10). Products winning movie auditions. *Advertising Age, 56*, 19-20.

Advertainment:
The Evolution of Product Placement
as a Mass Media Marketing Strategy

Susan B. Kretchmer

SUMMARY. This essay explores the issues implicated by entertainment vehicles created solely to spotlight specific advertisers. From the contemporary exemplar of this paradigm in the highly successful 1990-1998 "Sophisticated Taste" campaign for Taster's Choice® instant coffee, in which viewers watched the sparks fly between the characters of Tony and Sharon in a continuing series of ads that functioned as television programming across multiple media platforms, to the most recent incarnation in advergames, online computer games that promote brands, this study considers the nature and implications of perhaps the ultimate evolution of product placement and blurring of the lines between entertainment and commercial persuasion. *[Article copies available for a fee from The Haworth Document Delivery Service: 1-800-HAWORTH. E-mail address: <docdelivery@haworthpress.com> Website: <http://www.HaworthPress. com> © 2004 by The Haworth Press, Inc. All rights reserved.]*

KEYWORDS. Advergames, advertising, commercials, entertainment, Internet, product placement, promotion, television

Susan B. Kretchmer is a writer, magazine editor for a publishing company, and student at The Johns Hopkins University in Baltimore.

Address correspondence to: 24620 Twickenham Drive, Cleveland, OH 44122 (E-mail: susankretchmer@yahoo.com).

[Haworth co-indexing entry note]: "Advertainment: The Evolution of Product Placement as a Mass Media Marketing Strategy." Kretchmer, Susan B. Co-published simultaneously in *Journal of Promotion Management* (Best Business Books, an imprint of The Haworth Press, Inc.) Vol. 10, No. 1/2, 2004, pp. 37-54; and: *Handbook of Product Placement in the Mass Media: New Strategies in Marketing Theory, Practice, Trends, and Ethics* (ed: Mary-Lou Galician) Best Business Books, an imprint of The Haworth Press, Inc., 2004, pp. 37-54. Single or multiple copies of this article are available for a fee from The Haworth Document Delivery Service [1-800-HAWORTH, 9:00 a.m. - 5:00 p.m. (EST). E-mail address: docdelivery@haworthpress.com].

INTRODUCTION

> The American apparatus of advertising is something unique in history . . . It is like a grotesque, smirking gargoyle set at the very top of America's skyscraping adventure in acquisition ad infinitum . . . The gargoyle's mouth is a loudspeaker, powered by the vested interest of . . . [the advertising] industry, and back of that the vested interests of business as a whole, of industry, of finance. It is never silent, it drowns out all other voices, and it suffers no rebuke, for is it not the voice of America? That is its claim and to some extent it is a just claim. For . . . generations of Americans . . . have listened to that voice as to an oracle. It has taught them how to live, what to be afraid of, what to be proud of, how to be beautiful, how to be loved, how to be envied, how to be successful. (Rorty, 1934)

As Rorty (1934) suggests, advertising has had a powerful impact on the American psyche and cultural milieu. While some contend that advertising has created the consumer mentality, others assert that, to be successful in appealing to a mass audience, advertising must simply mirror the society of the time. Whatever the cause and effect relationship may be, it is indisputable that there is an interplay of influence between advertising and American culture.

Consider, for example, the case of one of the most important icons of popular culture, Santa Claus. The story of Santa Claus has been passed down through the centuries in legend and folklore. The image of Santa, while steeped in tradition, also owes a heavy debt to commercialization. The Coca-Cola Company, which began its famous Christmas advertising in the 1920s, transformed Santa into the enduring warm, friendly, jolly, plump (and Coke-drinking) image we recognize today (Coca-Cola Company, 2002).

Indeed, the goal of much promotion is to closely tie the product to central aspects of everyday life and shared human experience. As a result, there have been $100 million stadium-naming deals that place hallmarks of American popular culture like basketball and football in the MCI Center and FedEx Field in Washington, D.C. and the United (Airlines) Center in Chicago, and nearly put Houston Astros' baseball in a new stadium named for Enron Corp., before it became the largest American company in history to file for bankruptcy (Farhi, 2001). Similarly, Fujifilm donated $7.8 million to the Smithsonian's National Zoological Park in Washington, D.C. to support the development of an exhibit, to be called the Fujifilm Giant Panda Conservation

Habitat, for two pandas from China (Fujifilm, 2000). The pandas, a major tourist as well as local attraction, share the public and media attention they receive with their corporate benefactor, who conveniently offers enamored consumers a free-plush-panda-with-Fujifilm-purchase promotion (Cohn, 2002; Fujifilm, 2002). Not to be outdone, the Eastman Kodak Company has set up an internet site to provide views of the construction of the international space station. As part of the agreement, the Russian Space Agency had two spacewalking cosmonauts replace a placard on the side of the station that displayed the Russian flag with one showing Kodak's logo (Janoff, 2001). And the list of examples goes on, from the race cars that zoom around the track for hours looking like boxes of Tide or the six-pill sample pack of Viagra, to the sports clothing and equipment logos that power athletes to victory.

Advertising and promotion have evolved to the point where the line between what can be considered strictly entertainment as opposed to what can be seen as commercial persuasion has become extremely flexible and blurred. Consequently, the traditional definition of product placement as the manipulation of features of television and movie material for commercial purposes has taken on new meaning and expanded into new media forms, such as the Internet. In addition to standard product placement, the American public is now inundated with ads masquerading as news or entertainment through infomercials, promotional music videos passed off as creative programming, and film and TV commercial tie-ins and cross-promotions, including support from the news divisions of vertically integrated entertainment companies.

The most recent incarnation of this trend is entertainment content that mimics traditional media forms but is created solely as a vehicle to promote specific advertisers–what we will term "advertainment." While the sophistication of this concept has evolved over time, there are essentially two manifestations of its use: (1) the advertisement is the entertainment, or (2) the entertainment is the advertisement. An example of the first pattern is Anheuser-Busch's Bud Bowls. Originating on TV in 1989 and then migrating to a promotional tool and internet contest, teams of bottles of Bud and Bud Light beer battled for gridiron glory, during Super Bowl commercial breaks, in ads that functioned as entertainment. The campaign was so successful that, as with the "real" main event that it paralleled and parodied, Las Vegas bookmakers set odds on the outcome and national newspapers reported the score, even on page one of *USA Today* (Russell, 2001).

A precursor to the second approach can be seen in interesting illustrations of product placements that reframe popular television shows as ads. For instance, when we are bombarded with commercials featuring Heather Locklear endorsing Preference during *Spin City*, or Katie Holmes pushing Garnier Lumia during *Dawson's Creek*, or Jessica Alba selling the virtues of Feria during *Dark Angel*, every time the actress appears in her respective program, we are primed to think of the brand of associated hair color and the character becomes a living billboard for the product. Likewise, in an ongoing deal with cellular phone maker Nokia, ABC premiered its new 2001 fall show *Alias* without commercial interruption. Nokia ads ran, however, before and after the program. Although ABC Entertainment Television Group co-chairman Stu Bloomberg asserted that there would not be blatant use of the phones ("Alias," 2001), the storyline of the premiere episode included very prominent cell phone use. In fact, the lead character's cell phone plays a pivotal role in the climactic scene in the program and is instrumental in saving her life. Even if the audience did not immediately recognize the phones as Nokia models, the placement of the two Nokia ads just before and just after the action sets the context for the program, spotlights the phones as the "stars" by clueing the viewer in to what to watch for, and cements the brand association; the product placement and sole sponsorship completely alter the meaning of the televisual text so that a viewer who saw the opening and closing Nokia ads would have a very different experience in reading the show than someone who had not seen the ads.

Thus, this essay explores the issues implicated by both versions of this form of product placement in which entertainment vehicles are created solely to spotlight specific advertisers. After briefly setting the historical context, we will examine the contemporary exemplar of this paradigm in the highly successful 1990-1998 "Sophisticated Taste" campaign for Taster's Choice instant coffee, in which viewers watched the sparks fly between the characters of Tony and Sharon in a continuing series of ads that functioned as television programming across multiple media platforms, and its most recent embodiment in advergames, online computer games that promote brands. The essay concludes by considering the nature, implications, and future of perhaps the ultimate evolution of product placement and blurring of the lines between entertainment and commercial persuasion.

THE HISTORICAL CONTEXT

To understand the place and significance of advertainment in the evolution of product placement, it is important to recognize that it is not a new phenomena. In fact, it is something of a return to the past. Elsewhere in this volume, Kathleen J. Turner discusses the role of single-sponsored programs in early radio and television broadcasting and the subsequent rise of the magazine concept involving multiple sponsors in segmented commercial participation. For our purposes, the essential point that requires consideration is the historical closeness of the link between advertising and entertainment.

In the 1920's, as advertising migrated into the new medium of radio, symbiotic business relationships developed between radio networks, advertising agencies, and sponsors to create content (Barnouw, 1970; Barnouw, 1990; Hilmes, 1997; Hilliard and Keith, 1997). At first, network programming departments originated programming and sought sponsors to support it. The NBC Program Department, for instance, placed the interests of the sponsor at the center of the program creation process: "This department secures suitable talent of known reputation and popularity, creates your program and surrounds it with announcements and atmosphere closely allied with your selling thought" (quoted in Hilmes, 1997, p. 97). Then, sponsors increasingly turned to the advertising agencies that had been handling their print ads to produce their radio programming. By the 1930s, the J. Walter Thompson Company, one of the largest and most active agencies, was producing more than thirty-three programs, representing a total of sixty hours of airtime per week, and at least half of each year's top ten shows. Moreover, the daytime schedule was filled with extremely popular serials, or soap operas, also supplied by agencies on behalf of sponsors, with nearly half of that programming coming from Blackett-Sample-Hummert alone. As a result, the agencies, which wrote the scripts, hired the performers, producers and directors, matched program types to products, and managed scheduling and marketing research, exercised dominant control and power in radio and, later, in television, too. In addition, whether the sponsors bought the airtime and/or contributed the program, the broadcast networks regarded the period to be the sponsors' property, to be used in any way they chose.

Advertising and entertainment were inextricably intertwined in the broadcast media content that resulted from this system of production. Perhaps the most prominent signal was the use of the sponsor's name in the title of programs, such as the *Maxwell House Hour*, *General Motors Family Party*, *Firestone Orchestra*, *Wrigley Revue*, *Palmolive Hour*, *Goodyear Television Playhouse*, *Kraft Television Theater*, *U.S. Steel Hour*, *Revlon Theater*, *Ford Theater*, *Colgate Comedy Hour*, *Pepsi-Cola Playhouse*, *Schlitz Playhouse of Stars*, and many more. Indeed, much programming worked to feed the success of broadcasting itself. For example, NBC was created by RCA, the world's largest distributor of radios, to develop quality programming that would drive the purchase of receivers, and the *Eveready Hour*, one of the most influential shows of the 1920s, was sponsored by radio battery-maker National Carbon Company. Likewise, sponsors preferred programs that provided them continuing identification with attractive actors, especially those willing to do commercials, and donated merchandise for quiz show prizes in exchange for the mention of their brand names.

Further, cross promotions of entertainment content between media outlets were utilized, as with the *Amos 'n' Andy* comic strip that ran in the *Chicago Daily News* as a companion to the popular show on WMAQ, the radio station owned by the newspaper, and the 10-minute *Behind the Cameras* infomercials about upcoming films that Warner Brothers inserted in the programs it produced for ABC-TV for the 1955-1956 season. In addition, promotional tie-ins were employed to great success. When Marion Davies' talk about *How I Make Up for Movies*, sponsored by cosmetic Mineralava, aired in January 1923, the thousands of listeners who wrote to request the free autographed photo of the actress offered during the program, validated the efficacy of radio as a vehicle for commercial promotion. Similarly, as a test of the value of its sponsorship of *Memory Lane*, General Petroleum issued a free edition of the newspaper from the fictional town in which the drama was set; so many listeners stopped by GP stations to get a copy (and purchased gas while they were there) that the company continued its investment in the show.

Traditional product placement within programs routinely occurred, with advertisers censoring dialogue and manipulating ideas to their advantage. Premiering in 1949, *Man Against Crime* provides a useful illustration of how the system functioned. Sponsored by Camel cigarettes, the show's writing and direction were correspondingly carefully controlled, with written directions distributed to the production team. Cigarettes were never to be associated with "bad" or disagreeable characters or plots; cigarettes were to be smoked gracefully and there was to be no suggestion of a narcotic effect; arson and fires were never to be mentioned, as they could be linked in the viewer's mind to cigarettes; no one was allowed to cough; and, since there were rumors of a forthcoming report on the health effects of smoking and doctors generally disapproved of the fictional depiction of their profession, doctor characters were to be avoided but, if absolutely necessary, they had to be portrayed in the most admirable light.

Moreover, advertisers worked to control the aura of programming, exorcising political implications, economic problems, and the distastefully "ordinary," to enhance their selling message. This powerful influence on content impacted news programming as well. The *Camel News Caravan* offers a journalistic parallel to Camel's *Man Against Crime* fiction. The newsfilms could never show shots of "no smoking" signs or of anyone smoking a cigar, except Winston Churchill, whose status on the world stage merited an exception from the cigarette company rules.

These links between advertising and entertainment content pale in comparison with the programs produced solely to spotlight specific sponsors. For instance, in 1928, at the behest of Chesebrough Manufacturing Company, NBC created *The Real Folks of Thompkins Corners*, a dramatic serial that provided "a fitting background of homely associations for 'Vaseline' products" that suggested "a quaint, simple personality to them, much in keeping with their plain old-fashioned effectiveness" (quoted in Hilmes, 1997, p. 104). In each episode, the audience eavesdropped on the "real" daily lives of Matt Thompkins, town mayor, newspaper editor, general store manager, postmaster and band leader, and his wife, Martha, who were surrounded by a cast of "typical" small-town characters and recommended myriad uses for Vaseline products as part of the plot. Whether Matt explained "how he spreads a little 'Vaseline' jelly over his face before shaving," or Martha "advise[d] Elmer to put some 'Vaseline' on that sore toe of his" (quoted in Hilmes, 1997, p. 104), the network and the sponsor believed that, because the selling message was concealed within the storyline, it would have more force and credibility than direct commercial appeals. Other advertisers saw the merit of this approach with, for example, the Log Cabin Company assuming sponsorship of *Real Folks* in 1932; the homemaker show hosted by fictional character Betty Crocker for General Mills; the *Cream of Wheat Menagerie* featuring the company's trademark black chef in a musical children's program; and the Quaker Oats-sponsored soap opera about its trademark Aunt Jemima character and her family, set on the "old Higbee plantation in Dixie–famous for miles around because of Aunt Jemima's cooking" (quoted in Hilmes, 1997, p. 80), that interwove the company's pancake mix into the plots.

As a result, the successful union of advertising and broadcasting that began in the 1920s generated an industry where advertising flourishes as entertainment, with lavish budgets, impressive talents, and its own version of the Emmy and Oscar awards. At the same time, from the culture and celebrity of salesmanship to the pervasive aura of product consciousness to the staccato, fragmented style that echoes clusters of commercials, entertainment has become advertising.

THE ADVERTISEMENT AS ENTERTAINMENT:
THE "SOPHISTICATED TASTE" OF TASTER'S CHOICE

Perhaps the ultimate contemporary exemplar of the advertisement as entertainment paradigm is the highly successful "Sophisticated Taste" campaign for Taster's Choice instant coffee. Faced with declining consumer demand for coffee, intense price competition, a small share of the market, and a fraction of the advertising budget of its competitors, Taster's Choice created a unique continuing series of ads that functioned as television programming across multiple media platforms (Kretchmer and Carveth, 1992). For eight years, from 1990-1998, viewers avidly watched the romance brew between the characters of Tony and Sharon (see Illustration 1) and wrote to the company applauding the ads. Within a year of the campaign's debut, Taster's Choice sales increased 10-12%, it became the number one selling brand of instant coffee in the United States, and, although the advertising budget decreased, the effectiveness and efficiency of the ad spending increased exponentially. The campaign became a popular culture icon, covered along with entertainment and celebrity features in the print media, such as *People* magazine; reported as news on CNN radio, the *CBS Evening News*, *Good Morning America*, and the *Today Show*; and parodied in television programming ranging from *Saturday Night Live* to *Coach*.

Premiering in November 1990 with a soap opera-style format, the series of commercials featured two single "fortysomething" neighbors who developed a relationship primarily based on their "good taste" in coffee. Over the course of 13 episodes, the sexual tension between Tony and Sharon built as they met by chance, dated, experienced jealousy, rendezvoused in Paris, and confronted the reality of Sharon's son and ex-husband, with each commercial employing Taster's Choice as the pivotal link and plot point. The campaign's denouement began on Sunday, October 26, 1997 when coffee drinkers nationwide were given the opportunity to vote for "Tony" (the neighbor) or "Andrew" (the ex-husband) by redeeming a Taster's Choice coupon/ballot in a Sunday supplement in 50 million daily newspapers across the country. The Taster's Choice insert ad proclaimed: "Who will win her undying love? Is it Andrew or Tony? Their destiny is in your hands." The viewers' choice

ILLUSTRATION 1

Taster's Choice.

The Romance Continues...

Courtesy of DeVries Public Relations, Inc.

(Tony) was then announced in the February 3, 1998 issue of *Soap Opera Digest*.

Both in the structure of the commercials and in the integrated multimedia promotional support, a number of strategies were utilized to elevate the campaign from the discourse of advertising to the discourse of entertainment. The most notable aspect of the commercials was their conscious mimicry of television programming through the use of a content-"commercial"-content format (Kretchmer and Carveth, 1992). Specifically, during each spot, viewers were introduced to the plot; the ad then shifted to a shot of the coffee being poured with the tag "Savor the Sophisticated Taste of Taster's Choice"; and then the ad resumed the plotline in conclusion. As a result, the appearance of Taster's Choice within the dramatic or content portion of the commercials operated as a standard television and film product placement, with the added benefit that the storylines demonstrated a variety of contexts in which coffee is consumed and communicated a positive attitude about Taster's Choice consumers as sophisticated, romantic, sensual beings. The original "programming" allowed the actual "commercial" to be very brief, yet brand information and product attributes were conveyed throughout, thus creating a rational appeal advertisement embedded within an emotional appeal. Paralleling entertainment program story-telling, the use of Taster's Choice within the "content" portion of the spots acknowledged and rewarded viewer participation through prior narrative dependence (Chisholm, 1991), serving as the key that reminded viewers of previous events and, especially, of what always brought the characters of Tony and Sharon together.

Further, the appropriation of the soap opera format turned a popular entertainment genre that had been merely a vehicle for promotion into a commercial genre used to make the appeal for the product directly. In addition, continuity in terms of color tones, filming, and mood was maintained between the "content" and "commercial" segments so that the "commercial" did not seem nearly as intrusive as the usual televi-sion ad. In fact, the curiosity generated by the serial format, as well as the entire promotional effort that surrounded the television ads, led to a consumer-instigated search for entertainment and emotional gratifica-tion via the commercials. Thus, rather than the typical commercial "event to avoid," the Taster's Choice ads were eagerly "chosen or in-vited in people's lives" (Gunther and Thorson, 1992, p. 577).

Self-referencing through cross-media executions reinforced the "So-phisticated Taste" advertising campaign's status as entertainment. For example, print ads designed like standard program promotions appeared in *TV Guide* to alert the audience when new Taster's Choice spots were to air during upcoming shows. Moreover, the *TV Guide* promotions suggested that the advertisements and the entertainment programming had comparable qualities and, consequently, that viewing the commer-cials was of equal or perhaps greater importance than viewing the tele-vision show: "Romance. Action. Adventure. Suspense. (Indiana Jones will also be on)." Similarly, the association between the commercials and entertainment soap operas was enhanced by the placement of ads supporting the campaign in *Episodes*, ABC's bimonthly soap opera magazine with a circulation of over a million, and on ABC's two soap opera 900-numbers. The Taster's Choice campaign further integrated executions to mirror entertainment program promotion through print media interviews and appearances on network morning shows by the "stars" who portrayed Tony and Sharon; adulatory articles in the news media that encouraged the public to talk and think about the ads; sponsorship of the MGM/UA 50th Anniversary commemorative edition of *Casablanca* on home video, with a Taster's Choice vignette at the beginning of the tape; and various contests and surveys tied to the commercials, including a "Most Romantic First Date" essay contest assignment and survey, that solicited and reinforced the audience's vicarious participation in Tony and Sharon's romance and were cross-promoted in newspaper Sunday Supplements, magazine ads and advertorials, in-store merchandising, and four different television vignettes that aired on ABC, featuring popular stars from each of ABC's soap operas. As such, the interactive effects of all the Taster's Choice "Sophisticated Taste" campaign-related communications strikingly transformed advertising into entertainment, allowing the television commercials to stand alone as complete entities, heightening consumer involvement and attention to the product, and transitioning from a product-as-commodity orientation to the use of advertising as an added-value, intangible brand benefit.

ENTERTAINMENT AS ADVERTISEMENT: THE NEW CYBERWORLD OF ADVERGAMES

The second form of advertainment that we will consider involves entertainment that functions as an advertisement. The most recent embodiment of this paradigm is advergames, online computer games that promote brands. Many companies have begun to use the Internet as part of their marketing mix. Banner ads were highly touted, but have produced a mere .5% click-through rate and, in general, most web surfers spend only 60 seconds at an average site and browse about nine in an online session (March, 2001). In response, advertisers have tried to make the online experience more entertaining. For instance, Levi's, Polaroid, and BMW created online short films that feature their products; Subaru of America added an outdoor life section to its web site, with information and events about the organizations and activities that interest their owners; and NASCAR.com developed a weekly animated dramedy web series that explores the world of professional stock car racing through the lives of a family that race the circuit.

Yet, a fairly new approach, advergaming, appears to offer the greatest promise for success. Games are the fastest growing segment of online entertainment, increasing 25% per year and surpassing total movie box office revenues (YaYa, 2002a). In 2002, 45 million people are expected to play online games, jumping to a projected 73 million in 2004. Game sites are 8 of the top 10 entertainment destinations on the Internet. Online gamers play for an average of 13 hours per week, which is greater than the amount of time spent reading newspapers or magazines and about equivalent to the time spent watching TV. The session length in gaming areas averages 28 minutes, or four times the general site average, and click-through rates have reached as high as 30% (Blockdot, 2001). Plus, 50% of online gamers are women, while 73% of computer gamers are over 18 years of age and 42% are over 35. Thus, games offer advertisers a powerful and dynamic medium to engage consumers, build brand interactivity, drive traffic, and capture market information in the guise of entertainment. As YaYa, one of the pioneers of this new media form, explains, the purpose of advergaming is to "expose consumers to products by engaging them in an addictive game-play experience while simultaneously reinforcing a positive brand impression" (YaYa, 2002b).

In the past, video games specialized in standard but virtual product placement. In contrast, the new generation of advergames crafts the entire entertainment experience around the sponsor's brand. Moreover, advergames, such as "Pepsi Racing" (see Illustration 2), can allow players to select a character for game play, thereby enabling consumer psychographic, as well as demographic, data collection. The 3-D console-quality advergames can be played on a web site, or distributed via e-mail in a message, sent to targeted demographics, that launches the game and promotes "viral compounding," the spreading of a promotion from one individual to another that capitalizes on the player's competitive spirit (e.g., sending a challenge to beat one's game score) or collaborative nature (e.g., invitation to join a multi-player game).

Although the advertising message is always central to game play, the level of brand immersion can vary from associative, to illustrative, to demonstrative. Advergaming can "drive brand awareness by associating the product with the lifestyle or activity featured in the game," "prominently feature the product itself in game play," or "leverage the full arsenal of interactivity by allowing the consumer to experience the product within the virtual confines of the gaming space" (Chen and Ringel, 2001). The "Dodge Speedway" game, for instance, is both associative and illustrative, with revving engines and throbbing music that puts the player behind the wheel of a virtual Dodge-sponsored stock car in a NASCAR race where every advertisement along the track's walls is for Dodge cars. Likewise, Proctor & Gamble's "Mission Refresh"

ILLUSTRATION 2

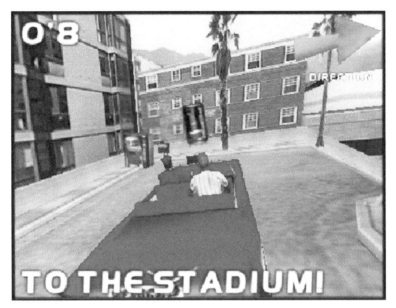

Courtesy of YaYa

invites players to help Captain Cool eradicate dandruff creatures with bubbles and bottles of Head & Shoulders shampoo. The "GM eMotion Challenge" exemplifies a demonstrative game; while players calibrate the virtual GM cars to perform better in different weather and terrain environments and work their way up from a Cavalier to a Corvette, the advergame teaches consumers about a new high-tech engine and transmission control system, called eMotion, available in its latest models. Similarly, "Spinopolis" (see Illustration 3), a trivia game, tests the player's knowledge of Siemens core businesses and enhances perceptions of their leadership role.

The success of advergames across a broad range of products is phenomenal–retention rates 10 times greater than for broadcast commercials, 16-45% of recipients play games received via promotional e-mail for an average of 25 minutes, 400% viral compounding with 90% of those who receive the pass-along e-mail responding (Pintak, 2001; Rodgers, 2002). In addition, advergames, whether for LifeSavers, or BBC America, or Miller Lite, build relationships between consumers

ILLUSTRATION 3

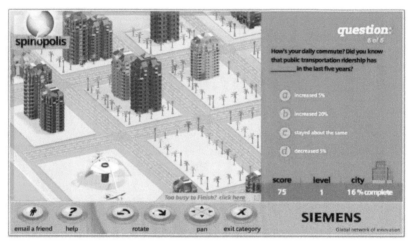

Courtesy of YaYa

and products by transferring the emotion of the game to the brand that is powering it and creating an engaging, rather than passive, experience. Conceived as entertainment and transformed into advertising, adver-games are being heralded as the future of promotion and are ensuring the continuation of the entertainment-advertising nexus in the new digital world of cyberspace.

CONCLUSION

In summary, from the beginnings of broadcasting to the forefront of Internet frontiers, entertainment and commercial persuasion have become intimately linked and, consequently, traditional product placement has taken on new meaning and force. The most recent and notable exemplar of this trend is entertainment content that mimics traditional media forms but is created solely as a vehicle to promote specific advertisers. This advertisement, as we have seen, can manifest as advertisements that function as entertainment, or entertainment that acts as an advertisement.

The entertainment-advertisement paradigm continues to grow. In television, for example, a new venture called Shine:M, led by the daughter of News Corp. chairman Rupert Murdoch, is planning to create and produce network series programming with advertising features fundamentally integrated into the content to "provide a new way for advertisers to connect with their consumers, by articulating their brand values through editorial content and creating platforms upon which they can extend their effectiveness" (Consoli, 2001). Online, with games as the enticement, marketers are working to initiate customer interaction that allows them to build and leverage databases to craft ongoing relationships with consumers.

All of the advertainment strategies–forging emotional, engaging connections with consumers, gaining "mindshare," advertisements appearing in the guise of entertainment, concealing selling messages within storylines, cultivating addictive game-play, turning consumers into instruments of viral brand advocacy–raise serious questions about the nature of this form of product placement and its implications for the American psyche and cultural milieu.

Critics have expressed concerns about subliminal persuasion, a general sense that advertising is ever more pervasive, and the dangers of overexposing unsuspecting youth to commercial messages. These are key issues that must be addressed as the targeting is clear. Consider the comments of the account director for the agency that handles Capncrunch.com for client Quaker Oats: "With kids, if you build a good (adver)game, you create a positive brand perception . . . If you can simply establish the brand as being cool and relevant you've cleared a major, major hurdle"; note that the web site captures names and e-mail addresses during registration and tracks consumer behavior and product preferences (Pintak, 2001).

Similarly, the Burger King "Rugrats in Paris: The Movie" racing game (see Illustration 4) was created in conjunction with the release of the film of the same name and challenged players to drive a character from the popular Nickelodeon cartoon show around the track without being captured by the Reptar monster from the series. Special toy watches available for children in Burger King restaurants contained a secret code that could be entered during the advergame for extra points. The reported results included eight minutes of brand immersion and high percentages of game players who had visited Burger King to obtain the secret code (YaYa, 2002c). Nevertheless, it is important to remember that these kinds of concerns are not new or unique in a media environment in which toymakers and merchandisers dominate Saturday morning TV programming blocks and *Harry Potter and the Sorcerer's Stone* sparks sales of everything from children's eyeglasses to the "junk beverages" manufactured by Coca-Cola, the movie's promotional partner.

ILLUSTRATION 4

Courtesy of YaYa

Perhaps the most troubling twist on advergaming is the use of freely-available open-source game software designed by commercial advergame pioneer Wild Tangent by Resistance Records, an arm of the National Alliance neo-Nazi group, to create "Ethnic Cleansing," a CD-ROM computer game that transforms racially motivated hatred and violence into entertainment (ADL, 2002). The object of "Ethnic Cleansing" is for the player, who can choose to wear virtual KKK robes or Skinhead attire, to patrol the streets and subways of a decimated city and kill "predatory sub-human" Blacks and Latinos and their Jewish "masters," who are portrayed as the personification of evil, to "save" the white world. The game features racist characterizations and slurs augmented with various National Alliance signs and racist rock music blaring on the soundtrack. As such, in the new media age, the "product placement" at this nexus of entertainment and advertising points to the crucial need for new media criticism and literacy to focus on the selling of ideas as well as the selling of commodities.

REFERENCES

"Alias" to premiere commercial-free (2001, July 22). Tribune Media Services. Available online at: *http://tv.zap2it.com/news/tvnewsdaily.html?19417.*

Anti-Defamation League (ADL) (2002). Racist groups using computer gaming to promote violence against Blacks, Latinos and Jews. Available online at: *http://www.adl.org/videogames/videogames_print.asp.*

Barnouw, E. (1990). *Tube of Plenty: The Evolution of American Television*, 2nd revised edition. New York: Oxford University Press.

Barnouw, E. (1970). *The Image Empire: A History of Broadcasting in the United States. Volume III: From 1953.* New York: Oxford University Press.

Blockdot (2001). Advergaming 101. Available online at: *http://www.blockdot.com/advergaming/stats.cfm.*

Chen, J., and Ringel, M. (2001). Can advergaming be the future of interactive advertising? <kpe> Fast Forward. Available online at: *http://www.kpe.com.*

Chisholm, B. (1991). Difficult viewing: The pleasures of complex screen narratives. *Critical Studies in Mass Communication, 8*, 389-403.

Coca-Cola Company (2002). Coca-Cola and Santa Claus. Available online at: *http://www2.coca-cola.com/ourcompany/cokelore_santa_include.html.*

Cohn, D. (2002, January 10). After a year, it's still panda-monium at the zoo. *Washington Post.* Available online at: *http://www.washingtonpost.com/wp-dyn/articles/A25866-2002Jan10.html.*

Consoli, J. (2001, November 5). For advertisers, it's showtime. *Mediaweek.* Available online at: *http://www.mediaweek.com/mediaweek/daily_news/print/article_display.jsp?vnu_content_id=1096111.*

Farhi, P. (2001, December 30). It's a whole new ballgame: Shaky economy hampers sports leagues, teams. *Washington Post*, A1.

Fujifilm (2002, January). Free offer! Plush panda with Fujifilm purchase. Available online at: *http://64.7.7.225/plushpanda/.*

Fujifilm (2000, December 18). Fuji Photo Film U.S.A., Inc., celebrates 35th anniversary in America. Available online at: *http://www.fujifilm.com/JSP/fuji/epartners/PressCenterDetail.jsp?DBID=NEWS_464779.*

Gunther, A., and Thorson, E. (1992). Perceived persuasive effects of product commercials and public service announcements. *Communication Research, 19*, 574-596.

Hilliard, R. L., and Keith, M. C. (1997). *The Broadcast Century: A Biography of American Broadcasting*, 2nd edition. Boston: Focal Press.

Hilmes, M. (1997). *Radio Voices: American Broadcasting, 1922-1952.* Minneapolis: University of Minnesota Press.

Janoff, B. (2001, October 16). Kodak tries other-worldly campaign. *Mediaweek.* Available online at: *http://www.mediaweek.com/mediaweek/daily_news/article_display.jsp?vnu_content_id=1080590.*

Kretchmer, S., and Carveth, R. (1992, August). Romancing the coffee: New trends in contemporary advertising. Paper presented at the Annual Convention of the Association for Education in Journalism and Mass Communication Annual Convention, Montreal, Canada.

March, T. (2001, Spring). How to bag the elusive human attention span. *Digitrends*. Available online at: *http://www.digitrends.net/marketing/13639_16525.html*.

Pintak, L. (2001, May 23). It's not only a game: Advergaming set to become a billion dollar industry. *TurboAds.com*. Available online at: *http://www.turboads.com/ richmedia_news/2001rmn/rmn20010523.shtml*.

Rodgers, A. L. (2002, January). Game theory. *FastCompany.com*. Available online at: *http://www.fastcompany.com/build/build_feature/yaya.html*.

Rorty, J. (1934). *Our Master's Voice: Advertising*. New York: John Day.

Russell, D. (2001, January 26). Time in a bottle: A bleary-eyed look back at Bud Bowls. *Daily News* (Philadelphia). Available online at: *http://dailynews.philly. com/content/daily_news/2001/01/26/features/FJOE26.htm*.

YaYa (2002a). Why games? Available online at: *http://www.yaya.com/why/index_ why.html*.

YaYa (2002b). YaYa creates viral internet games that build brands and drive revenue. YaYa online press kit. Available online at: *http://reports.yaya.com/presskit.pdf*.

YaYa (2002c). Case studies. Available online at: *http://www.yaya.com/clients/index_ clients.html*.

Merchandising
in the Major Motion Picture Industry:
Creating Brand Synergy
and Revenue Streams

Charles A. Lubbers
William J. Adams

SUMMARY. To help guarantee a profit in a very risky industry, major motion picture studios have dramatically increased movie production and marketing budgets. While advertising is the traditional emphasis in the movie marketing mix, in recent years the budget for promotion has equaled the advertising budgets. This essay discusses two areas of movie promotion that studios have increasingly turned to for additional revenues: merchandising and promotional/partner tie-ins. These two elements of the promotion mix generate billions of dollars in revenue for studios each year, but they are generally overlooked by the general population and academic researchers. *[Article copies available for a fee from The Haworth Document Delivery Service: 1-800-HAWORTH. E-mail address:*

Charles A. Lubbers (PhD, University of Nebraska) is Associate Professor in, and Chair of, the Public Relations Sequence, A. Q. Miller School of Journalism and Mass Communications, 105 Kedzie Hall, Kansas State University, Manhattan, KS 66506-1501 (E-mail: lubbers@ksu.edu). William J. Adams (PhD, University of Indiana) is Associate Professor of Radio-Television in the same institution (E-mail: wadams@ksu.edu).

[Haworth co-indexing entry note]: "Merchandising in the Major Motion Picture Industry: Creating Brand Synergy and Revenue Streams." Lubbers, Charles A., and William J. Adams. Co-published simultaneously in *Journal of Promotion Management* (Best Business Books, an imprint of The Haworth Press, Inc.) Vol. 10, No. 1/2, 2004, pp. 55-63; and: *Handbook of Product Placement in the Mass Media: New Strategies in Marketing Theory, Practice, Trends, and Ethics* (ed: Mary-Lou Galician) Best Business Books, an imprint of The Haworth Press, Inc., 2004, pp. 55-63. Single or multiple copies of this article are available for a fee from The Haworth Document Delivery Service [1-800-HAWORTH, 9:00 a.m. - 5:00 p.m. (EST). E-mail address: docdelivery@haworthpress.com].

Digital Object Identifier: 10.1300/J057v10n01_05   *55*

<docdelivery@haworthpress.com> Website: <http://www.HaworthPress.com>
© 2004 by The Haworth Press, Inc. All rights reserved.]

KEYWORDS. Brand, economics, films, licensing, merchandising, motion picture industry, movies, product placement, promotion

INTRODUCTION

Sony spent $125 million to make *Godzilla*. Is it any good? Does it really matter? The studio has marshaled another $200 million to invade the public's imagination and make sure the movie's a hit. . . . 'Size does matter' is the slogan that Sony is using to promote its big summer release, *Godzilla*, but you already knew that. Indeed, you may not even have noticed, but you've probably seen the slogan three or four times today, given that it's been plastered on billboards and buses, buttons and T-shirts, caps and toys, batteries and Taco Bells, saturating the public consciousness like a deceased princess. (Carvell, 1998, p. 162)

Godzilla is one of numerous examples every year of movies with large production costs and equally massive marketing efforts. Carvell's quote above provides examples of the two major areas of movie marketing–advertising and promotion. While advertising has received some attention from scholars (for example, Zufryden, 1996), little attention has been paid to the growing importance of movie promotion through merchandising and promotional/corporate tie-ins.

Sony's efforts for *Godzilla* are consistent with the rapid increases in movie costs. Jack Valenti, head of the Motion Picture Association of America, noted that movie budgets in 1997 averaged a record $75.6 million (Schatz, 1999). Earnest (1985, p. 4) notes that, "In an age of rapidly spiraling media costs, it is now the rule-of-thumb that media expenditures to launch a motion picture average two-thirds the cost of the movie. The break-even point is calculated as 2.5 times the cost of production." Zufryden (1996, p. 29) notes that "Marketing costs for domestic movie releases have more than quadrupled in the last 15 years and averaged nearly $18 million dollars per film in 1995." Carvell (1998) added that just two years later, 1997, marketing costs had increased to an average of $22 million.

Promotion is an element of the overall marketing efforts for a movie. Two other major elements of the marketing efforts are advertising and distribution. While advertising has been the traditional mainstay of movie marketing efforts, recent trends have seen a growth in promotion to the point where it is becoming as important as advertising. In 1997, Friedman observed that "some analysts say annual promotional dollars for movies could at least equal that of studio movie advertising. That means more than $4 billion per year" (p. 38).

Carvell (1998) notes that to create public awareness of *Godzilla,* Sony spent an estimated $50 million in marketing and its promotional partners have committed an additional $150 million. These promotion figures lead one to wonder why a major studio, such as Sony, and its partners would commit over $300 million to a gamble that may or may not appeal to the public. The answer is simple, one major hit can mean the survival of the studio. Baird (1999) says major studios try to get one massive hit each year. A major hit like *Titanic* or *Forest Gump* is known as a tent-pole movie because it can hold up everything else at the studio. One financial success can support other box office failures. Carvell (1998) notes that increasing marketing expenditures is a gamble, but the rewards are commensurate: "The profits from licensing, spinoffs, TV sales, sequels, and merchandising from a smash–a *Lion King*, a *Batman*, a *Jurassic Park*–can easily top $1 billion."

The increase in production and marketing costs has meant that revenue must be generated from sources other than box office receipts. Decades ago, a movie garnered most of its revenue from a traditional system that began with the first-run box office revenues and were followed by revenues from second runs, television and overseas distribution. The growth (primarily in the 1980s) of the videocassette recorder and cable television ushered in new profit potential. However, the growing revenue opportunities through alternative distribution of the movie was not sufficient to help guarantee success. As a result, alternative revenue generation opportunities (including product placement, merchandising, licensing, and promotional partners) received greater attention.

A tent-pole movie can create the entertainment industry version of corporate synergy. "Synergy" is a buzzword in business circles. The general idea of the concept is to have all the parts of an organization working in unison to achieve an overriding goal–usually a profit. Nowhere is synergy more apparent than in the movie industry. The role of product placement has been discussed by others in this work. The remainder of this essay discusses the role of merchandising and the associated promotional tie-ins. For a more complete discussion of movie promotions, see Lubbers and Adams (2001).

MERCHANDISING

Merchandising involves creating or licensing others to create merchandise that is based upon the movie. While most moviegoers pay little attention to this aspect of modern movie promotion, it offers large financial rewards for studios and their licensees. Countless examples of merchandising exist, but perhaps no organization does it better than Disney, which produced 186 items of merchandise associated with the movie, *The Lion King* (*Business*, 1998).

The recent release of the first *Harry Potter* movie offers additional insight into the scale of merchandising associated with major movies. Warner Brothers owns the movie, merchandising and other media rights to the four *Harry Potter* books that have already been written. According to Jardine (2001), some industry estimates are that *Potter* merchandising may be worth $1 billion, including a $95 million deal with Coca-Cola. Other licensing agreements include deals with major corporations, such as Sears Roebuck & Co. as a principal retail partner, toy licensee Mattel, and Electronic Arts videogames (Dolbow, 2001).

Licensing other organizations to produce merchandise is a major portion of the activity in merchandising. Desjardins (2001, p. 4) noted that characters from the entertainment industry "are the driving force in a licensing industry that generated more than $5.8 billion in revenue in 2000." Charles Riotto, President of the Licensing Industry Merchandisers' Association (LIMA), noted at the opening of the annual International Licensing Show that "Entertainment and character licensing continued to be the strongest category last year, generating nearly $2.6 billion in royalty revenue to property owners" (Desjardins, 2001, p. 4). A study reported that licensing revenues in 2000 increased to $5.847 billion. Entertainment characters accounted for 44.3% of the market share with trademarks/brands and fashions a distant second with 16.8% (Desjardins, 2001).

Chris Dixon, an analyst at PaineWebber in New York, says that these new media organizations no longer just make films or books, now "'they make brands.' The brand is a lump of content–such as . . . Time Warner's *Batman* or Viacom's *Rugrats*–which can be exploited through film, broadcast and cable television, publishing, theme parks, music, the Internet and merchandising" (*Business*, 1998, p. 57). Soter (1992) noted that while the movie *Batman* earned its then-owner, Warner Brothers, $251.1 million in its initial theatrical release, "Warner was able to double that–earning an additional $500 million–from the sale of licensed t-shirts, coffee mugs, soundtrack albums, cereal and other gimmicks tied into the movie" (p. 10).

In another example, Freeman (1999) says that public demand for movie soundtracks has led to a new Hollywood profit center. The proof is in the numbers. In 1998, of the 711 million units of music sold in the United States, 61 million (8.6%) were soundtracks. Additionally, two of the top ten albums of the year were soundtracks (Freeman, 1999).

While merchandising appears to be a great asset to the studio's bottom line, the same cannot be said for all the merchandise licensees. In fact, licensees for *Harry Potter* merchandise were waiting patiently to determine if *Potter* merchandise would sell. Licensees worry that they ". . . put up extremely high guarantees and fees for a phenomenon that may not in fact be such a huge hit, thus leaving them in the red" (Dolbow, 2001, p. 1).

Friedman (1999) notes that after toy ventures for *Godzilla* and *Babe II* were flops, that major toy licensee, Equity Marketing, is getting out of show business merchandise. David Lieboweitz of Burnham Securities offers a concise reason for Equity Marketing's failures, "if you don't succeed on the silver screen, it's very hard to have merchandise jump off the shelves" (Friedman, 1999).

Finnigan (2001, June 11) says that humbled major movie studios are trimming their licensing staffs and paying more attention to the licensees after a period with no major big hits for licensees. Finnigan quotes Peter Byrne, new head of licensing and merchandising at 20th Century Fox, as saying that the retail trade in theatrical merchandise is getting tougher.

Fox's leaner licensing division is emblematic of staff reductions that have recently befallen Disney, Universal Pictures and Warner Bros., all once possessing over-populated licensing units that failed to deliver on expectation. Movie merchandise did not move nearly fast enough off Disney and Warner Bros. studio store shelves, with a disappointing run stringing from *Batman Returns* and *Hercules* (1997) to *Wild Wild West* (1999) followed by *101 Dalmatians*, and even the more recent and highly anticipated *Harry Potter and the Sorcerer's Stone*. Many argue that Warner stores also carried too much licensed stuff on relatively obscure Looney Tunes characters such as Foghorn Leghorn.

The current trend in the licensing arena can best be described as one of caution. Desjardins (2001) notes that after the success of *Lion King* merchandise in 1994 other studios jumped on the bandwagon. Very quickly the market became flooded with merchandise that led to a string of merchandising failures. Studios are now being more selective in the number of licensees and the amount of merchandise placed into the market. The largest merchandising story for 2001, *Harry Potter*, had 85 licensees. While this is a large number, it is approximately one-half the number of licensees for some of the *Batman* films in the 1990s.

In addition to reducing the number of licensees, studios are being more selective about the amount of merchandise distributed. Al Ovadia, Executive Vice President of Sony Pictures Consumer Products said "The reality is that the marketplace has changed. Now, the idea is to put a reasonable amount of product out there and make sure none of the categories overlap or get confused with others" (Desjardins, 2001, p. 33).

In his article on the decline in licensed toy sales associated with movies, Lacter (2001) notes that many of the merchandising flops after *The Lion King* illustrate the risk of taking on a movie license. The risks include both royalty fees for up to 20% and minimum guarantees based on revenue projections.

PROMOTIONAL TIE-INS/PARTNERS

Closely allied to merchandising is the use of promotional tie-ins. Such tie-ins are partnerships developed with other organizations that are designed to promote both of the organizations. Friedman (1997, p. 37) says that, "the summer traditionally brings out the heavyweight dollars when it comes to tie-in promotions." He adds that ". . . industry estimates are that $750 million to $1.5 billion in consumer promotions will be tied-into movies between Memorial Day and Labor Day."

While summer is the traditional season for tie-ins, the holiday season is another major period for movie release and tie-in activity. The 2000-2001 holiday season saw the success of a major motion picture with several new and unique promotional tie-ins. Beth Goss, Senior Vice President of Promotions for Universal Pictures, led the studio's promotions of *How the Grinch Stole Christmas*, the previous last year's top movie. Part of the marketing success came from her efforts to attract blue-chip tie-in partners and her success at uncovering unseen opportunities (Podmolik, 2001). Finnigan (2001, March 26) summarizes the tie-ins for *The Grinch*. "It was Goss . . . who sent *Grinch* on a trajectory to earn more than $260 million in worldwide box office to date via a Santa's bag of partnerships with Kellogg's, Sprite, Nabisco, Hershey and Wendy's. Together with Universal and Imagine Entertainment, the partners combined on some $75 million in marketing support that sprayed more than 105 million packages of Ritz Bits, Oreos, Chips Ahoy!, Fruit Loops, Apple Jacks and Frosted Flakes with movie graphics, and saw the grinning title character peer out from millions of green cans of Sprite, which spent $10 million in ads and merchandising behind its first movie promotion."

In addition to convincing Sprite to participate in its first-ever movie promotion, Goss is credited with finding new venues for promotional tie-ins. The most impressive may have been her agreement with the U.S. Postal Service to identify the Grinch's fictional town of Whoville with cancellation stamps reading "Happy Who-lidays from the U.S. Postal Service" on over 6 billion pieces of holiday mail (Finnigan, 2001, March 26).

Product tie-ins are most common between film studios and fast food or beverage companies. For example, Richard Taylor, Vice President of Marketing Services for Burger King, says that Burger King's tie-in with the first *Rugrats* movie led to significant increases in kids' meal sales (Play Food, 1999). This success follows an earlier successful tie-in with the movie, *The Lion King*. The eight-week Burger King-*Lion King* promotional tie-in, ". . . gets scored as one of the most profitable events in BK history: total customer traffic up 19%; kids' meal unit volume up 25% and sales up 10%; and a whopping 50 million premiums blown out the doors" (Benezra, 1995).

There is no guarantee that the relationship between promotional partners will be harmonious or will be beneficial for all parties involved. Studios often have rules for the promotional tie-in, which bind or limit the type of marketing done by their partner. One example of this was Sony's Tristar studio's requirement that Taco Bell or any of their other partners not actually show what *Godzilla* would look like before the release of the movie.

Kaeter (1998) notes that Taco Bell was able to build a successful promotional campaign within the bounds of their agreement. She also notes that even though the movie *Godzilla* had lackluster ticket sales, the Taco Bell tie-in was very effective. The same can be said of Subway's tie-in promotion with the movie *Coneheads* in 1994 (Stanley, 1995). In this case, the film's popularity was not tied to the promotion's success. Stanley notes, "marketers at some of the largest fast-food chains and package-goods companies across the country relate similar experiences: even though the films they partnered with were duds, their associated promos were not" (p. 21).

While the risks are clear, major brands continue to take the gamble. PepsiCo's 1999 $1.25 billion deal with Lucasfilm is the largest worldwide promotion deal. It is only reasonable that the largest promotional deal would be for a new movie in the *Star Wars* series, since sequels (and by their nature–prequels) are considered more of a "sure-thing" (Miller, 2000).

SUMMARY

As major movie studios have been taken over by larger corporate parents, the need to show continuous and significant profit has become even more important. This trend occurred as movies became even more expensive to create and to market. Movie studios have attempted to bolster their bottom lines by generating new lines of revenue. While product placement can reduce the costs of production, as well as adding revenue and "realism" to the movie, it is not sufficient to offset the large increase in costs. With greater frequency, studios are turning to merchandising and promotional tie-ins. Merchandising bolsters the bottom line and helps to establish a product brand. Promotional tie-ins create awareness that increase box office revenues and support the merchandising efforts.

REFERENCES

Baird, R. (1999, January 21). Head for the hills. *Marketing Week, 21*(45), 26-29.
Benezra, K. (1995, March 20). Burger King/*The Lion King. BrandWeek, 36*, 21-22.
Business: Size does matter. (1998, May 23). *Economist, 347* (8069), 57-59.
Carvell, T. (1998, June 8). How Sony created a monster. *Fortune, 137*(11), 162-170.
Desjardins, D. (2001, July 9). Popularized entertainment icons continue to dominate licensing. *Dsn Retailing Today, 40*(13), 4, 43.
Desjardins, D. (2001, June 4). Studio approach to licensees puts quality before quantity. *Dsn Retailing Today, 40*(11), 33, 40.
Dolbow, S. (2001, June 11). Wary over Harry. *Brandweek, 42*(24), 1, 10.
Earnest, O. J. (1985). *Star Wars*: A case study of motion picture marketing. In Bruce A. Austin, editor, *Current Research in Film: Audiences, Economics and Law, Volume 1*. Norwood, NJ: Ablex Publishing Corporation, 1-18.
Finnigan, D. (2001, June 11). Hollywood gets humble. *Brandweek, 42*(24), 28-34.
Finnigan, D. (2001, March 26). Marketers of the next generation: Beth Goss. *Brandweek, 42*(13), 32.
Freeman, L. (1999, February 1). Soundtracks send loud message to bottom line. *Advertising Age, 70*(5), S12.

Friedman, W. (1999, January 11). Saying goodbye to Hollywood. *Advertising Age, 70*(2), 12.

Friedman, W. (1997, May 19). Films for all seasons. *BrandWeek, 38*(20), 37-46.

Jardine, A. (2001, November 15). Marketing magic. *Marketing, 20,* 20.

Kaeter, M. (1998). Moviemaker's strings didn't tie Taco Bell down. *Potentials in Marketing, 31*(8), 10.

Lacter, M. (2001, February 5). Trouble in toyland. *Forbes,* 98-99.

Lubbers, C. A. & Adams, W. J. (2001). Promotional strategies utilized by the film industry: Theatrical movies as product. *Journal of Promotion Management, 6*(1/2), 161-180.

Miller, R. (2000, January 20). The box office retains its draw. *Marketing,* 19-20.

Play food. (1999, January 15). *Restaurants and Institutions, 109*(2), 16.

Podmolik, M. E. (2001, March 26). *Grinch* nothing but smiles for Universal. *Advertising Age, 72*(13), S18.

Schatz, T. (1999, April 5/12). Show me the money: In search of hits, the industry may go broke. *The Nation, 268*(13), 26-31.

Soter, T. (1992). At the movies: Marketing lessons from tinseltown. *Management Review, 81*(11), 10-15.

Stanley, T. L. (1995, January 30). Movie goes bust . . . Promo goes boom. *BrandWeek, 36*(5), 20-24.

Zufryden, F. S. (1996). Linking advertising to box office performance of new film releases: A marketing planning model. *Journal of Advertising Research, 36*(4), 29-41.

The Extensions of Synergy: Product Placement Through Theming and Environmental Simulacra

Scott Robert Olson

SUMMARY. Building brand identity becomes more difficult in a media-saturated culture, making it difficult to get a commercial message through to its audience, and requiring marketers to develop evermore omnipresent devices for reaching consumers. Corporations use synergy as a way of conveying consistent brand messages through multiple venues. Those venues have expanded beyond our conventional notions of the mass media, however, and increasingly rely on physical environments such as theme parks, casinos, and even residential communities to communicate and reinforce brand messages. These places, artificially constructed *environmental simulacra*, obscure the distinctions normally made between the cinematic world and the real world. The transformation of space into a new advertising medium has significant cultural implications. *[Article copies available for a fee from The Haworth Document Delivery Service: 1-800-HAWORTH. E-mail address: <docdelivery@haworthpress. com> Website: <http://www.HaworthPress.com> © 2004 by The Haworth Press, Inc. All rights reserved.]*

Scott Robert Olson (PhD, Northwestern) is Vice President for Academic Affairs at Minnesota State University-Mankato, 315 Wigley Administration Center, Mankato, MN 56001 (E-mail: scott.olson@mnsu.edu).

[Haworth co-indexing entry note]: "The Extensions of Synergy: Product Placement Through Theming and Environmental Simulacra." Olson, Scott Robert. Co-published simultaneously in *Journal of Promotion Management* (Best Business Books, an imprint of The Haworth Press, Inc.) Vol. 10, No. 1/2, 2004, pp. 65-87; and: *Handbook of Product Placement in the Mass Media: New Strategies in Marketing Theory, Practice, Trends, and Ethics* (ed: Mary-Lou Galician) Best Business Books, an imprint of The Haworth Press, Inc., 2004, pp. 65-87. Single or multiple copies of this article are available for a fee from The Haworth Document Delivery Service [1-800-HAWORTH, 9:00 a.m. - 5:00 p.m. (EST). E-mail address: docdelivery@haworthpress. com].

KEYWORDS. Advertising, brand, marketing, movies, product placement, simulacra, synergy, television

INTRODUCTION

Illusion is no longer possible, because the real is no longer possible. (Baudrillard, 1983, p. 38)

Critics of product placement often focus on the artificial world
of logos and consumption it creates in movies and television shows
that employ the practice. Mark Crispin Miller, for example, claims
in the documentary video *Behind the Screens: Hollywood Goes Hypercommercial* (Soar, 2000) that "there's a very big difference between a
world of products that looks like the world we live in, and the world of
products that's based on placement." The idea that advertising somehow is far removed from the real world is a reassuring bromide, but unfortunately the world we live in is coming to resemble the world of
product placement. The reason for this is that media companies are extending placement beyond the movie screen and into the environments
we inhabit. This blurring of the distinction between real and artificial
space and between commercialized and non-commercialized environments is an advanced stage of corporate strategy, the extension of synergy. The danger of this strategy is that it compromises our ability to
separate the real from the artificial. In order to understand the effect
of this new advertising medium on U.S. culture, it is important to understand synergy and two of its strategies: theming and environmental
simulacra.

SYNERGY

Synergy is the practice among media conglomerates of using one
medium to promote products in another, using each to sell the other.
Synergy is the prima facie logic behind corporate consolidation and
mergers, and is for the most part admired by Wall Street. It works like
this: because of its broad media holdings, the Disney Company can
cross-promote a product like *The Lion King* in cinemas, on the ABC
television network, in Disney Stores, on CD records, in video games, on
the Broadway stage, and in magazines. AOL Time Warner, the biggest
media conglomerate in the world, displayed one of the most coordi-

nated synergy-exploiting roll-outs of a product by promoting the Warner Brothers film *Harry Potter and the Sorcerer's Stone* (Crowe, 2001) on the cover of *Time* and *Entertainment Weekly* magazines, on the Cable News Network, through albums on Warner Bros. Records, and through the America Online Internet service. All of these outlets exist within a single corporate umbrella. Placing the film *Harry Potter* as a consumable product in *other* media created an unprecedented blockbuster that earned $116 million in its first week of release (*Variety Box Office*, 2001), rivaled the film *Titanic* for overall box office, and became "the acme of corporate synergy" (Harris and Dawtrey, 2001). Each medium helps sell the other.

There is some reassurance, however, in the knowledge that these are, after all, just items in the media. Each is just a media product. Each is something we can buy or not buy, watch or turn off, and not something inescapable, not something which surrounds us and seems natural or real. So far, consumers can hold them at bay. This may be changing: advertisers and media companies are developing ways for the communities in which we live to become an extension of the media, an extension of synergy.

The primary tools that corporations and media companies use to extend marketing synergy into the physical environment are the related strategies of (1) theming and (2) the *environmental simulacrum* or simulated place. Theming is the coordination of a single simple concept, such as a logo, across platforms that address all the human senses. Simulacra are synthetic creations designed to seem real and natural, and include robot presidents at DisneyWorld, faux Eiffel towers in Las Vegas, and (increasingly) residential communities. These environments serve as gigantic, immersive placements of products, primarily through brand association. When considering environmental simulacra, it becomes important to distinguish between product placement and its variation, brand placement. Products are usually placed in movies and television programs, and the placement involves the characters. Movies and television also feature brand placement, in which a logo or image designed to reinforce a company or product is displayed instead of the product itself. Movie and television shows can throw out a product for a moment or two and then move on. Environment simulacra, on the other hand, prefer brand placement. Brands are, after all, much more ambiguous and polysemic than products, making them well-suited to the frequent and persistent strategies found in environmental simulacra. In the physical environment, the placement is not thrown out and left behind as it is in the movies; rather, it lingers and produces an accumulating effect, as all brand imaging intends to do.

Simulacra are not new. Chinese emperors cherished automaton birds, for example. Corporate use of simulacra as a means of brand placement, however, is a relatively new phenomenon, and it transforms the nature of the simulations themselves. Simulations built for corporate synergy remove the semiotic referent. Their signifiers refer not to real persons or places, but to products and slogans. Over time, the real world–or at least our perception of it–is replaced by a corporate, commercialized world. Baudrillard (1983) described a "precession of simulacra" through which this process takes place:

> Whereas representation tries to absorb simulation by interpreting it as false representation, simulation envelops the whole edifice of representation as itself a simulacrum. This would be the successive phases of the image:
>
> - It is the reflection of a basic reality
> - It masks and perverts a basic reality
> - It masks the absence of a basic reality
> - It bears no relation to any reality whatever: it is its own pure simulacrum. (p. 11)

In other words, with the emergence of electronic media and a global economy, images have moved away from correspondence with nature and toward self-reference. Automaton birds did not have a Nike swoosh on their wings.

The goal of synergy marketing is to construct a culture in which our lives gain meaning through the brands we consume. This is not easy to do, but is pursued systematically by advertisers and marketers. For example, the 2001 American Advertising Federation annual convention in Cleveland featured numerous speakers who addressed the challenges of cutting through media clutter, of delivering a message in an environment that is usually ad-free. One of the strongest synergy devices is product placement, which, according to the keynote address by Joe Cappo of Crain's Chicago Business is a multibillion-dollar business (Cappo, 2001).

Media corporations use synergy because it makes brand a part of everyday experience. In fact, it is difficult to conceive of postmodern Western culture without the experience of personal identity development through brand consumption. Marketers strive to create a situation in which the typical consumer behaves as though "who I am is what I buy." This makes products easier to sell. As McChesney (1997) points out, "firms without this cross-selling and cross-promotional potential are simply incapable of competing in the global marketplace" (p. 21).

The Western economy has changed, and with it the type of product being placed and the sophistication of the placement. In the 1940s, radio situation comedies would write consumer products into the script, so that *Fibber McGee and Molly* might carry on a conversation about the virtues of Glo-Coat Floor Wax. But the postmodern American economy is driven more by the consumption of leisure products than household items, in particular the consumption of media events like sports, movies, and television. Glo-Coat had little room to return the promotional favor and cross-promote *Fibber McGee*, but ESPN can promote Michael Jordan, who promotes Gatorade, which sponsors ESPN, in an endless loop of cross-promotion. This is the essential flavor of the most current phase of synergy: products are placed and brands are reinforced using an entirely new medium of commodification, and this medium is the simulation and replacement of real life and real environments.

Synergy Strategies

Synergy is carefully planned and controlled to create multifaceted marketing opportunities. Elsewhere (Olson, 1999), I have discussed in detail the five synergy-strategies of the media. To summarize, they are:

1. *Merchandising*, the creation of consumer goods based on a media narrative or brand idea, such as T-shirts or toys;
2. *Intertextuality*, the linking together of two different media narratives, such as the appearance of characters from one situation comedy on another television program;
3. *Placement*, the insertion of consumer products or brands into a movie or television program for marketing purposes, such as when a character drinks a Coca-Cola and displays the logo prominently;
4. *Theming*, the coordination of a single, simple idea into a plethora of visual puns and other iterations, such as using a corporate logo for the shape of a swimming pool; and
5. *Simulacra*, the creation of artificial persons and places meant to promote a positive association with a media or brand experience, such as a *Batman* ride at a theme park.

These strategies are obviously interrelated. For example, a simulacrum is a variation on theming and also a placement of product into the physical environment, and merchandise plugging a movie may be a product placement in the movie itself, and so on. Usually, two or more of these strategies are exploited in a coordinated cross-media marketing effort. Disney typically uses all five in rolling out a new animated feature.

The point here is that it is not enough to talk about how products are placed in movies. This is merely the most obvious strategy in a five-front assault. The commodity value of movies and television is extended beyond their own dimensions by being rendered and product-placed into our physical environment, and in that sense extended beyond the screen. The media product is product-placed into our physical environment.

The five synergy-strategies identified here make it seem as though audiences are passive receptors of marketing messages. Why do audiences submit to this? Why are they willing to link their identity and experience to brand marketing? These are obviously complex questions beyond the scope of this analysis, but one possible explanation is worth considering. Contemporary reception theory and analyses of the polysemic aspects of media texts make clear that audiences are generally active and engaged in their experience of texts, including movies and television (Ang, 1985, 1988; Bacon-Smith, 1992; Bourdieu, 1993; Burton-Carvajal, 1994; Fish, 1980; Fiske, 1986, 1987; Gillespie, 1995a, 1995b; Hall, 1980, 1992; Jauss, 1982, 1988; Jenkins, 1992; Liebes, 1988; Liebes and Katz, 1993; Miller, 1995; Morley, 1993; Smoodin, 1994; Tompkins, 1980).

Audiences, therefore, engage the media text in active ways; they are not all couch potatoes, but are willing to tolerate tremendous volumes of advertising. This willingness can be partially explained by the theories of Blumenberg (1985) and Kubey and Csikzentmihalyi (1990). Blumenberg's concept of "the Absolutism of Reality" is the idea that life is full of inexorable chaos and misery, and that this reality is absolute. Everyone has to confront the fact that one will die, and that life in the meantime can be full of many awful things. Such a state of being is indisputable, hence the "absolutism of reality." According to Blumenberg, the reason we seek myths and stories so incessantly is that they deny the absolutism of reality. In myths and movies, the good guys win, suffering has a purpose, life has meaning, and the protagonists live happily ever after.

A similar concept is found in Kubey and Csikzentmihalyi (1990), who rely on empirical data rather than philosophical tradition to postulate "negentropy" as the primary reason why heavy users consume the media. The media negate the entropy they see in the world around them, thus providing a "negentropy" effect. The essential idea here is that real life cannot satisfy the expectations that capitalism creates for us, so the media step into that role. But the expectations in turn become so great that the infrequent use of television or movies is insufficient to satisfy the consumptive desire, so media products must be placed into the environments we inhabit as reminders of satisfaction.

Product placement or any other synergy strategy helps to combat the "absolutism of reality" and to equip viewers with a "negentropy" defense. Brands are familiar and reassuring. The whole idea of brands relies precisely on that consumer comfort–consumers choose the brand name over the cheaper yet identical generic because the brand is consistent and familiar. This is as true of a series of movies (*Rocky V*) as of a consumer product (Bayer aspirin), and of all entertainment products: movies, television programs, and theme parks, for example. All of them encourage consumers to use familiarity with a prior consumption experience as a negentropy strategy. What other reason can there be for visiting a Hard Rock Café in a far away city that replicates the one close to home except that it provides a predictable experience? Or for an American visiting EuroDisney? Or for watching *Lethal Weapon IV*? Such places hold chaos and confusion at bay by providing a ready-made, thoroughly familiar simulated environment. Product placement in movies or television programs similarly constructs and then satisfies consumer worries about eating the right food, drinking the right cola, wearing the right shirt. Reality is not so absolute when one can easily purchase relief from its horrors.

Product placement in movies or television programs is one way advertising accomplishes this negentropy effect, but as has been described above, product placement is not restricted to that venue. Two recent marketing developments may accomplish the goal just as well: *theming* and simulacra branding.

Theming

Theming is designing buildings, product packaging, or physical environments around a single idea or icon, such as a corporate logo. Theming is the brand image or identity as a product to be placed, brand-placement becoming an increasingly common practice in the media (Galician and Bourdeau, 2004, in this publication). The idea behind theming is to overwhelm the consumer with the omnipresence and omnipotence of a given brand identity. No one does this better than Disney, whose synergy strategies are calculated to reinforce many aspects of the company's brands and products. The best example of theming is the very symbol of Disney itself: three intersecting circles in an inverted pyramid recognized around the world as Mickey Mouse's silhouette. This simple image is iterated in numerous ways, including:

1. The shape of the lake at Walt Disney World;
2. The Michael Graves-designed housewares sold at Target stores;
3. The crown on the water tower at MGM Studios Florida;
4. The Disney channel logo;
5. The archway at a Disney office building in Florida, etc.

The idea of this Mickey Mouse logo is visually and conceptually simple, but semiotically complex. After all, what does Mickey Mouse *mean*? The answer to that question has more to do with the cultural projections of a viewer than with any inherent signification. Mickey Mouse means what one wants him to mean, but that just makes mouse products easier to sell. The mouse is a semiotic black hole pointing back to consumption.

Michael Graves is the preeminent themer for Disney. He is essentially the house architect for the company, designing such landmark venues as the Team Disney headquarters in California, a Greek temple in which the entablature is made up of the Seven dwarves; the Dolphin Hotel at Epcot, a massive cartoon fish that looks like a forgotten Disney character but which serves as the branding agent for the hotel; or the Celebration, Florida Post Office, a small but utterly distinctive public service building in a Disney utopian community. All of these are simulations, but all are used in practical ways, as real buildings inhabited by real people. Brand name is everything in theming.

Simulacra Branding

Theming is the multi-platform, multimedia approach to cross-referencing a corporate brand. Environmental simulacra are specific instances of theming in which a physical environment is used to do the theming and product or (usually) brand placement. The defining characteristic of brand placement in both cases is the seamlessness with which television, film, radio, the recording industry, advertising, merchandising, manufactured products, theme parks, and technology work together toward a single marketing synergy. Theming is the broader concept. Environmental simulacra are the specific renderings of a media commercial idea into a particular place and time.

Environmental simulacra have numerous characteristics that work with a synergy theming strategy to assert brands and products. These traits include:

1. *Artificial déjà vu.* Environmental simulacra are new and synthetic, but designed to be familiar and comfortable. This serves the negentropy function;
2. *Postmodernism.* As with most aspects of postmodernism, environmental simulacra put a new face on something that otherwise holds the absolutism of reality and is therefore frightening, mysterious, and new. The distillation of American history into a single, simple fable told by a robot Mark Twain and a robot Ben Franklin at The American Experience in EPCOT is an example. This also serves the negentropy function, because it reduces the perception of chaos;
3. *Narratized space.* The earliest forms of human habitat developed in an organic way, and form followed function. Experiments in urban planning such as the Place de la Concorde or the Washington Mall are examples of planned, inorganic space, but the goal of these was symmetry, not narrative. Environmental simulacra attempt to tell a story, and to reveal, conceal, and put into sequence aspects of their design in order to enhance a narrative experience. The story is generally about the virtues a corporate brand or consumer product, such as the value of AT&T telecommunications services as found in the history of communication fable that unfolds in the great sphere at EPCOT. The story structures are familiar, and in many cases sequels or peripheral narratives to movies or television programs consumed previously.
4. *Mythic Displacement.* Within a culture, myths are the substrata of narrative. Across cultures, the building blocks of myths–mythotypes (Olson, 1999)–enable different cultures to make different meanings out of polysemic texts. Myths serve important cultural functions, including the propagation of purpose, wonder, awe, and participation. All of these are obviously negentropic. Because they follow the conventions of the American media, and are therefore inherently mythotypic, environmental simulacra make use of myth and mythotype in the narratives they portray. This further reinforces the cultural logic of the experience, and reifies the system that creates it.

5. *Repurposed Mythology.* The myths found in environmental simulacra or in any synergy strategy serve different purposes than the
myths found in religion. As mentioned above, spiritual myths exist to instill a sense of purpose, the experience of awe and wonder,
and the value of community participation, among other things.
They function to define values and promote assimilation. Mytho-
logical narratives constructed for the purpose of consumer product sales or corporate synergy make use of participation, awe,
wonder, and purpose, but not as the ends in themselves but rather
as a means to a different end. That end is product sales, so mythology that has been repurposed to serve corporate synergy and product placement has as its primary virtues:

   a. Commodification,
   b. Commercialization, and
   c. Consumer values.

Corporate brand replaces divine spirit in the product placement mythology. Environmental simulacra put the consumer in an artificial location
that is a commercialized, advertising environment construed as a natural one–myth made to seem real.

Consumers tolerate these environments because they resist the absolutism of reality and promote negentropy. They accomplish this in sophisticated ways, by being safe but adventurous and an opportunity for
vicarious thrilling experiences of the type described by Cawelti (1976).
They are both dangerous and comforting, and consequently they reduce
the sense of chaos and confusion found in the "real" world. Finally, environmental simulacra allow us to relive fond media memories by being
a product placement that we can actually step inside. This is why consumers seek out environmental simulacra and tolerate the heavy-
handed brand placement they engender.

Brand Placement Advantages

It is easy to see why media companies appreciate environmental
simulacra as a means of placing brand and product. These environments
afford many advantages over conventional advertising and product
placement:

1. They break through advertising clutter. Consumers are inundated
   with television commercials that they can easily avoid using a remote
   control, with pages of advertisements in newspapers and magazines,

with billboards, and even with conventional product placement in movies and television. Environmental simulacra provide a completely different medium for brand and product placement.

2. They immerse consumers in a situation designed to sell them something. Unlike other advertising media, environmental simulacra engage the entire range of the senses. Most advertisements are restricted to sight and possibly sound.
3. They control our experience. In an environmental simulacrum, everything that is seen, heard, smelled, touched, or tasted is tightly controlled. In other advertising media, the control is considerably less: one can look away as one passes a billboard, or go to the bathroom during a station break, but once one is in an environmental simulacrum, one is inside it, and under its control. The controlled environment primes the consumer for consumption, and then (as often as not) puts the consumer in a gift shop immediately after the experience to position consumption as the best way to memorialize the experience.
4. They reach consumers who have already selected them, and are therefore inclined toward the placement. Everyone inside an environmental simulacrum chose it as a destination, and therefore is predisposed to its message of consumption. In fact in most cases, the consumer has actually paid to have the simulacrum experience, already associating it with consumption.
5. They encourage consumers to go on desiring and consuming a particular cultural experience, within the scope of the experience but also through future and subsequent iterations of it.

Admittedly, the environmental simulacrum is an extremely expensive medium in which to place a brand or product, and therefore not appropriate for most advertising messages. It is difficult to conceive of "The Glo-Coat Experience" as a successful simulacrum, for example. On the other hand, no other medium gives such control and focus to a consumer message. When a corporation has the scope, clout, and resources to sponsor a simulacrum, companies such as Disney or Viacom or AOL Time Warner, they are given a powerful and unique medium through which to deploy a synergy strategy.

EXAMPLES

Many corporations have succeeded in this medium, and the best examples come from Paramount/Viacom, Las Vegas, and Disney. One of the most familiar examples of an environmental simulacrum that serves all five of the functions listed previously is the Cheers Bar found in many U.S. airports. These make use of the popular television program *Cheers* to create a familiar environment, one that looks very much like the pub from the show, right down to the chubby accountant and moustache-wearing postal worker seated at the bar. These two fellows look very much like the characters Norm and Cliff from the show, but in the case of the airport version of the Cheers Bar, these are simulacra, robots who chat with each other and with the guests, who order drinks, and who otherwise make the place seem all the more like the one we know from television. These robots are sufficiently life-like that George Wendt and John Ratzenberger, the actors who played Norm and Cliff on the show, brought a lawsuit against Paramount over their right to their own likenesses.

The advantage the Cheers Bar presents to Paramount/Viacom is clear—it is another opportunity to promote the television program and sell products associated with it, such as T-shirts and mugs. What might be less clear is the advantage the Cheers Bar presents to consumers in airports. Travel is a source of anxiety for most people, and airports signify comings and goings and, therefore, chaos and uncertainty. The Cheers Bar represents an oasis of comfort and familiarity amidst this chaos, a stiff drink of negentropy. The pub appears to be a very familiar place even if the travelers have never seen it before for the simple reason that it has been seen on television, repeatedly, in their own living room. That familiarity holds at bay the absolutism of reality, pushing back the fear that airplanes are often late, sometimes crash, and bring separation as often as they bring reunion.

Another example is *STAR TREK: The Experience* in Las Vegas. *Star Trek* is itself a sort of cottage industry for Paramount, yielding five live-action television series, one animated television series, ten feature films, and a bewildering variety of merchandise that includes toys, apparel, collectibles, novels, comic books, magazines, websites, and even Klingon-language instructional materials. Each cross-promotes the other in a holistic and synergistic product placement strategy rivaled only by the *Star Wars* franchise. In fact, one of the most distinctive features of these two media phenomena is that the product placements they engage in are almost exclusively for other products *within* the brand. There are no shots of Captain Kirk drinking Pepsi or Jar Jar Binks enjoying a Domino's pizza.

Yet, despite the amazing degree of cross-promotion in the *Star Trek* line, all of these devices are familiar media, media that struggle with advertising clutter, and media that engage only one or two of the senses. *STAR TREK: The Experience* solves that problem by rendering the brand as an environmental simulacrum. Located in the Las Vegas Hilton, *STAR TREK: The Experience* charges patrons $25 to give them access to a synthetic environment that simulates those found on the television programs. After touring a museum that shows a "history" of the future, consumers go on a simulated space mission inside a starship shuttle-craft. Guests can then dine in Quark's Bar or shop for *Star Trek* jewelry, clothes, glassware, models, and other souvenirs on the Promenade, both locations from the television series *Star Trek: Deep Space Nine*. This being Las Vegas, visitors can even be married on the deck of the Starship Enterprise. Taste, smell, and touch join sight and sound in creating a totalized brand placement experience.

STAR TREK: The Experience is honest with consumers about how it really is little more than a multi-sensory advertisement for *Star Trek* media and related merchandise. The website for the simulacrum claims:

> STAR TREK: The Experience™ at the Las Vegas Hilton is ready to transport you to the 24th century where you can become a part of the most popular space adventure of all time . . . STAR TREK: The Experience is not an exhibit, nor is it a convention. It is a one-of-a-kind, multi-million dollar attraction that will permanently reside in the North Tower of the Las Vegas Hilton. The attraction includes the opportunity to see, feel, touch and live the 24th century via a 22-minute voyage through space and time–and themed shopping and dining. (Star Trek, 2001)

In this controlled product placement environment, the *Star Trek* brand and merchandise are sold and cross-promoted in almost every manner conceivable, with consumers consenting to pay $25 for the privilege.

STAR TREK: The Experience is in Las Vegas, a place that has always been a kind of environmental simulacrum, an oasis of unreality and simulation constructed in the middle of nowhere. But one can quickly see the nature of its simulacra has become increasingly oriented toward corporate synergy and product placement. The Bellagio Hotel and Casino, for example, uses the cache of fine art to present an upscale image, but one more suited to glitz than to dignity, in which "paintings jumped out at you, gleaming and surprised, as from a bath of varnish" (Fenton, 2001, p. 83). Given that Bellagio is an environmental simulacrum of a museum rather than a museum itself, it is as likely to exhibit motorcycles as Renaissance masters. The Luxor Hotel and Casino features a similar simulation of a museum, in this case purportedly of treasures from an Egyptian tomb, but, in fact, mere simulations of antiquities.

There are many other examples of environmental simulacra in Las Vegas, and in some cases, the brand or product being placed is subtle and savvy to the postmodern audience. The MGM Grand, for example, pushes Hollywood-style movie musical glamour and the familiar MGM lion logo. The Paris Hotel, The Venetian, and The New York New York Hotel all promise a vicarious experience of something many Americans consider exotic and distant, with the result of culture and cities becoming other products to be placed. The Luxor Hotel is essentially a replica of the Novus Ordo Seclorum eye-in-the-pyramid Masonic symbol found on U.S. one dollar bills, rendering the hotel itself as an enormous product placement for capitalism.

Las Vegas does not have a monopoly on environmental simulacra, however. Theme park rides are another great example of placing a product or brand by using an environmental simulacrum. Traditionally, the referentiality has only gone in one direction, so that the ride is a way of reliving a thrilling experience from the film, placing the film product again in the consumer's mind and providing a new way to consume it, not only through the ride but through the inevitable gift shop that goes with it. That had been the model until the 1990s, and resulted in original Disneyland simulacra like *Mr. Toad's Wild Ride* and culminating in clumsy assertions of synergy such as roller coasters called *Batman* that otherwise have little to do with that film series. Although it is not a ride, perhaps the apex of the traditional form is the *Indiana Jones Adventure*, which allows an audience to experience in person what it enjoyed on a screen.

A newer form of theme park ride emerged in the 1990s, however, and instead of being an off-shoot or spin-off, it is co-designed with the movie, the two becoming a single cross-referential experience. Rides of this type include *Terminator II in 3D*, a kind of supplement to the film *Terminator II* using new footage shot in 3D with the same cast. An even better example is the *Jurassic Park* ride, which was so closely designed in concert with the movie property it cross-plugs that the ride and gift shop more-or-less appear in the film. This is an important divergence from past practice, because the environmental simulacrum, rather than being an after-thought, now affects the design of the film, from screenplay, to storyboard to final cut.

Theme park rides are merely other forms of entertainment, though, and, therefore, somewhat benign. But product placement does not limit itself to entertainment experiences. Disney Wedding Planning is one of the most postmodern of environmental simulacrum product placements. For a fee, Disney will arrange a "fantasy" wedding at Disney World or Disneyland. As the website states:

> Once upon a time, in an enchanted land, there was a place where wedding dreams and honeymoon wishes came true every day. Today, such a place actually exists–at the Walt Disney World Resort. Since 1991, over 15,000 couples have sealed their promise to each other here in uniquely magical ceremonies. And happy honeymoon couples from around the world have made us one of the most popular vacation destinations on the planet . . . here, romance has wings and imagination is unbounded. Here, all it takes is a dream to make a dream come true . . . fairy tales do come true. (Disney, 2001)

The wedding is all-inclusive, from the guest accommodations, to the meals, to the venue for the ceremony, and even to the honeymoon, which is also enjoyed at Disneyworld. One example is the Cinderella Package, in which couples can enact the wedding from that film, including replica costumes for bride and groom and "ugly stepsister" costumes for the bridesmaids. In this example, the corporation has successfully placed a product–in this case, a movie–into one of the most important "real" events in a person's life. A wedding becomes another commodity, and one with another product to sell in the process. Environmental simulacra replace the chapel, and movies are apparently the ascendant religion.

It should not be surprising that Disney pioneered using weddings as a venue for product placement given that Disney is the leading manufacturer of environmental simulacra. In addition to the Fairy Tale Wedding, every theme park ride at the seven major Disney parks around the world serves a product placement function. The rides at EPCOT, for example, all have corporate sponsors, and each one uses the ride as a platform to promote their own corporate message, from Exxon to AT&T to Kraft Foods. Consistent with Las Vegas venues that situate culture as a sort of brand identity, the World Showcase pavilions at EPCOT present Norway and China and Canada as environmental product placements. This setting provides some superficial advantages over the real cultures they are meant to replace because, in Disney fashion, it is cleaner than the real thing, speaks a familiar language, is closer to home, and is cheaper than traveling abroad. Baudrillard (1983) spoke of the precession of simulacra in which the artificial comes to replace and efface the real, a process apparently well under way in Orlando.

Perhaps the most extreme example of theming and environmental simulation is the town of Celebration, Florida, a place that was built by Disney as a real community but that does double duty as a Disney brand intensifier. The best way to describe Celebration is a 21st century, high-tech version of the town Mayberry R.F.D. (from *The Andy Griffith Show*). But this is not a movie set–it's real. How could a simulated town like Celebration succeed if not because of the brand? As Rybczynski observes, "one reason people wanted the [Celebration] houses was that they were *Disney* houses" (1996, p. 37, emphasis original). The town provides negentropy, escape from the absolutism of reality found outside its peaceful confines, and at the same time serves as a life-size, live-in simulation of the Disney corporate message.

Celebration is a utopian community of sorts, which is not surprising given Walt Disney's interest in building a perfect community. Somewhere along the way, Walt's vision was distorted, though, because Celebration is more about corporate brand and product placement than about solving urban problems. Celebration epitomizes theming: it engenders all the elements that allow theming to function as an omnipresent ghost of brand placement. Celebration is a simulation–an environmental simulacrum of an imagined past, and a platform for further iteration of the Disney brand.

DISCUSSION

What does the introduction of this new product placement medium, the environmental simulacrum, mean for American culture? This question can be divided into many aspects, but the ones that will be under consideration here will be the moral and ethical dimension of corporate synergy and the effect on social organization that it apparently produces. Do corporate synergy and product placement violate ethical norms? Are they in any way immoral? Are they changing American culture in ways we can perceive from a contemporary vantage point? Can audiences do anything to resist synergy and environmental simulacra, or are consumers helpless against their onslaught?

To the extent that ethics and morality can be seen as different approaches to human interaction, there seems to be no ethical constraints on environmental simulacra, theming, or product placement generally. Obviously, there is and ought to be an ethical constraint on the use of journalism for synergy, and this is sometimes abused. Journalists have a detailed code of ethics, and they chafe at corporate strategies that ask them to compromise their independent ideals. AOL Time Warner often wants CNN to promote a story that will be in the next issue of *Time*, an example of cross-media product placement within the AOL Time Warner corporate umbrella, and one of dubious ethics to the extent that it affects news content. Were AOL Time Warner to insist that CNN cover the opening of *Harry Potter*, a Warner Brothers film, or on *Time* giving the film a good review, it would be clear breaches of journalistic ethics. Apart from situations related to journalism, and because of the code of ethics basis to Journalistic practice, most examples of product placement are not issues of ethics. Perhaps this specific problem will become moot as Time Warner emerges again without AOL control, although the problem remains where any group owner controls multiple media that intersect (and perhaps dominate) commercial concerns over journalistic ones.

The example of journalism aside, one can find few ethical codes that constrain the use of media synergy, theming, or environmental simulacra as an advertising medium. The ethics of advertisers and marketers do not prohibit it, and neither do those of film and television producers, studios, or networks. Codes of ethics are not the whole story, though. Synergy may present issues of morality, especially as it attends product placement and its use in theming and environmental simulacra. These moral issues include:

1. *Control.* Does the synergy strategy exert an undue amount of control over the consumer, and is that control exerted beyond the boundaries of what the consumer expected?
2. *Choice.* Does the consumer have alternatives? Is there any space that has not been converted into an environmental simulacrum? The answer to that so far has been yes, and so citizens do have options, but ever since the introduction of the shopping mall and the shift from the town commons from political and communal space to being commercial and consumer space, alternatives have been disappearing. So far, viewers and consumers aren't utterly defenseless.
3. *Consent.* Has the consumer willingly submitted to the synergy environment, or has participation been the result of deception or coercion?

Moral considerations such as these may not be reflected in the specific ethical codes found in the Advertising Federation's guidelines, but they ought to guide the conversation within a culture about the appropriate role and scope of synergy marketing.

What is needed is a set of moral parameters that can be brought to bear on the extensions of synergy. In the interest of moving the debate to such a level of structure, here are some preliminary suggestions to help evaluate the morality of a particular product placement practice:

- Is the practice causing harm? Specifically:

  - Is the practice of product placement causing artistic harm? Is it limiting the forms of artistic expression available to filmmakers, urban planners, architects, writers, designers, and other artists?
  - Is it causing cultural harm? Is it causing children to learn less, or is it squelching diversity, or causing social dislocation?
  - Is it causing economic harm? Is it causing prices to be set unfairly, or caused gouging? Has it redirected the economy in unsustainable and therefore harmful directions? Has it made independent voices, those outside the corporate synergy strategy, too expensive or otherwise economically unappealing, therefore silencing them?

- Is the practice getting worse? Is it progressing? Are more and more communities and environments becoming opportunities for marketing? Does more and more apparel display a logo? Is theming the dictating logic of ever more corporate projects?
- Is there room for films, television programs, and environments that do not make use of theming or product placement? Will the market tolerate them?
- Has creativity been colonized, so that artists and designers can no longer conceive of films, television programs, or environments that do not make use of theming or product placement?
- Has American culture also been colonized? Have the identities of Americans and citizens of other cultures around the world become so entwined with consumption that synergy is becoming an inherent characteristic of the culture?
- How will the process of digitalization, which enables the realistic insertion of advertisements into places where they do not actually appear, affect the gathering omnipresence that advertisements seem to have in American culture? Already, digital advertisements are

inserted onto the backboard of baseball games so that they are seen to home viewers but not to those in the stadium. How far will this practice extend? Will it next add advertisements to old movies? To political events?

This list is not meant to be comprehensive, but rather a starting point for analysis and discussion of corporate synergy practices, of product placement proliferation, and of revealing the progression of theming and environmental simulacra as corporate branding practices.

The answers to these questions are not easily found, of course, which explains in part why consumers are not rising up to resist synergy. The main reason is that consumers either haven't noticed it or actually like it. Marketers have been fairly successful at linking American identity to shopping, so synergy hardly stands out. As shopping has come to be the dominant trait in American culture, and as what I buy has come to define who I am, synergy has seemed more like an opportunity than a problem. The economy has changed along with this shift. Glo-Coat wasn't meant to be an idea or a lifestyle, but Coca-Cola is, and Disney is–they are ideas and they are lifestyles, and in those examples can be seen the transformation of the economy and of its strategies for selling products.

CONCLUSIONS

What we see in the precession of simulacra and the precession of products placed is an evolution of the American economy, from mundane household goods to the culture itself as just another consumer product. Along the way, shopping has been rendered into a kind of secular religion. Corporate synergy has become a kind of worship, a worship of product placement. Consider the parallels between synergy and religion. Religion exists to provide purpose, awe and wonder, and participation. In religion, purpose is conveyed by faith and doctrine, awe and wonder are conveyed by pilgrimage, and participation conveyed by intentional faith communities. In corporate synergy, consumer products come to be seen as the primary conveyors of meaning in life, the pilgrimage is taken to visit an environmental simulacrum, and participation means sharing a commodified event with other consumers. Perhaps the most powerful proof that this is happening is that environmental simulacra are living advertisements that consumers are willing to pay to participate in, and which encourage further consumption of the product through an endless self-referential cycle of cross-platform merchandising, culminating in a cultural environment in which consumers are willing to use the most meaningful days of their lives, such a weddings, as opportunities for corporations to do further product placement.

Product placement works because of the culture of consumption. The power of shopping as a central pillar of American culture is not mere assertion, but is given witness by the failure of e-commerce and the crash of the dot-coms. On-line purchasing clearly provides tremendous convenience, efficiency, and cost advantages over traditional brick-and-mortar businesses. For consumers, on-line purchasing saved time and reduced price. The failure of e-commerce was purely cultural: for many if not most Americans, shopping is the preferred leisure activity. The engineers and designers who built the e-commerce website in many cases were of the personality type that wanted to avoid shopping whenever possible, so it may have been difficult for them to imagine that most people actually *want* to shop. The reason they do is that shopping largely defines who they are.

Some citizens have noticed the extensions of synergy, however, and do want to resist the pressures of the culture of shopping. In line with the schemata developed by de Certeau (1984), these activists have developed numerous tactics to combat corporate strategy. These tactics include media jamming, fan-made media, and media literacy. Media jamming, sometimes also called "culture jamming" (Dery, 1993), is the practice of defacing billboards, intercepting satellite signals, creating mock ads, or staging embarrassing special events to disrupt corporate marketing. Examples include doctoring Nike billboards from saying "Just Do It" to saying "Do It Just" or a Joe Camel cigarette billboard to be "Joe Chemo," the TRUTH campaign against smoking, and the Adbusters organization's subversive doppelganger ads (Collins, 1997).

Fan-made media is a milder form of resistance. Audiences sometimes feel such a strong affinity for a media product that the official, authorized narratives prove unsatisfying or insufficient, and the fans take matters into their own hands, creating their own movies and stories. This is particularly true of *Star Trek* but is found with other media programming as well (see Jenkins, 1992, for examples). While essentially affectionate toward the media product, and therefore much less radical than media jamming, fan-made media obviously defy the wishes of the holder of the copyright and create extensions of the media experience *without* synergy. A recent example is a digital film called *Star Wars–the Phantom Edit* which is essentially a shorter, tighter version of the cinematic feature *Star Wars Episode I: The Phantom Menace* with the character Jar Jar Binks edited out (see Gaslin, 2001, for numerous examples).

Finally, media literacy in the form of audience sophistication about the strategies behind corporate synergy is another way for audiences to counter with a resistant tactic. Knowing what the media are trying to accomplish and how they go about it is at least some defense against synergy strategies. There are certainly abundant opportunities for media consumers to educate themselves on how the media work, from magazines and television programs that cover the industry with the devotion of a war correspondent to university-level courses on the subject. In many countries, but not in the U.S., media literacy is part of the elementary school curriculum.

Despite these clever tactics, the media mutate quickly and adapt to audience resistance and sophistication, developing a new strategy to confound each tactic. To resist media jamming, media strategists have begun to employ "corporate jujitsu," a practice that anticipates jamming and uses it to create a media event that actually promotes the product. For example, Nike itself staged a jamming operation against its own ads in Australia, engendering extensive media coverage for a new cleated boot that might otherwise have gone unnoticed (Lappin and Grierson, 2001). Disney, Paramount, and Lucasfilm have been extremely aggressive in resisting some of the fan-made media through the deployment of lawyers issuing cease-and-desist requests on the basis of infringement of copyright and trademark. Finally, to resist media literacy, media companies have adopted a strategy of enabling the audience's deconstructive tendencies while delivering consumerist messages all the same. The spoofing of product placement while actually placing products in the film *Wayne's World* is an example of how the film industry stays one step ahead of the audience. Ironic self-reflexivity and postmodern pastiche such as those found in the film are the latest adaptation of consumer capitalism.

Limited resistance aside, the extensions of synergy cement the notion that the primary defining characteristic of American culture is shopping, and that consumers want products placed everywhere, and placed all the time. Theming and environmental simulacra are large-scale, multisensory advertisements that consumers willingly choose to inhabit. All time and all space become media for product placement and corporate marketing. The extensions of synergy are almost absolute.

REFERENCES

Ang, I. (1985). *Watching Dallas.* London: Methuen.

Ang, I. (1988). (Not) coming to terms with *Dallas.* In C. Schneider and B. Wallis, editors, *Global Television.* New York: Wedge Press, 69-77.

Bacon-Smith, C. (1992). *Enterprising Women: Television Fandom and the Creation of Popular Myth.* Philadelphia: University of Pennsylvania Press.

Baudrillard, J. (1983). *Simulations.* New York: Semiotext(e).

Blumenberg, H. (1985). *Work on Myth.* Trans. R. Wallace. Cambridge, MA: MIT Press.

Bourdieu, P. (1993). *The Field of Cultural Production.* New York: Columbia University Press.

Burton-Carvajal, J. (1994). "Surprise package": Looking southward with Disney. In E. Smoodin, editor, *Disney Discourse: Producing the Magic Kingdom.* New York: Routledge, 131-147.

Cappo, J. (2001, June). Address to the Advertising Federation. Paper presented at the Conference of the American Advertising Federation, Cleveland, OH.

Cawelti, J. (1976). *Adventure, Mystery, and Romance.* Chicago: University of Chicago Press.

Certeau, M. de (1984). *The Practice of Everyday Life.* Trans. S. Rendell. Berkeley: University of California Press.

Collins, R. (1997, Winter). Goodbye, Joe. *Adbusters, 19,* 53-55.

Crowe, C. (Director). (2001). *Harry Potter and the Sorcerer's Stone.* [Film]. (In theatrical release in 2001 and available from Warner Home Video in 2002).

Dery, M. (1993). Culture Jamming: Hacking, Slashing, and Sniping in the Empire of Signs. Westfield, NJ: Open Magazine Press.

Disney Corporation. (2001). Disney's fairy tale weddings and honeymoons. *Disney.com.* Available online at: *http://Disney.go.com/vacations/disneyweddings/ index1.html.*

Fenton, J. (2001). From Florence to Las Vegas. *New York Review of Books, 48*(20), 81-83.

Fish, S. (1980). *Is There a Text in This Class? The Authority of Interpretive Communities.* Cambridge, MA: Harvard University Press.

Fiske, J. (1986). Television: Polysemy and popularity. *Critical Studies in Mass Communication, 3*(4), 391-408.

Fiske, J. (1987). *Television Culture.* New York: Routledge.

Galician, M.-L., and Bourdeau, P. G. (2004). The evolution of product placements in Hollywood cinema: Embedding high-involvement "heroic" brand images. In this volume.

Gaslin, G. (2001, June 1). "Star" turns. *Entertainment Weekly,* 92.

Gillespie, M. (1995a). *Television, Ethnicity, and Cultural Change.* New York: Routledge.

Gillespie, M. (1995b). Sacred serials, devotional viewing, and domestic worship: A case-study in the interpretation of two TV versions of *The Mahabharata* in a Hindu family in West London. In R. Allen, editor, *Speaking of Soap Operas . . .* New York: Routledge, 354-380.

Hall, S. (1980). Encoding/decoding. In S. Hall, D. Hobson, A. Lowe, and P. Willis, editors, *Culture, Media, Language.* London: Hutchinson, 128-138.

Hall, S. (1992). The question of cultural identity. In S. Hall, D. Held, and T. McGrew, editors, *Modernity and its Futures.* Cambridge, England: Polity Press, 273-326.

Harris, D., and Dawtrey, A. (2001, November 26). Can B.O. postman "ring" twice? New Line hopes to emulate "Harry" hoopla. *Variety Weekly,* 1.

Jauss, H. (1982). *Toward an Aesthetic of Reception.* Trans. T. Bahti. Minneapolis: University of Minnesota Press.

Jauss, H. (1988). *Aesthetic Experience and Literary Hermeneutics.* Minneapolis: University of Minnesota Press.

Jenkins, D. (1992). *Textual Poachers: Television Fan and Participatory Culture.* New York: Routledge.

Kubey, R., and Csikzentmihalyi, M. (1990). Television and the quality of life: How viewing shapes everyday experience. Hillsdale, NJ: Lawrence Erlbaum Associates.

Lappin, T., and Grierson, B. (2001, December 9). Corporate jujitsu. *New York Times Magazine,* 64.

Liebes, T. (1988). Cultural differences in the retelling of television fiction. *Critical Studies in Mass Communication, 5*(4), 277-292.

Liebes, T., and Katz, E. (1993). *The Export of Meaning: Cross Cultural Readings of "Dallas."* Cambridge, MA: Polity Press.

McChesney, J. (1997). *Corporate Media and the Threat to Democracy.* New York: Seven Stories Press.

Miller, D. (1995). The consumption of soap opera: *The Young and the Restless* and mass consumption in Trinidad. In R. Allen, editor, *Speaking of Soap Operas . . .* New York: Routledge, 213-233.

Morley, D. (1993). Active audience theory: Pendulums and pitfalls. *Journal of Communication, 43*(4), 13-19.

Olson, S. (1999). *Hollywood Planet: Global Media and the Competitive Advantage of Narrative Transparency.* Mahwah, NJ: Lawrence Erlbaum Publishers.

Rybczynski, W. (1996). Tomorrowland. *New Yorker, 72*(20), 36-39.

Smoodin, E. (1994). Introduction: How to read Walt Disney. In E. Smoodin, editor, *Disney Discourse: Producing the Magic Kingdom.* New York: Routledge, 1-20.

Soar, M. (Producer), and Soar, M. and Ericsson, S. (Directors). (2000). *Behind the Screens: Hollywood Goes Hypercommercial.* [Film]. Northampton, MA: Media Education Foundation.

Star Trek. (2001). STAR TREK: The experience. *Las Vegas Hilton: Startrekexp.* Available online at: *http://www.ds9promenade.com/startrek/index.html.*

Tompkins, J., editor (1980). *Reader-Response Criticism: From Formalism to Post-Structuralism.* Baltimore, MD: Johns Hopkins University Press.

Variety box office (2001, November 26). *Variety Weekly,* 9.

CONTROLS ON PRODUCT PLACEMENT

Product Placement and the Law

Paul Siegel

SUMMARY. Consumer activists who propose regulations either banning certain product placements or requiring their affirmative disclosure in motion picture closing credits generally assert that such regulations would not violate the First Amendment because product placements are commercial speech, which receive far less constitutional protection than core political speech. This essay reviews the evolution of the Supreme Court's commercial speech doctrine and concludes that product placements would likely not be considered commercial speech at all; moreover, the essay argues, even if they were found to be commercial speech, the Court's evolving doctrine would likely protect the placements from regulation. *[Article copies available for a fee from The Haworth Document Delivery Service: 1-800-HAWORTH. E-mail address: <docdelivery@haworthpress.*

Paul Siegel (PhD, Northwestern University, 1982) is Professor of Communication Studies at Gallaudet University, 800 Florida Avenue, N.E., Washington, DC 20002 (E-mail: Paul.Siegel@Gallaudet.edu).

[Haworth co-indexing entry note]: "Product Placement and the Law." Siegel, Paul. Co-published simultaneously in *Journal of Promotion Management* (Best Business Books, an imprint of The Haworth Press, Inc.) Vol. 10, No. 1/2, 2004, pp. 89-100; and: *Handbook of Product Placement in the Mass Media: New Strategies in Marketing Theory, Practice, Trends, and Ethics* (ed: Mary-Lou Galician) Best Business Books, an imprint of The Haworth Press, Inc., 2004, pp. 89-100. Single or multiple copies of this article are available for a fee from The Haworth Document Delivery Service [1-800-HAWORTH, 9:00 a.m. - 5:00 p.m. (EST). E-mail address: docdelivery@haworthpress.com].

KEYWORDS. Advertising, commercial speech, First Amendment, motion pictures, product placement

INTRODUCTION

Could the practice of product placements in motion pictures be forbidden, or otherwise regulated? This is a question not easily answered by an examination of existing case law. Indeed, to date no published decisions, state or federal, have addressed the matter.

Social critics have sought government intervention or industry self-restraint since not too long after E.T.'s famous trek along the Reese's Pieces trail (Adler, 1999; Center for the Study of Commercialism, 1992; Product Placements, 1993; Snyder, 1992). As early as the late 1980s, bills were introduced in Congress that would have required movie studios to affirmatively disclose, on-screen, the names of all companies that had made payments in exchange for having their products appear in a film (Snyder, 1992, p. 302). No federal legislation emerged. Moreover, both the Federal Trade Commission and the Federal Communications Commission declined to engage in any rule-making aimed at restrictions on product placement in movies (Federal Trade Commission, 1993; Snyder, 1992, 311-2). While the tobacco industry claims to have created self-regulations prohibiting product placements of their product in motion pictures (Federal Trade Commission, 1999), producers of TV programs are statutorily required to disclose to viewers the names of companies that have paid for product placements (Announcement, 2001). The federal law requiring such disclosure has survived a court challenge (*Capitol Broadcasting*, 1971).

Space limitations prevent a thorough explication here of the more narrow issue of placements in movies of tobacco products. Suffice it to say that for about a decade or so, beginning with the Court's *Posadas* decision (1986), it appeared as if the government would be given an added measure of freedom to regulate advertising for legal, but "dangerous" products and services, such as casino gambling, alcohol, and tobacco products. More recent decisions, however, have suggested the Court's retreat from this stance (*Rubin*, 1995; *44 Liquormart*, 1996). Still, part of the Master Settlement Agreement (1998) that effectively ended dozens of state attorney generals' suits against the major tobacco companies commits the companies to refrain from placements of their products in movies and several other media. Even here, however, there is substantial disagreement about the real scope of those promises (Adler, 1999; Kline, 2000; Siegel, 2002, p. 373).

Analogies to television, however, will not help us determine the constitutionality of product placement regulations applied to other media, even though product placements, both real and "virtual," have crossed over onto TV screens (Askan, 2000; National Public Radio, 2001c; Schlosser, 2001; Walker, 2002) and to other media (National Public Radio, 2001a, 2001b). The Supreme Court has made clear on a number of occasions that broadcast content may be regulated in a host of ways that would surely be unconstitutional if applied to other communications media, owing to continued allegiance to the notion that the airwaves belong to the public (see generally, Siegel, 2002, 433-435).

DEFINING AND REGULATING ADVERTISING

This essay contends that government-imposed regulation of product placements in movies would likely be found unconstitutional. In that product placements may seem at first blush to be instances of commercial speech–which can be more strictly regulated than most other kinds of speech–it begins by reviewing the complicated history of the Supreme Court's commercial speech doctrine. Building on that review, the essay next demonstrates that there is substantial doubt as to whether product placements would ever be considered commercial speech. Finally, the essay considers what the legal status of product placement might be even if we assume for argument's sake that it is commercial speech. Even here, it will be argued, the Court's most recent statements about the place of advertising in the constitutional schema would suggest that most product placements could not be constitutionally subject to regulation.

Evolution of the Supreme Court's Commercial Speech Doctrine

In the summer of 1940, F. J. Chrestensen sailed into New York harbor on a surplus Navy submarine, hoping to charge Battery Park passersby 25¢ (15¢ for children) to take a tour. The entrepreneur's attempts to draw attention to the submarine were stymied by a local ordinance forbidding the distribution of *commercial* leaflets on city streets.

Undeterred, Chrestensen went back to the printing press, quite literally, and produced a new leaflet, the reverse side of which boasted a political message (a complaint about the anti-leafleting ordinance!). The Supreme Court was unimpressed (*Valentine*, 1942, 55). Justice Jackson's opinion reaffirmed that "purely commercial advertising" is wholly unprotected by the First Amendment, and assessed Chrestensen's leaflet as a crude attempt to evade a legitimate statute.

It was not until 1976 that the Supreme Court explicitly overturned *Valentine* (*Virginia State Board of Pharmacy*, 1976). On at least two occasions in the intervening 34 years, the Court had to adjudicate controversies involving messages which, like Chrestensen's, included both commercial and non-commercial elements. The first of these was the landmark libel case, *New York Times v. Sullivan* (1964). Often overlooked is the fact that the artifact resulting in *New York Times* was not a news story or an editorial, but a paid political advertisement placed by civil rights workers seeking financial donations. Their message was "not a 'commercial' advertisement" like Chrestensen's, the Court concluded, in that it "communicated information, expressed opinion, recited grievances, [and] protested claimed abuses" (pp. 265-6).

More than a decade later, the Court confronted the case of a student newspaper editor in Virginia who ran–in violation of state law–an advertisement placed by a New York abortion clinic *(Bigelow v. Virginia,* 1975). Here the Court, in the course of overturning the editor's conviction, again emphasized that defining "commercial" speech is not a simple task. That the abortion clinic's message "reflected the advertiser's commercial interests" and "involved sales or solicitations" was not enough to disqualify it from First Amendment protection, nor was the fact that the newspaper "was paid for printing it." The specific ad was protected, the Court told us, because it "contained factual information of clear public interest."

In its very next term after *Bigelow*, the Court confronted another controversy from Virginia, this time in the form of a state law forbidding pharmacists to advertise the price of prescription drugs (*Virginia State Board of Pharmacy*, 1976). Here was a regulation aimed at purely commercial speech, messages that do "no more than propose a commercial transaction" (in this case, "I will sell you the X prescription drug at the Y price"). The Court could no longer evade the question of *Valentine*'s continued usefulness, and the majority opinion soundly rejected the earlier decision as it invalidated the Virginia law.

As to clarifying the scope of constitutional protection for commercial speech, however, the *Virginia Pharmacy* decision is a bit less helpful.

"Speech does not lose its First Amendment protection because money is spent to project it, as in a paid advertisement of one form or another," we learn from Justice Blackmun's majority opinion. We are told too that "speech is protected even though it is carried in a form that is sold for profit," such as motion pictures, "and even though it may involve a solicitation to purchase or otherwise pay or contribute money" (p. 761). Justice Blackmun added that "if there is a kind of commercial speech that lacks all First Amendment protection, therefore, it must be distinguished by its content." But nowhere does he indicate what kinds of commercial speech content would lie beyond the constitution's protection.

A related complication in the *Virginia Pharmacy* case is Blackmun's unnecessary attribution of strong political elements to that which he had just emphasized was purely commercial speech (Siegel, 1990). For many people, he pointed out, access to prices of consumer items may be of more pressing urgency than "the day's most urgent political debate" (p. 763). One can almost imagine a chorus humming *The Battle Hymn of the Republic* to the following, also from Blackmun's opinion:

> So long as we preserve a predominantly free enterprise economy, the allocation of our resources in large measure will be made through numerous private economic decisions. It is a matter of public interest that those decisions, in the aggregate, be intelligent and well informed. To this end, the free flow of commercial information is indispensable.

And if it is indispensable to the proper allocation of resources in a free enterprise, it is also indispensable to the formation of intelligent opinions as to how that system ought to be regulated or altered. Therefore, even if the First Amendment were thought to be primarily an instrument to enlighten public decision making in a democracy, we could not say that the free flow of commercial information does not serve that goal (p. 765).

In its very next term (*Linmark*, 1977), the Court continued its tendency to emphasize the political elements of purely commercial messages. At issue was a Willingboro, New Jersey town ordinance–designed to stem the flow of "white flight" and to retain its integrated community–which forbade the use of "FOR SALE" and "SOLD" signs on residential lawns. The Court unanimously struck down the ordinance, in part because it stifled the flow of information "of vital interest to Willingboro residents, since it may bear on one of the most important decisions they have a right to make: where to live and raise their families" (p. 96). Here too, we see the elevation of the commercial ("I have a house for sale here") to the political (a statement about racial harmony?). Justice Marshall's opinion is especially ironic in that, in a racially charged atmosphere of unscrupulous realtors inducing panic selling, the presence of a "FOR SALE" sign would not necessarily signal to a black family that this was, indeed, a place where *they* could live.

That distinguishing commercial and more political speech is a difficult task for jurists was emphasized again in a concurring opinion from Justices Blackmun and Brennan (*Metromedia*, 1981). The Court, without being able to settle on a majority opinion, had invalidated a San Diego ordinance that forbade most billboards, but that made an exception for on-site commercial signs, thus manifesting the fatal flaw of giving commercial speech more protection than political speech. But what is political, and what is commercial, Blackmun and Brennan wondered. They asked that we consider the following four messages:

"Visit Joe's Ice Cream Shoppe."

"Joe's Ice Cream Shoppe uses only the highest quality dairy products."

"Because Joe thinks that dairy products are good for you, please shop at Joe's Shoppe."

"Joe says to support dairy price supports: they mean lower prices for you at his Shoppe."

While the difference among these various messages is the text itself, Blackmun and Brennan also wondered about how the text interacts with the identity of the speaker. If the message is "Support the San Diego Padres," does it matter if the speaker is the team's owner, its players, or some fans with no connection to the team? What about a billboard imploring viewers to buy only American cars? Does it matter if the advertiser is Chrysler, or the UAW, or simply a group of public-spirited citizens (pp. 538-9)?

Are Product Placements Commercial Speech?

Even this highly truncated history of the Supreme Court's commercial speech doctrine makes clear that there is nothing at all clear about the construct. Not all advertising is commercial, we saw in *New York Times* and in *Bigelow*. That a specific product is mentioned in a message, that the message is an inducement to part with money, and that the speaker has economic interests in promulgating the message, also cannot alone determine the proper category. In a case striking down a federal law that prohibited the mailing of unsolicited advertisements for contraceptive devices (*Bolger*, 1983), the Court allowed that the *combination* of these elements *might* properly result in a message's being categorized as commercial speech.

What of product placements? Focusing first upon the content of the typical product placement, one would be hard pressed to suggest that a traditional advertising message is present at all. Most product placements take one of two forms–either a simple reminder that a product line exists (Superman hurling a villain into the air so hard that he destroys an electronic Coca-Cola billboard), or a narrative suggesting that a given (fictional!) character prefers a specific brand (Cher's character ordering "a fifth of Mumm's" in *Moonstruck*). Neither kind of message includes an explicit inducement to buy a product. Indeed, in this respect, product placements are similar to the kinds of image ads that even tobacco companies regularly place on TV–e.g., the one depicting a victim of domestic violence thanking the Phillip Morris conglomerate for funding her local battered women's shelter–maddening, perhaps, but not at all violative of federal law prohibiting the advertising of tobacco products in that medium.

The content and overall intended effect of product placements differs in another significant way from those of traditional advertising. Advertisements in most other media are designed to catch viewers' attention sufficiently so as to break the flow of the narrative. Viewers are supposed to take note of the fact that a commercial message is upon them, even to the point of planning an "action step." The step might be to "look in the frozen food aisle" for the advertised product the next time the viewer is at the supermarket, or it might be to "talk to your doctor" about whether you might be a candidate for the prescription drug being advertised. By contrast, product placements are seen as most effective the less they intrude upon a movie's story line. The ideal placement is one that injects itself unobtrusively into a film's overall atmosphere, rather than calls overt attention to itself. Moreover, from the filmmaker's perspective, most stories demand an atmosphere thoroughly permeated by commercial logos if they are to have any verisimilitude. After all, in the typical home, dozens of product brand names confront us every waking hour.

The Court at least sometimes has focused upon the speaker's economic motives in determining whether a message is commercial. The typical product placement certainly involves someone's economic motives, but is it that of the speaker? Is the speaker the company that has paid for the placement? Or is the movie studio, which has the final say in what over-all message is sent to viewers, more properly considered the speaker? Unlike the two-sided leaflets announcing Mr. Chrestensen's subma-rine—wherein a non-commercial message was artificially added to a pri-marily commercial one, a movie is a primarily noncommercial message to which some arguably commercial speech (the product placements) has been added (Snyder, pp. 321-2).

What if Product Placements Are Commercial Speech?

The Supreme Court's commercial speech doctrine is complex and sometimes contradictory. As such, it is at least plausible that consumer advocates might make a convincing case for the genre's commercial na-ture. After all, a court just might consider the companies who place products the true speakers, rather than the movie studios. Moreover, such advocates would correctly point out that sophisticated advertising campaigns almost never include overt inducements to buy a product. "Call now—operators are standing by!" is the watch cry of a low-budget huckster, not a Fortune 500 company. Since most product advertise-ments, regardless of medium, nonetheless fall into the category of com-mercial speech, why not product placements as well? Suppose, then, that product placements did fall within the purview of the Supreme Court's commercial speech doctrine. Would their regulation or prohibi-tion be constitutional?

Our inquiry begins with a case decided 4 years after the landmark *Virginia Pharmacy* decision. If the *Virginia Pharmacy* case tells us that even purely commercial speech enjoys *some* First Amendment protec-tion, this later case represents the Court's first attempt to tell us *how much* protection (*Central Hudson*, 1980). The *Central Hudson* test—as later revised in the *Board of Trustees* decision (1989)—consists of four inquiries lower courts must conduct in adjudicating commercial speech cases. Courts first ask if the advertisement is deceptive, or if it is pro-moting an illegal product or service. If so, any law regulating or prohib-iting it is constitutional. If not, courts pose three queries about the state's interest in regulating this kind of speech: (1) Is that interest a sub-stantial one? (2) Does the regulation really further that interest? and

(3) Is there at least a "reasonable fit" between the regulation and the state's interest?

It is interesting to note that in more recent years some members of the Court have suggested discarding *Central Hudson* altogether and treating truthful commercial speech as fully protected by the First Amendment *(44 Liquormart,* 1996; *Greater New Orleans,* 1999). Although many commentators see the Court moving in this direction, the view has not yet been embraced by the Court's majority, and it may not be. So until the Court rules otherwise, *Central Hudson* stands.

To be sure, some critics have suggested that product placements should fail the *Central Hudson* test at the very outset. After all, how can an ad that is cleverly designed to not look like an ad be anything but deceptive (Miller, 1990)? Such an argument might have made sense when product placements were new to the scene–say, 15 years ago. But nowadays, audiences are keenly aware of their existence, and Hollywood even confirms viewers' sophistication with such comedic send-ups of product placements as seen in *The Truman Show* and *Wayne's World.*

What of *Central Hudson*'s second query–do governments have a substantial interest in regulating product placements? Consumer activists have argued in favor of regulation on two grounds–the already-discredited claim that the entire genre is inherently deceptive, and the fear that it is part and parcel of an unhealthy "hyper-commercialism" infecting discourse in America generally (Bernard, 2000). While there certainly is merit to the latter argument, it is one that the Supreme Court has at least implicitly rejected over the years through its tendency to attribute strong political elements to even purely commercial speech. Critics will rightly point out that it is the rare motion picture whose message is predominantly political. We go to the movies to be entertained, don't we, not to be proselytized?

Here, too, the argument will likely fail, in that the Court has on a number of occasions indicated that speech designed merely to entertain–the Court has equated this with "artistic speech"–enjoys the same level of First Amendment protection as core political speech (*National Endowment,* 1998; *Schad,* 1981; *Southeastern Promotions,* 1975). Sometimes, the Court has suggested that artistic speech should be protected precisely because to some audience members it may carry political significance (*Burstyn, Inc.,* 1952), while at other times, the Court has made clear that art is protected as a wholly independent First Amendment entity (*Turner Broadcasting,* 1994). Moreover, the Court has explicitly recognized motion pictures as deserving of full First Amendment protection for over half a century (*Burstyn, Inc.,* 1952).

Almost certainly, a state-imposed prohibition of product placements would fail the *Central Hudson* test's first or second step. But what of an affirmative requirement to disclose the existence of such placements as part of each film's ending credits? Such a schema would fly in the face of long-standing Supreme Court doctrine to the effect that freedom of speech entails a constitutional right *not* to speak (*Cook*, 2001; *Wooley*, 1977). But there is a countervailing tendency for courts to permit regulations requiring commercial speakers to make prescribed disclosures to customers. In the dozen or so cases the Supreme Court has heard involving lawyer advertising, for example, only one regulation has ever been upheld–an Ohio rule requiring attorneys who solicit cases on a contingency fee basis to make clear in their advertisements whether clients will have to reimburse their lawyer for out-of-pocket expenses and court fees (*Zauderer*, 1985). Moreover, the Federal Trade Commission has within its arsenal the power to demand advertisers engage in affirmative disclosures. Nonetheless, both the FTC powers and the Court's *Zauderer* holding were predicated on the fear that consumers would be deceived in the absence of the required disclosures. It would be highly unlikely for a court to find that contemporary film audiences are deceived by the very practice of product placements.

CONCLUSION

A highly unscientific online poll conducted by the British firm, Filmscape–its website describes itself as "the global film trivia portal" (Poll Archive, 2001)–asked respondents to indicate their overall assessment of product placements in movies. The results: 25% view them as "a nifty way" for movie producers to raise money, 30% saw them as "interesting cultural markers," 25% found them "distracting," and for 18%, placements were deemed "evil." By comparison with equally unscientific results culled from this author's probing his own media law students' concerns about the phenomenon, Filmscape's results seem positively alarmist. If my students' reactions are at all typical, moviegoers know that studios depend upon product placements, and they frankly don't care. Indeed, they would find it jarring if film characters were to resort to using generic consumer items–drinking "COLA" instead of "Coke" or "Pepsi."

The use of real products on screen lends movies a feeling of reality, my students report, so why chastise the studios for accepting money in return for the "strategic placement" (Solman, 1988) of that reality? For better or worse, this review of the relevant case law suggests that the government is unlikely to do anything to protect moviegoers from the particular kinds of reality imposed on movie producers by the advertisers who place their products on the big screen.

REFERENCES

Adler, R. (1999). Here's smoking at you, kid: Has tobacco product placement in the movies really stopped? *Montana Law Review, 60,* 243-284.

Announcement of payment for broadcast (2001). 47 U.S.C.S. 317.

Askan, D. (2000). Sports broadcasting and virtual advertising: defining the limits of copyright law and the law of unfair competition, *Marquette Sports Law Journal, 11,* 41-86.

Bernard, J. (2000, December 10). Why I'm fed up with Fed Ex, *Daily News,* 18.

Bigelow v. Virginia, 421 U.S. 809 (1975).

Board of Trustees of the State University of New York v. Fox, 492 U. S. 469 (1989).

Bolger v. Youngs Drug Products Corporation, 463 U.S. 60 (1983).

Joseph Burstyn, Inc., v. Wilson, 343 U.S. 495 (1952).

Capitol Broadcasting Company v. Mitchell, 333 F. Supp. 582 (D.D.C. 1971), aff'd mem., 405 U. S. 100 (1972).

Center for the Study of Commercialism (1992, December 11). Press Release: FTC denies CSC's petition to promulgate rule on product placement in movies.

Central Hudson Gas & Electric Corp. v. Public Service Commission of New York, 447 U. S. 557 (1980).

Cook v. Gralike, 531 U.S. 510 (2001).

Federal Trade Commission (1999). *Cigar Sales and Advertising and Promotional Expenditures for Calendar Years 1996 and 1997.* Report to Congress. Washington, DC: Author.

Federal Trade Commission (1993, April 1). Press Release: Departing FTC official Cutler pounds agency's chest, exhorts commission critics to focus on real-life issues.

44 Liquormart, Inc. v. Rhode Island, 517 U.S. 484 (1996).

Greater New Orleans Broadcasting Association, Inc. v. United States, 527 U. S. 173 (1999).

Kline, R. L. (2000). Tobacco advertising after the settlement: Where we are and what remains to be done, *Kansas Journal of Law and Public Policy, 9,* 621-634.

Linmark Associates, Inc. v. Township of Willingboro, 431 U.S. 85 (1977).

Master Settlement Agreement (1998, November 23); online at: http://naag.org/tobac/cigmsa.rtf.

Metromedia, Inc. v. City of San Diego, 453 U.S. 490 (1981).

Miller, M. (1990, April). Hollywood: The ad. *Atlantic Monthly,* 41-68.

National Endowment for the Arts v. Finley, 524 U. S. 569 (1998).

National Public Radio (2001a, September 3). Product placement in classic literature, *All Things Considered.*

National Public Radio (2001b, August 3). Cracker Jack: The ultimate example of product placement, *All Things Considered.*

National Public Radio (2001c, May 17). New technology allowing TV viewers to by-pass usual commercials forces advertisers to find new ways of keeping their products in view, *All Things Considered.*

New York Times v. Sullivan, 376 U.S. 254 (1964).

Poll Archive (2001). Online at: http://www.filmscape.co.uk/interact/polls. Visited 24 December 2001.

Posadas de Puerto Rico v. Tourism Company, 478 U.S. 328 (1986).

Product placements (1993, July). *Entertainment Law & Finance*, 5.

Rubin v. Coors Brewing Company, 514 U. S. 476 (1995).

Schad v. Mount Ephraim, 452 U.S. 61 (1981).

Schlosser, J. (2001, January 29). Advertisers say product placement is alternative to spots, *Cahners Business Information*, 34.

Siegel, P. (2002). *Communication Law in America*. Boston: Allyn & Bacon.

Siegel, P. (1990). Smart shopping as patriotism: Avoidance, denial and advertising. *Communications and the Law*, *12*, 37-58.

Snyder, S., (1992). Movies and product placement: Is Hollywood turning films into commercial speech? *University of Illinois Law Review*, 301-337.

Solman, P. (1988, August 9). Product placement. *MacNeil/Lehrer News Hour.*

Southeastern Promotions, Ltd., v. Conrad, 420 U.S. 546 (1975).

Turner Broadcasting System, Inc. v. FCC, 512 U.S. 622 (1994).

Valentine v. Chrestensen, 315 U.S. 52 (1942).

Virginia State Board of Pharmacy v. Virginia Citizens Consumer Council, Inc., 425 U. S. 748 (1976).

Walker, J. (2001, August 1). Product placements thrive on TV, *Jack O'Dwyer's Newsletter, 34*(30), 3.

Wooley v. Maynard, 430 U.S. 705 (1977).

Zauderer v. Office of Disciplinary Counsel of the Supreme Court of Ohio, 471 U.S. 626 (1985).

On the Ethics of Product Placement in Media Entertainment

Lawrence A. Wenner

SUMMARY. This study examines the ethical propriety of current trends in product placement in television and film entertainment. Historical background for the product placement concept and practice is provided. Changes in the marketing climate that have provided a push for product placement are outlined. A characterization of the product placement industry as it stands today, and the ethical issues raised by the practice frame the analysis. Three distinct "genres" of contemporary product placement are analyzed: (1) Product Placement, (2) Product Integration, and (3) Video Insertion. First, the rise of Product Placement, strategic changes in use, and increased dependence on revenues in production will be discussed. The second section examines a newly mounted form of Product Integration, whereby product placement plays a key role in content development and support of production in television and film. Third, the origins of Video Insertion will be traced to the Princeton Video Image invention of its proprietary L-VIS product. The ethical efficacy of

Lawrence A. Wenner (PhD, University of Iowa) is Von der Ahe Professor of Communication and Ethics, School of Film and Television, College of Communication and Fine Arts, Loyola Marymount University, One LMU Drive, MS 8345, Los Angeles, CA 90045 (E-mail: lwenner@lmu.edu).

An earlier version was presented to the Inaugural International Media Ethics Conference on "Ethics, Media Credibility, and Global Standards," Old Parliament House, Canberra NSW, Australia, July 2002.

[Haworth co-indexing entry note]: "On the Ethics of Product Placement in Media Entertainment." Wenner, Lawrence A. Co-published simultaneously in *Journal of Promotion Management* (Best Business Books, an imprint of The Haworth Press, Inc.) Vol. 10, No. 1/2, 2004, pp. 101-132; and: *Handbook of Product Placement in the Mass Media: New Strategies in Marketing Theory, Practice, Trends, and Ethics* (ed: Mary-Lou Galician) Best Business Books, an imprint of The Haworth Press, Inc., 2004, pp. 101-132. Single or multiple copies of this article are available for a fee from The Haworth Document Delivery Service [1-800-HAWORTH, 9:00 a.m. - 5:00 p.m. (EST). E-mail address: docdelivery@haworthpress.com].

Digital Object Identifier: 10.1300/J057v10n01_08   *101*

placing "virtual advertisements" in space and times that do not naturally exist will be examined. The article closes with summary assessments and consideration of recommendations for action. Ethical issues focused on in the assessment include deception, artists' rights, and excess commercialism. Recommendations consider the climate for full and advance disclosure of product placements in media entertainment, the prospects for a voluntary rating system, and the threat of reclassifying product placement infused media entertainment as commercial speech. *[Article copies available for a fee from The Haworth Document Delivery Service: 1-800-HAWORTH. E-mail address: <docdelivery@haworthpress.com> Website: <http://www.HaworthPress.com> © 2004 by The Haworth Press, Inc. All rights reserved.]*

KEYWORDS. Commercial speech, ethics, media, movies, Princeton Video Image, product integration, product placement, television programming, video insertion, virtual advertising

INTRODUCTION

Within the wheelings and dealings of Hollywood filmmaking–where top talent is paid millions of dollars to star in movies with budgets in the tens [now hundreds] of millions–a humble bottle of soda and a simple candy bar wouldn't seem to warrant much attention. But if the pop and chocolate in question are going to be swigged and munched quite deliberately by one of those top stars in one of those major features–brand-name labels visible to all–then the sweet little snacks do indeed become big business. Specifically, the business of product placement. (Crisfulli, 1995, p. 4)

" 'Survivor' is as much a marketing vehicle as it is a television show," [producer Mark] Burnett noted in the July issue of 'Esquire' magazine. "My shows create an interest, and people will look at them, but the endgame here is selling products in stores–a car, deodorant, running shoes. It's the future of television." (as cited in Kern, 2001, p. 166)

Virtual product placement technology allows products or images to be retrofitted into or removed from existing programming, Mr.

[Paul] Slagle [Vice-President of Sales and Marketing at Princeton Video Image] says. 'It gives the seller the flexibility to sell the same program over and over again,' he says. (as cited in Friedman and Neff, 2001, p. 4c).

Is it going to get to the point where the tail wags the dog? All of a sudden, it's not about character and story, it's about, 'I have to mention this product three times because it's helping to pay for this show.' It becomes the proverbial slippery slope. (NBC Vice President of Standards and Practices Alan Wurtzel, as cited in Stanley, May 13, 2002, p. 38)

We live in an age of ubiquitous advertising. "Zapping" commercials with our remote controls and "zipping" through them as we playback prerecorded television programs are just two of the more common responses that citizens have to what has become an increasingly commodified environment. There is no doubt about it: We live in a time of "commercial clutter." While consumers zip, zap, duck, and cover in an attempt to cope with the situation, advertisers find they have an even larger problem with commercial clutter. The advertisers' problem is of course one of how to "break through the clutter" and get the attention of the consumer. And, in age-old tradition, their problem becomes our problem. In today's advertising-propelled media environment, we may try to run, but we can't hide. Advertising is more and more being embedded into the entertainment vehicle itself. Programming has become the Trojan horse, with product placements playing the role of the armed warriors lodged inside.

The Product Placement Concept

Product placement is a fairly simple concept. In the classic arrangement, stemming from the feature film model that began the practice, it "involves incorporating brands in movies in return for money or for some promotional or other consideration" (Gupta and Gould, 1997, p. 7). Commonplace in television programming as well, brands are featured in three primary ways (Smith, 1985). First, the product itself can be seen either in the background or, more desirably, actually being used. Second, a corporate logo, insignia, trademark or other identifying feature may be shown. Third, an advertisement, such as a billboard or television commercial, may be placed into a scene as "ambiance" in the background. In addition, direct verbal mentions of the brand name or product may be made in the dialogue or the brand may be creatively alluded to, without actually mentioning the brand, as was the case with the "computing machine" with "the fruit" reference that signified Apple in *Forest Gump*.

It is often assumed that corporations pay a considerable fee for the privilege of placing their brand into media entertainment. While this is done on occasion, the "pay for placement" model is the exception rather than the rule, accounting for perhaps 10% of product placement transactions (Harrison, 1999). More typical is some type of barter arrangement, where goods are supplied for use on- or off-screen, in trade for (or in the hopes of) being placed into the entertainment vehicle (Crisafulli, 1995). When a direct payment model is used, "visual exposure is the least expensive, verbal mentions are moderately priced, and character usage is the most costly" (DeLorme and Reid, 1999, p. 72). Such a hierarchy of valuing placements pertains regardless of how the "promotional consideration" has come about. Miller (as featured in Jhally, 2000) has gone so far as to anoint a film placement where a star actually mentions the brand name and is enthusiastically seen using the product as the "plug deluxe." Indeed, social science evidence suggests that consumer memory and evaluation of products are enhanced when a star uses a clearly identifiable product in a way that makes sense in the scene (d'Astous and Chartier, 2000).

Historical Background

Product placement in film and television has been with us far longer than many might think. Companies have always been ready to make their story part of the story on the screen. While identifiable instances may be found earlier, common practice dates from the 1930s feature films. Here, we saw the early cooperation of the automobile companies willing to help out a studio that might need a car for a scene or two and the strategic encouragement that the DeBeers company gave to include diamonds "as a girl's best friend" as a cap to a golden age Hollywood love story. The practice continued, often providing opportunities for products, such as alcohol or tobacco that elicit special ethical concern. From Humphrey Bogart's disdain at Gordon's Dry Gin being pitched overboard in *The African Queen* to Joan Crawford belting down Jack Daniels in 1945's *Mildred Pierce*, branded "sin" products paid to become part of the scene. In the 1950s and 1960s, the practice continued as occasional, but consistent. In 1982, the spotlight shined brightly on product placement with the attention given to Reese's Pieces candy as the peace offering in Steven Spielberg's *E.T.* After M&Ms said no to the placement, which ironically did not involve a fee, Reese's stepped in and their sales skyrocketed 66% (Crisafulli, 1995).

As a consequence of E.T. "phoning home," product placement took off in the late 1980s and became standard operating procedure in the 1990s. As a result, Pampers cleaned up for a $50,000 fee in *Three Men and a Baby*, Mel Gibson was seen swigging Cuervo Gold as a result of the $150,000 placed on the table for *Tequila Sunrise*, and Esso gas pumps fueled *Days of Thunder* for $300,000 (McCarthy, 1998). More blatant attempts to build movies around products in the 1980s often flopped. Notably, Columbia Pictures, then owned by Coca-Cola, featured Bill Cosby, the product's ad spokesperson in a spy spoof *Leonard Part 6* that reeked of Coke and McDonald's and attempted to cash in on the alien craze with *Mac & Me*, which critics saw as a "feature length commercial" (Lovell, 1998). In 1998, with AOL paying between $3 and $6 million to become the Internet service provider (ISP) linking Tom Hanks with Meg Ryan in *You've Got Mail*, this increasing tendency of product placements to drive the plot reached a head with critics particularly offended by AOL's smiley face logo being used in the film's trailers (Govani, 1999; Jhally, 2000). Some brands, such as Fed-Ex, believing that they could take product placement to the bank, stepped into the role of financial backer, funding 80% of *Cast Away* which featured Fed-Ex packages prominently saving the star stranded on a remote island (Shaw, 2001).

The Push for Placement

In today's media entertainment environment, product placement has come to play such a starring role because the strategy of integrated marketing communications (known as IMC) has fostered an awareness of how pieces of public perception can complement each other. As a result, product placement has become part of the overall advertising and public relations mix, integral to building brand awareness and positive associations (Chabria, 2002). This, combined with increased interest by advertisers in "breaking through the clutter" and catching the consumers in a moment of pleasure, as opposed to when their defenses are up–as they are when seeing an advertisement–has driven the development of product placement in the marketplace ("Movies may carry . . .," 1999). The occasional "rags to riches" success story has also played a role in fueling the product placement myth. In addition to the surge in

Reese's Pieces sales, often cited are the tripling of sales for Ray Ban sunglasses after being donned by Tom Cruise in *Risky Business*, the doubling of the market for little known Red Stripe beer after being featured in *The Firm*, and the resuscitation of the Slinky novelty from being seen in *Toy Story* (Buss, 1998; Crisafulli, 1995; Mueller, 2001).

Rising interest in the practice is also fueled by pressures on entertainment producers. Here, increased interest in product placement is often attributed to the rising costs of film and television production (Branswell, 2002). To stem costs, producers have always sought to "borrow" a car, hotel lobby, or department store as a prop or site for a scene. Understandably, willing cooperation came from businesses pleased to see their brands, products, and services immortalized, hopefully positively, on screen. A more realistic appraisal might admit that feature films and television programs have always cost a good deal to produce. It might be fairer to say that in today's marketplace, the multinational conglomerates with media holdings are looking more strategically at maximizing profits. It is not so much an issue of keeping production costs down, but offsetting them with revenue streams that capitalize on synergies that have market value (Paul, 2002). Nonetheless, it is clear that any "cost savings" that have resulted from product placement have not been passed on to consumers, either in the form of lowered admission prices to feature films or to fewer sponsored breaks in commercial television fare (Gupta et al., 2000).

INDUSTRY AND ISSUES

The practice of product placement has begun to be so widespread that it has fostered an industry of its own. While the size of the industry is hard to measure, observers have pegged industry size to be in a range between $50 million and $1 billion a year (Harrison, 1999; Mueller, 2001). Annual retainer fees paid to specialty product placement agencies range from tens of thousands of dollars a year for a small or emerging brand to a few million a year for a major automobile maker (Klayman, 1998). The industry has its own trade association, the approximately decade-old Entertainment Marketing Association (EMA) [formerly Entertainment Resources and Marketing Association (ERMA)] (see *www.erma.org*). EMA is made up of three hand-in-glove constituent groups that each have a vested interest in the practice: (1) the corporations and manufacturers that are looking to get their brands placed into entertainment vehicles, (2) the studios and production companies that are looking to defray costs by having products "comped" or placed into their projects, and (3) the product placement agency, which may be either a specialty agency representing a cadre of corporate clients looking for placements or a more general advertising or public relations firm that offers placement services to its clients. According to a past-president of the organization, the purpose of EMA is "to promote the profession and to ensure that it has a high standard of ethics" (as quoted in Harrison, 1999). Indeed, EMA offers a 12 point "Code of Standards and Ethics" to guide its members. (See Table 1.) Unfortunately, the points of concern over ethical behavior center on "rules of conduct" for the business transaction that occurs between the corporate entity, the studio or producer, and the product placement agency. Broader efficacy issues that might hint at responsibilities to the audience are notably left out, as are statements that explicitly recognize the rights of artists in the creative process.

While EMA's Code does not directly address social responsibility or artistic rights issues, it is clear that their membership has a vested interest in product placements being done in a sensitive and responsible way. In their pamphlet "Product Placement 101" (and on their website *www.erma.org*), it is clearly stated that, in the course of pitching a placement: "If the placement opportunity in any way jeopardizes the creative integrity of the film, it will be dismissed as a possibility at this time" (ERMA, "Product Placement 101," n.d.). From the EMA perspective, a good product placement doesn't make a lot of noise by calling attention to itself. Advocates for the responsible use of product placement pose that the practice is most appropriate if it is "seamless" or "organic" to the story or situation (Merrill, 2001). Just exactly what this means is of course open to a good deal of interpretation. It is part of an overall argument that product placements advance realism. Support for this claim comes on evidence that our contemporary environment is populated by products that are branded rather than having a generic "beer" or "corn flakes" label slapped on them. Of course, it is its quiet footsteps in approaching us, its nimbleness in blending into the background below the threshold of perception, that raise key questions about the deceptive nature of product placement in media entertainment (Berkowitz, 1994).

Beyond this core concern over deception, the issues surrounding artist's rights and the influences on creative integrity need to be more carefully examined. When directors and screenwriters are pressured to "make room" for product placements in their script, even if they "theoretically" have veto power, the rights of the artist and the climate for creativity may have been impinged upon. The mere fact that product

TABLE 1. Entertainment Marketing Association (EMA)*: Mission Statement and Code of Standards and Ethics (from Organizational Website *www.erma.org*) [*Formerly Entertainment Resources and Marketing Association (ERMA)]

MISSION STATEMENT

We will uphold and promote the highest level of conduct and present a professional image of our industry and its members. This will be accomplished by advancing the knowledge and education of our members and communicating information about our industry to the public and the media.

CODE OF STANDARDS AND ETHICS

1. A member shall exemplify high standards of honesty and integrity while carrying out obligations to a client or employer.

2. A member shall deal fairly with past or present clients or employers and with fellow practitioners, giving due respect to the ideal of free inquiry and to the opinion of others.

3. A member shall adhere to the highest standards of accuracy and truth, avoiding extravagant claims, unfair comparisons, or taking credit for ideas and projects borrowed from others.

4. A member shall not knowingly disseminate false or misleading information and shall act promptly to correct erroneous communications for which he or she is responsible.

5. A member shall not guarantee the achievement of specified results beyond the member's control.

6. A member shall not represent conflicting or competing interests without the express consent of those concerned given after full disclosure of the facts.

7. A member shall not accept fees, commissions, gifts or any other consideration from anyone except clients or employers for whom services are performed, without their express consent, given after full disclosure of the facts.

8. A member shall scrupulously safeguard the confidences and privacy rights of present, former, and prospective clients or employers.

9. A member shall not intentionally, or knowingly, damage the professional reputation or practice of another practitioner.

10. If a member has evidence that another member has been guilty of unethical, illegal, or unfair practices, including those in violation of this code, the member is obligated to present the information promptly to the proper authorities within the Association, for investigation and possible action.

11. A member called as a witness in a proceeding for enforcement of this code is obligated to appear, unless excused for sufficient reason by the authorities of this Association.

12. A member shall, as soon as possible, sever relations with any organizations or individuals if such relationship requires conduct contrary to the articles of this code.

Used with permission of Entertainment Marketing Association (EMA).

placements routinely play a key role in the budgetary process and thus, are expected, make this issue deserving of ethical scrutiny (Elliott, March 29, 1999; Paul, 2002). The issues of deception and risks to artistic integrity contribute to an overarching ethical issue that surrounds product placement. This, of course, concerns the claim of "overcommercialization" and its consequences. It is generally argued, given the present state of product placement, that an ethical line has been crossed. Reliant on a virtue ethics logic, such excess is deemed harmful in that it enmeshes entertainment, storytelling, and consequently the imagination in the logic of commodity culture (Govani, 1999; McCarthy, June 19, 2001).

In the next sections of the article, these and other ethical implications of current practices in film and television entertainment are considered more carefully. Three related variants of the product placement phenomenon are assessed: (1) product placement in its original form, as it has been used in feature films for years and is being used now, on a stepped-up basis, (2) product integration, which is a more strategic approach where products drive the creative form and content of media entertainment, and (3) video insertion, a new, technologically driven variant on the scene that allows for virtual placements in program content. The examination of each of these will begin with a basic discussion of how the technique works. This will be followed by consideration of arguments made for the technique, in order to assess whether the stated benefits contribute to a greater good or might mask a harm. Lastly, consideration is given to criticism that has been voiced about each technique, in order to evaluate the ethical contours of the concerns that have been voiced about the practice. After giving consideration to each of the three practices, the final section assesses the ethical efficacy of product placements in media entertainment and presents recommendations for action.

POPP: (PLAIN OLD) PRODUCT PLACEMENT

The basic form of product placement stems from the need to have realistic props in movies or television programs. Historically, a studio or film producer examines a script and makes assessments of the kinds of products or props they need in the course of shooting. From this, they may contact specific manufacturers or producers directly to see if a deal can be worked out. In the more modern version, a list of product types that are needed may be made by the producers and put out to bid to corporations and to product placement agencies. It is typical in today's marketplace to find that product placement agencies are more proactive: They solicit scripts prior to production and comb them for possibilities for their clients and use them as opportunities to pitch to potential clients. It is not uncommon for companies or placement agencies to get in even earlier in the development process or to lobby writers to feature their products in the script itself (Crisafulli, 1995; Paul, 2002). Still, the general goal of the original conception of product placement is to help "present a realistic picture of life as we've lived it, but not to the point of intruding into the dramatic content of the film," according to EMA Past President Eric Dalquist (Mueller, 2001, p. 61).

The packages that result not only offer the producer the rights and use of the brand in the work, but may offer fees as compensation for the placement. While less typical than a barter transaction, these fees can range from small to large, depending on the type of product, competition in the marketplace, and nature and duration of the placement that is anticipated. Guarantees sometimes factor in, adding to the cost of the placement. As Paul (2002, p. 22) reports:

> Manufacturers will sometimes pay a lot to guarantee that their product is used, and not a competitor's. Product placements usually cost between $10,000 and $1 million, though they often average about $50,000. Carmaker BMW reportedly paid $3 million to get James Bond to switch to one of its cars in the 1996 movie *Golden Eye*.

The corporate "partner" can pay for the placement in other ways. Cross-marketing deals often require the brand to contribute to underwriting significant portions of the advertising costs for a film. While these ads sell both the movie and the product, they tend to sell the movie first, burying the true cost of the placement elsewhere, and often making involvement a more expensive proposition. Such cross-marketing deals and tie-ins can run up promotional budgets considerably. For the U.S. marketing alone for the James Bond adventure *Tomorrow Never Dies*, the placed brands of "Smirnoff, Omega, and BMW spent $77 million on marketing tied to the film" (Cowlett, 2000, p. 29).

Benefits

While the advantages of product placement to moviemakers and to corporate brands are clear, the benefits to consumers are more elusive. At the basic level, the studio or producer may reduce prop costs by a quarter to a third through a simple trade of product use for the placement. Arguments are often made that these savings allow for improvements in "production values," through supporting longer shooting schedules or enhancing lighting, sound quality, or musical scoring (Branswell, 2002).

For the marketer or corporate brand, product placements offer a series of related benefits. Foremost is that the product's appearance in the film is that it is an "ingrained message" that is not expected by the audience, and thus received in a "happy, receptive state of mind" (Shaw, 2001, p. 36). The general "inobtrusiveness" of placements squelches the call for the mute button in television viewing. In the movie theater, where there is no mute button, the audience is captive, drawn to the screen and placement in a darkened environment. Related to its inobtrusiveness, an added advantage of the placement context is that it may be interpreted as "implied endorsement" by the stars or celebrities using the product in a film or program ("When is a prop . . .," 2001).

Putting aside the occasional instances of cross-marketing participation and underwriting of advertising campaigns that can be an expensive way to insure a premium placement position, a key benefit of product placements is that they are relatively low cost or no cost beyond the "borrowed" use of the prop. The cost efficiencies are considerable in comparison to paid advertising. The paid placement, which again is not the most common form, averages $50,000, a fee that might not even buy a one-time 30-second placement on prime-time television. Beyond cost efficiencies, placements offer good value. They can often be "high profile" by generating excitement in the marketing roll-out of the entertainment product. Further, value can be long-lasting and far reaching. Films and television programs are often distributed to global audiences and can often have remarkably long shelf-lives in reruns and video distribution. These factors conspire to make product placement a tantalizing bargain for those looking to build their brand (see ERMA, n.d.; "When is a prop . . .," 2001).

Criticism

There are few benefits to consumers in the basic product placement. Tastefully done, they may add a realistic "ambiance" to a scene or situation. They allow attention not to focus on a trivial detail in a scene by having an "unbranded" or "generic" product call attention to itself. Indeed, as John Barnard, CEO of the UK's largest placement agency, the New Media Group, has said, "You are trying to sink messages into consumers' minds subconsciously, if you are too obvious, the danger is that an audience may feel it is being plugged, or just see the deal" (Cowlett, 2000, p. 29). Of course, when subliminal burying of the placement puts the "plug" below the threshold of perception, deception is a necessary outcome. More risky, however, is that the branded product will call attention to itself by being positioned in a way that the label can be clearly read or having the camera linger a little too long. This relates to the common complaint that product placements can easily "overpopulate" a film or television program, turning the entertainment vehicle into series of commercials (Govani, 1999). Saturation of placements cause harm in two distinct ways. First they corrupt any artistic work that did not set out to be a commercial in the first place. Second, they draw the ire of the audience. There is much evidence that excessive placement cause perceivable "discontinuities" in consuming media narratives and are resented by the audience (c.f., d'Astous and Chartier, 2000). Similar reactions come from placements that are inappropriate to the story's context, such as Disney's use of "Air-Hercules" sandals that puts Nike up close and personal or the UPS truck showing up in backcountry Africa in *George of the Jungle* (McCarthy, 1998; Thompson, 1997). Put in ethical terms, overly saturated and inappropriate use of product placements in media entertainment does not convey "other respecting care" for the audience and their experience.

Beyond the dangers associated with subliminalism and overcommercialism, realism is inherently compromised in another way. Because companies seek to protect the public goodwill towards their brands, placements, almost without exception, show usage in a positive light. Consequently, the broken whiskey bottle that is used in a scene to kill someone will undoubtedly be generically unidentifiable as opposed to say, Jack Daniels. As Chabria (2002, p. 18) puts it, "a toy company wouldn't want a toddler choking on its latest rattle in a TV drama." Moviemakers who don't show products placed in a favorable light, risk legal action, as was the case when Reebok was surprised by the line "Fuck Reebok, all they do is ignore me, always have, always will" in the sport marketplace drama *Jerry Maguire* (McCarthy, 1998, p. 8). Thus, the marketer's goal in placements is to find those that are "positive and appropriate," as one executive put it (Leith, 2000, p. 1P). Of course, realism that tends toward "positive and appropriate" is necessarily a false realism, and thus one that is, by definition, deceptive.

Clearly, the cost savings advantage attributed to product placement is not passed on to the consumer. When placements proliferate, movie ticket prices don't go down and there aren't fewer commercials in a television program. Thus, the observation made by one television executive that "product placement is like prostitution" (Ryle, 2001, p. 5) is a useful analogy. Not only does it put artists involved in the creation of media entertainment into a compromised position, but the larger benefits go to corporate overseers who play the role of the pimp. The "press for prostitution" may be the more serious issue. While practitioners associated with EMA may indeed stop when creative personnel say placement is inappropriate or objectionable, it is not so easy to "just say no" and probably just as effective as the strategy has been in combating the war on drugs. When writers are approached by corporations before scripts are even completed, and when films in development are more likely to receive Hollywood's "green light" when opportunities for placements and tie-ins are built-in, the climate for creativity has been structurally changed. Producers, directors, writers, actors, and other creative personnel come to learn that the likelihood of their being hired is linked to their willingness to be friendly to products being placed in their work. In a business where the "clout" to say no is fragile and elusive, "uncooperative" or "difficult" creative workers can be replaced by others who "see the light."

PRODUCT INTEGRATION

If the original impetus for product placement came from opportunities that were "already in the script," then it might be said that the locus has shifted in a refinement known as "product integration" to "becoming the script." As a *Time* magazine report (Poniewozik, 2001, p. 76) noted:

> Product placement used to be simpler. Jerry Seinfeld gave shoutouts to Snapple and Junior Mints (gratis) to give his sitcom verisimilitude. The *Price is Right* still pitches bedroom sets and floor wax. But after *Survivor's* success, "product integration" (a step past mere placement) is taking in-show advertising to a new level of sophistication and stealth. Products are becoming part of the show, be it the Taco Bell that's the site of a "murder" investigation on a new reality show or an SUV used in a TV-staged transcontinental race. And producers and advertisers are getting cozier than at any time since the days of *Texaco Star Theater*.

Largely, but not exclusively, a television phenomenon, product integration ups the ante on product placement. With softness in the advertising market over the last few years, television sponsors have had new leverage to place demands on networks: "They have asked for and received integration into the content of television shows in return for their spending" (Stanley, April 29, 2002, p. 12). This represents a "sea change," as Rob Donnell, an executive with J. Walter Thomson has put it, because "[t]he networks didn't used to want us" (as quoted in Brown, 2002, p. A1). Much of the change is fueled by evidence that viewers are finding more and more ways to avoid commercials, through zapping, zipping, and muting–strategies that have been advanced further with personal video recorder technologies such as TiVo and Replay TV (Neff, 2001).

Minus these new technologies, this changed environment evokes memories of the early days of television when the sponsor was more firmly in control. Here, shows like *Kraft Television Theater, Coke Time*, and the *Schlitz Playhouse of Stars* populated prime-time. And of course soap operas, sponsored by soap companies, had a vested interest in creating a domestic setting where their products could "shine brightly." While the old model often had "named" advertisers as the sole sponsors of "their" programs, such an approach would be prohibitively expensive in the new product integration environment. As well, in the 1950s, most title sponsors were content with "bringing the show" to the audience, rather than becoming a key feature of the show's plotline. In today's market, integral placements are traded for subsidized production costs and/or commitments to advertise in a given show (Stanley, May 13, 2002).

Intregration Planning

The current turn to product integration has taken a variety of forms, with brands intervening in the "integration planning" at various stages from the ground level concept of a series to plot twists and themes that put their product hand-in-glove with the show. The networks themselves are out there, drumming up business on Madison Avenue. Pressed for cash in developing a summer replacement reality show, NBC Entertainment President Jeffrey Zucker enlisted a large ad agency to underwrite the $750,000 an episode production cost and buy large advertising blocks in a show called *Lost*. NBC and Zucker had nothing to lose as Coca-Cola, Johnson & Johnson, Lowe's, and Marriott International all "secured roles for their products in a series that's supposed to be unscripted" (Wells, 2001, p. 131).

Product integration has been spurred in good part by the possibilities of structuring such "reality" shows around a regularized sprinkling of products (McCarthy, July 23, 2001). The opportunities have clearly been mutually beneficial, and there certainly has been a quick learning curve. During *Survivor's* first season, about a million dollars of advertising was linked to product placements. As the show moved to its second season in *The Australian Outback*, product integration had become so essential to the program's design that Mark Burnett, the show's executive producer, suggested that the products had become the adventure's "17th character." Some $12 million dollars in advertising had the carrot of having their products integrated into the storyline. As Burnett put it, "You'd better make [advertisers] feel they're selling product, or they're going to find new places to advertise" (Poniewozik, 2001, p. 76). Product integration was used as a carrot not only for advertisers; contestants on the show were rewarded with integrated products such as Bud Light, Mountain Dew, and Doritos for surviving stages of battling the Outback. Initial internal resistance to this hypercommercialism was successfully overcome:

> *Survivor's* host, Jeff Probst, said he initially was a little concerned about stuffing real-world products into an otherworldly setting. "It seemed so foreign," Probst says. "But then I realized it's a legitimate use of the product. It plays a part in the show." (Stanley, May 13, 2002, p. 36)

Money talked in other reality shows as Fox's *Murder in Small Town X* and ABC's *The Runner* built on the model of *Survivor* by designing elements in the plotlines of these shows to showcase sponsors like Nokia, Jeep, Taco Bell, McDonald's, and Sears (Poniewozik, 2001; McCarthy, July 23, 2001). With product usage and locations tailored to sponsor's desires, television programming, like negotiating a commercial lease in a shopping mall, had moved to a "built-to-suit" model.

While networks were out there pitching business for product integration, so too were advertisers. A noteworthy move was made by the Ford Motor Company in developing a show called *No Boundaries*, a title which echoed the Ford brand's current marketing slogan. Ford, offering to underwrite production costs and agreeing to "control the ad inventory during the show's run," found a willing taker in the upstart WB network (Stanley, May 13, 2002, p. 38). While a ratings casualty, thirteen episodes of the adventure reality show were shot, showcasing contestants competing in Ford sport utility vehicles. According to an ad executive overseeing the Ford account, the appeal of the concept is clear: "With *No Boundaries*, we get to spend an hour presenting the value of the Ford brand, and an ad that airs during the show is more effective, it spikes the spot" (Brown, 2002, p. A1). Ford has also integrated itself into the *Tonight Show with Jay Leno* by proposing "The Lincoln Garage Concert Series" as a regular Friday feature in the program in trade for some $9 million in advertising commitments to NBC. As part of the agreement, Ford builds the concert stage set which will feature Lincoln Navigators and other vehicles in a "gritty" garage setting for the youthful bands that will appeal to the brand's target market (Stanley, May 13, 2002).

Scripted programs are also being included in the product integration mix. A notable example has been Revlon's involvement in the ABC soap opera *All My Children*. The show's producers conceived an idea whereby Revlon would be cast as a "named" arch-rival to Erica Kane, the show's protagonist, and her cosmetics company, Enchantment. Even with being cast as the villain, Revlon "bit the apple" and signed up for a three month "story arc" that featured them in the soap. Although they would even be called "vultures" in the script, Revlon saw value, guaranteeing $3 and $7 million in advertising purchases to ABC over the run of the storyline. In a variant on "call me anything, but remember my name," Revlon doesn't mind being disparaged in the show as it characterizes them as a "formidable player" in the cosmetics business and because it gets them out of the commercial clutter (Flint and Nelson, 2002; Stanley, May 13, 2002).

Benefits

For advertisers, product integration is a step forward that allows them to respond to consumers' rising avoidance of commercials and to get out of the usual clutter of competing messages. The weak advertising market has allowed them to more forcefully leverage an advantage they have always had. Money just talks in a different way. In "blending a commercial message with a program so that the program is the message," Robert Riesenberg, Vice-President of the Universal McCann agency has observed, product placement offers "a perfect marketing fit" (as quoted in Brown, 2002, p. A1). Part of the reason the fit is so good, is that there's an enhanced "credibility factor" in integration that "makes the product benefit seem more plausible" (Ebenkamp, p. S10). Because brands get in on "ground floor" discussions, the placements can be more sensibly "integral" than a product placement opportunity that is merely "tacked on," as is the case with the original conception of placing products in existing scripts.

For networks, product integration has become a major chip to play in attracting elusive advertising dollars by "adding value" beyond the commercials themselves. This makes them more attractive in a fragmented and competitive marketplace for ad dollars. A related benefit is that program development and production costs are not only "outsourced" but subsidized by advertisers, who move from being merely clients to becoming partners. In many of the product integration deals, networks retain controlling interest in the shows as properties that can be moved to global and syndicated markets. The net result is that for networks, both risks and costs are tempered (Stanley, May 13, 2002).

For creative personnel and for viewers, the benefits of product integration are more difficult to identify. For producers, director, and writers, about the best that can be said is that with product integration, as opposed to just product placement, they necessarily enter the marketplace with their eyes wide open when considering a project dependent on the practice. For viewers, there is one upside that so far has gained little steam. This is the press by certain advertisers to develop "family friendly programming" that is consistent with the values that these advertisers want associated with their brands. Fed up with television saturated with gratuitous violence and sexual explicitness, the Family Friendly Programming Forum of the Association of National Advertisers provides development funds and advertiser support for family-oriented shows. The first success to come out of this effort has been the WB Network's *Gilmore Girls*. While the goal of the forum is not to integrate products in the explicit way that product integration practices seem to be moving, their strategy shares the trend for sponsors to get involved in development, tune content to the goals of their brands, and to make commitments to provide advertising support (Neff, 2001).

Criticism

Current product integration trends sound a loud alarm over acceptable tolerances for commercialism. Critics recognize that television has always been a commercial medium:

> Since television has always been in the service of advertising, this kind of art meeting commerce is inevitable, according to industry executives. How far it goes will depend on how well it's done. "There is a model somewhere between network prime time as we know it now and QVC," [marketing executive Mark] Stroman says. "But no one's figured it out yet." (Stanley, May 13, 2002, p. 36)

The temptations, however, are considerable. As Pennington (2002, p. G-3) suggests: "Integrated advertising might also be a slippery slope in which greedy networks and their corporate owners couldn't resist making every show an infomercial, packed with product plugs at the expense of storyline and character development." She goes on to ask "[w]hat will it mean for television if we can't tell the ads from the show?" This is a fair enough worry: when deception becomes routine in the stories that we tell to each other, how might we argue that we are better off for it?

The effects of the practice on the storytelling function are an artists' rights issue as well. With network licensing fees covering less and less of the production costs of programming, the pressures for producers and writers to integrate products to offset these shortfalls is considerable. In the course of the interaction, we may have pitted "free speech" in a losing battle with "commercial speech." As Robert Thompson, Director of Syracuse University's Center for the Study of Popular Television put it:

> It makes me nervous if creators will be told to integrate a brand into a story because someone's paying for it. Maybe other stories won't be told because they aren't as amenable to product placement. If I'm a writer, the last thing I want is a list of products that I have to integrate into a script. Will we get bad storytelling because of these constraints? (as quoted in Stanley, May 13, 2002, p. 38)

Once such expectations become routine, a moderate mid-point may become elusive because tolerances expand as the practice ceases to be perceived as deviant. This has often been likened to the dripping faucet that is disturbing at first, but quickly blends into the background. We are at a point now where advocacy organizations, such as the Center for Digital Democracy and the Center for Science in the Public Interest, clearly hear the drips. They see product integration as "blatant commercialization" and as a "betrayal" to viewers (Stanley, May 13, 2002). How loudly viewers hear these drips and how long they will hear them is difficult to say.

VIDEO INSERTION

Elvis may have left the building, but if the possibilities of newly emerging video insertion technologies play out, he will soon be appearing regularly on screens large and small, in movies and television programs, in new releases and in reruns, and in different languages to be understood across the world's markets. Elvis is how Princeton Video Image's L-VIS, or live-video insertion system is pronounced. Princeton Video's L-VIS is the industry's leading technology, able to put a digital Elvis or a digital "anything else" into film and television programs, while they are being produced or after the fact. The possibilities make purists, who were up-at-arms about the colorizing of movie classics, livid. The features offered by Princeton Video, and its competitors Orad Hi-Tech Systems IMadGINET technology and Symah Vision, allow placing "virtual ads" virtually anywhere ("Pressure Mounts . . .," 2000).

These technologies, refined over the last decade or so in sports broadcasts (and occasional repair jobs in feature films) can put something where there isn't anything or replace something that's there with something else. At first, value was added to football broadcasts by adding inserted first down lines. Later, virtual billboards were added to baseball telecasts that were nowhere to be seen in the stadium. Overseas, insertion technology is regularly used in rugby and cricket, and FIFA has endorsed its use in soccer broadcasts without reservation (Goddard, 2000; "Pressure Mounts . . .," 2000). However, it was the moving of the technology to prime-time television that meant a new era was upon us. As Stuart Elliott (October 1, 1999, p. C11) of the *New York Times* said:

> Another frontier is being crossed in the commercialization of culture as digital technology has been used for the first time to "virtually" place products in a prime-time television entertainment program watched by American viewers. That milestone interpolation of advertisements where they had not been before is being carefully studied by Madison Avenue as part of its never-ending effort to wrap consumers in a cocoon of sponsored images that range from the mentioning of brand-name products in children's textbooks to the renaming of stadiums for huge corporations.

By using complex software algorithms, the technology has evolved so that the video image that is inserted sufficiently adjusts tracking and perspective so that it is indistinguishable from actual objects (Berger, 1999).

The possibilities for this, as well as the marketing and pricing models, are just now beginning to take shape. UPN gave the technology a trial in their series *Seven Days*, "when it digitally inserted a Wells Fargo Bank sign, Kenneth Cole shopping bags and bottles of Coca-Cola and Evian into the show after it was finished" (Berger, 1999, p. 14). In another test, Princeton Video inserted a Snackwell's cookie box into the 1960s kitchen of a *Bewitched* rerun, even though the Snackwell's brand didn't exist at that time (Poniewozik, 2001). Virtual product placement has been sold for a number of Warner Bros. shows in syndication, including *Friends, The Drew Carey Show*, and *Suddenly Susan* (Friedman and Neff, 2001). The most extensive trial to date has been in exploring the international market for telenovelas produced by Mexico's Televisa Network. Here the network has charged "advertisers about $4,500 to $6,000 for three shots each lasting about 10 seconds in one episode" (Berger, 1999, p. 14). When the telenovela plays again or moves to another market, the virtual placement is sold again.

Benefits

A number of key benefits come from video insertion, when compared to other product placement strategies. Foremost is the portability of the technology. As Dick Robertson, President of Warner Bros. Domestic Television Distribution has pointed out: "Product placement is nothing new to television. This [virtual placement] is just a better way of doing it, so the product placement doesn't have to live in the show's negative forever" (Ross, 1999, preceding p. 1). Thus, that Coke can shown in the refrigerator of an original show can be bought by Pepsi for rerun syndication, and sold again to 7-Up for foreign markets. Video insertion has strong advantages in being able to tailor virtual ads to different markets. The packaging for say, a cereal box, can shift from English to Spanish to French to Chinese "to read" more easily in different markets. Or that billboard seen in the background of a scene can be sold to one company that has distribution in one region, while it might feature a completely different product from another company when seen in other parts of the world. The combined ability to resell placements and to segment markets where products are placed is a compelling benefit to marketers and sponsors alike. Television reruns and the latest release of a film can update their placements. No longer will we have to see a placement for a product that has ceased to exist in the marketplace. However, on the flipside, we may end up seeing products inserted into content that didn't actually exist at the time of shooting or exist in the era being portrayed on screen. This latter risk is most perplexing, in that it may suggest that a product "always existed" when it is actually a recent market invention (Friedman and Neff, 2001; Poniewozik, 2001).

In television, virtual placements promise an ease in entering the integrated digital marketplace. With the interactive television that is just around the corner, consumers will able to "click" on virtual placements and buy the products in one fell swoop. This may run the gamut from buying a jersey of a star player when a goal has been scored to ordering a pizza when a scene triggers hunger. Advocates argue that such features offer convenience to consumers (Goddard, 2000). Technological advances have also been made to remedy an early complaint about video insertion technology expressed by product placement specialists. As opposed to a real placement, virtual placements couldn't allow stars to actually handle and thus, be seen using, products (Elliott, March 29, 1999). This obstacle appears ready to fall, as Princeton Video is already developing new software that will allow actors to be seen handling virtual products in a way that will be perceived no differently than the real thing (Ross, 1999).

Criticism

A key criticism of video insertion technology mirrors one of its main strengths: It makes insertions look like something that was there all along. As Dennis Wilkinson, President of Princeton Video put it: "The goal is make them real [and to] look as if they were there when the show was originally produced." Framed as an ethical assessment, the goal is to deceive. It is not surprising that the technique has been called "the Harry Houdini of the media business" (Elliott, October 1, 1999). Critics such as Jeff Chester, Executive Director of the Center for Digital Democracy argue that virtual placement is a "deceptive marketing practice" and can't see that there is an "appropriate manner of inserting digital ad images into a TV show because it blurs a line that ought to separate editorial content from paid peddling" (Elliott, May 23, 2001, p. C6). He worries that the "click to buy" capabilities of virtual placements point to an "Orwellian" future that will make advertisers' intrusions into 1950s television look like small potatoes because now "the TV begins collecting information on you" (Poniewozik, 2000, p. 76). Media critics are "terrified" by the possibilities of virtual advertising adding to already plentiful threats of privacy invasion and see its ability to add "sneaky advertising" ad infinitum to "places where you wouldn't expect it and where you can't avoid it" as pushing commercialism over yet another threshold (Littlefield, 2000, p. C-10). Advertising insiders, such as John Muszynski, an investment executive with an arm of the Leo Burnett Company concur with this fear about overuse: "I would just hope that the networks will be very careful with this and don't allow it to become a runaway train" (Elliott, March 29, 1999).

Beyond fears over virtual placements becoming a "Houdini" or "runaway train" of ad intrusion, there are a number of artist's rights issues raised by video insertion technology. While Princeton Video works on technology that will allow actors to hold and use virtual products, it seems clear that "acting" with inserted products will require both an awareness and a requisite delicacy that is not required of an ordinary prop on the set (Elliott, March 29, 1999). As such, it necessarily constrains and changes dramatic action and flow. However, marketing models, the setting of price points, and legal issues also cloud the rights of artists. As Elliott (October 1, 1999, p. C1) reports:

> Virtual ads, however, face some real obstacles, particularly in entertainment programming. One is the vexatious issue of rights, particularly how to reimburse the creators and producers of series if their work is changed. Even though virtual ads represent a new source of revenue for the Hollywood studios that produce TV programming, many describe the rights issue as a drawback that will impede the widespread appearance of virtual ads.

Clearly old contracts with writers, producers, directors, and actors did not anticipate the possibility of products being retroactively being placed into finished works. Thus, it is likely a very gray legal area.

However, this market of entertainment product "already in the bank" will be the source of the greatest temptation for marketers and owners of this product. There are indicants that when technological changes promise to open new markets, accommodations can be made. The move to colorization of black and white films provides one example of tampering with completed work that has come to be accepted. Of course, putting virtual ads into classic and not-so-classic product is a much higher bar. But as Michael Jacobson, Executive Director of the Center for Science in the Public Interest has cynically put it: "People will object to the sneakiness of this, and then they'll get used to it" (Littlefield, 2000, p. C-10). Moving into the future, it is clear that media conglomerates will command their legal staffs to protect their future rights to virtual placements in entertainment produced from this point forward. Just how much "clout" the creative community and its guilds have in combating such a push remains to be seen.

ASSESSMENT AND RECOMMENDATIONS

The basic idea of product placement has been with us for a long time and undoubtedly will be with us in the future. It seems likely that, given rising advertising clutter and increases in ad avoidance strategies by consumers, marketers will advance their reliance on product placement and other strategies that get advertising into our line of sight. When these factors combine with a softness in the advertising market, corporate interests have more leverage to influence and become part of the stories we tell ourselves as a culture. Historically, drama, comedy, and other of the arts have offered a way for artists to reflect on culture's priorities, values, and assumptions. That free artistic expression can indeed be powerful and influence social thought and organization was in good part at the center of Plato's worries over the poets.

Putting the arts patronage system aside, people provided support for the arts by attending a play, seeing a movie, or buying a book. Part of what we were buying was the artist's vision, or at the very least, an opportunity to engage with that vision and to respond. This is not to say that such vision was unfettered or uninfluenced by marketplace realities and making the product attractive to an increasingly mass audience, but rather that the vision was not one infused with a side concern about "goodness of fit" as a product showcase. The creative product had a key locus in the artist's imagination. A product placement infused arts necessarily filters cultural observations. In such an environment, the likelihood of something being produced necessarily begins to correlate with the synergies that the product demonstrates in being conducive to and compatible with marketing displays. Perhaps this is a harsh realization for those advocates of product placement who argue that placements merely add realism. But the fact of the matter is that once the product placement door is opened, there is great temptation to put a larger wedge in, with the net result being that the viability of mass art becomes judged based on its abilities to serve as a Trojan horse for products, product tie-ins, and as an uncontested site for the logic of commodity culture.

In framing this study, three overarching ethical issues concerning product placement in media entertainment were advanced. While these issues–deception, artists' rights, and excess commercialism–are not mutually exclusive of one another, and there are probably many other ethical issues, such as privacy concerns, that could be raised in association with product placement strategies in contemporary practice, they are the most frequently raised concerns about the phenomenon. While ethical implications of these issues have been commented upon throughout the article, some summary judgment and recommendations are in order.

Deception

That product placement qualifies as deception seems clear. As advocates of the practice have reiterated in defense of the practice, a good product placement should be "seamless" and "organic" to the script. Simply put, the goal of the practice well done is for it to fall below the threshold of perception. Of course, herein lies the industry's "Catch-22." If a product placement is done sensitively, it blends in, isn't "cognitively" flagged as a placement, and as a consequence tends to be misinterpreted, and thus deceives.

More significantly, the argument that product placements add realism is suspect. Products that are placed in entertainment vehicles, are, almost without exception, positively cast. A reality that shows the branded portion of our world in unyielding positive light is a false one. To only "name names" when the angel's halo appears above is disingenuous. We know from our experience with cigarette brands, automobile brands, fast food brands, and the like that brands do not necessarily correlate with health, safety, or happiness. So to say that product placements enhance reality is necessarily a fallacious claim. It is akin to saying that television commercials reflect reality. What is reflected is of course a highly selective vision of the world that is in the best interests of the sponsoring party. While product placements may not be so forthright, there are laws to protect people from deceptive practices in advertising, while product placement largely passes under the radar screen.

When the issue of deception in product placement comes up, advocates of the practice very often counter that consumers are increasingly "savvy" and aware that placements and other marketing approaches are likely to be buried anywhere (Ebenkamp, 2001). Indeed, social science surveys confirm that many consumers are both readily aware of product placement as a technique and have no strong objection to seeing brands in film and television programming, as long as it isn't "overdone" or "inappropriate" (d'Astous and Chartier, 2000; DeLorme and Reid, 1999; Gould et al., 2000; Gupta et al., 2000). However a consumer that is "aware" in the general sense, is not necessarily the same as "buyer beware." After all, just because many people were aware that cigarettes weren't particularly healthy for them, didn't mean that the clearly marked "disclaimer" that they "may be hazardous to your health" was not in order.

Even though some consumers may indeed be wise to the product placement ploy, this does not mean that once the lights go down in the movie theater, for example, that their defenses remain up over the course of the film. As a matter of fact, this argument defies plausibility. We go to films for different reasons than to defend ourselves from product placements. We go to immerse ourselves in a fantasy world that stands apart from our everyday worlds, where we are coming to expect commercial assaults at every turn. Thus, there is a clear pattern that when the economy or politics turn sour, movie attendance rises. A related problem is that even if defenses did "stay up" for some, one cannot be so sure that "defenses are up" for consumers across the board. Evidence suggests that older viewers have both less awareness of product placements and are more annoyed at the practice than younger adults (DeLorme and Reid, 1999). As well, there is much evidence to suggest that children have difficulty separating the creative wheat from the marketing chaff when product placements are used (cf. Lewis, 2001).

Artists' Rights

In mass art, the rights of artists are always subject to being negotiated away. Artists need to work just like everyone else to make a living and thus are dependent on employers to hire them and foot the bill for their work. As was alluded to in the analysis section, particularly with regards to virtual placement, artists' rights as an ethical and legal issue sit in a very gray area. This is compounded by the marketplace realities of working in the Hollywood dream factory, which of course, is not limited geographically to that area's zip code. The entertainment business has always been a fragile place to work. It is a climate of both "who you know" and "what have you done lately?" Being regularly out of work or "between jobs" is a fact of life for many writers, directors, and other creative personnel. As has been argued for before, this leaves creative personnel in a tenuous situation. Yes, they can "just say no" to or exercise considerable selectivity in using product placement in their work, but such "flexing of the creative muscles" must be done in the context of considerable risk. In a business where many people have heard the threat "you may never work in this town again," being finicky about product placements may come at the cost of one's career. As a result, it is not surprising that product placement usage has advanced at a rapid clip.

Nonetheless, one can argue that, with "plain old" product placements, writers, producers, and directors have knowingly struck their bargain for commercial scatterings that are consistent or appropriate to a situation or storyline. Here, these creative personnel know that some accommodation for these kinds of things is the "cost of doing business" in Hollywood. But, what seems pretty clear is that those "costs" are rising quite disproportionately to the rise of inflation that would drive increased production costs. Hence, we have seen the "logical extension" of product placement, product integration come to dominate the logic of prime-time as a "sea change." The push to product integration has moved significant portions of the television schedule to a "build-to-suit" model. However, this is no "patron of the arts" model, it is a "patron of commerce" model. As a consequence, product integration and its new technological sibling, video insertion have moved the creation of media entertainment from a climate of selective accommodation to one that is increasingly compromised, so tilted to corporate interest that now the tail is wagging the dog. The net result may be that the pairing of the artist with corporate partners will become so normalized that they cease to be thought of as "strange bedfellows." As the tensions between art and commerce have always played a role in keeping values in perspective, it is hard to see how this new arrangement has much promise in offering a greater good to a greater number.

Excess Commercialism

Product placement as a deceptive practice and structural harms inflicted on artists' rights in the creation of media entertainment combine to exacerbate concerns over heightened commercialism. There is a key difficulty in making an argument stick that product placement pushes commercialism over some edge. Commercialism obviously exists on varying socially-defined conceptions of a continuum of excess and deficiency. Understandably, there is a great deal of difficulty in reaching agreement about what the end-points of the continuum should be, let alone a temperate middle. This dilemma is compounded by a lack of certainty about what the consequences of commercialism, let alone excess commercialism, will be. It is more profitable to take, as Carroll (2000) has, the anti-consequentialism arguments about mass art in stride, and focus instead on the "activations" encouraged by the text and engagement in that text. In the case of product placement in media entertainment, his arguments are particularly compelling:

> Questions about the direct behavioral consequences of the artwork need not arise in order for the ethical critic to be in a position to approve or reprove an artwork. Rather the ethical critic can focus on the probity of the moral experience that an artwork shapes or prescribes as a condition for correctly assimilating it. Do those interactions cultivate our moral powers, or do they deform them? As

we read, view, or listen to an artwork with a significant ethical dimension, our consciousness is occupied by content that has been shaped in a certain way–that prescribes and facilitates moral responses. Without claiming anything about the likely behavioral consequences of the work, we can nevertheless comment on the moral value of the pathways that we are invited to follow. (Carroll, 2000, p. 370)

Thus, in looking at product placement in media entertainment, regardless of what we may make of the consequences, there can be little doubt of structural encouragement and facilitation of what might be called a "commodified imagination." The pathway we are invited to follow becomes one where a branded world and all its "imaginings" are argued to be necessarily better than one not so circumscribed.

The situation is compounded further by the fact that in a product placement-infused media entertainment, the possibility of "imagining" a world that is not branded or one where the values associated with brands are distinctly different than the brand purveyors would like us to believe, becomes something that is beyond the pale. In evaluating product placement then, we need to ask ourselves are we better off, morally enriched, by a circumscribing of cultural imagination in an unchallenged, and increasingly supersaturated logic of commodity culture? If the lens through which we come to see social worth and happiness is filtered through brands in the stories we tell to ourselves, on what terms does it become possible to argue that we are better off for this? Only if the greater good for the greater number is interpreted as "consumer choice" can the logic of such an argument proceed. For others, who see citizens as more than consumers, such an argument fails miserably.

These arguments put aside others about excess commercialism. A fundamental argument posed by critics throughout this study is that product placement, in its very technique and its increasing saturation, represents a betrayal to the audience that is not demonstrative of "other respecting care." Indeed, it becomes difficult to think "caringly" about an audience as an audience when you are foremost thinking of them as consumers. Even when pigeon-holed as consumers, little care or benefit can be found. The cost-savings argument advanced for product placement promises better scripts, sets, and production values. Still, it is hard to see how the "blockbusters" that have resulted from such infusions into production budgets are verifiably better "art." Certainly, this Hollywood trend and the rise of reality programs on television with "hyper" product integration have not been anointed by critics as "better works" thrust before the public. And if the cost savings demonstrated some kind of care for the audience, there would be at least some limited "pass-through" of the savings in reduced ticket prices for movies or commercial clutter on television. This money simply hasn't been put where their mouths have been. Finally, it is difficult to see where a greater good lurks around our digital "click-to-buy" future that surely will come with virtual placements. With this, we only ease access of products to consumers at a time when consumers are already besieged by such access and worried, quite fairly, about privacy incursions that already seem structurally stacked in the favor of marketers.

RECOMMENDATIONS

The analysis and arguments in this article point to product placements in media entertainment as a complex and far-reaching ethical problem. It is hard to see a "going back in time" where the logic of the basic practice would be prohibited. Practical solutions begin with answering a very basic question: "Do viewers have the right to know when they are being appealed to on a commercial level?" (Avery and Ferraro, 2000, p. 24). A fairness assessment, following the logic of laws limiting deceptive practices in advertising, would answer this question with an unqualified "yes." However, the terms and conditions of moving to action will surely be hotly debated. While an advertisement must be identifiable as such to consumers, placements and other cross-marketing practices fall into a grayer area. The question becomes one of how and when such practices should be disclosed to the consumer. Presently, in television, paid placements are technically illegal. As a result, product props can be donated, and the FCC stipulates that this must be disclosed. Hence, we see the "promotional consideration given to . . ." disclaimer buried in the increasingly unintelligible credit roll at the end of programs. The FCC prohibition of paid placements has, in one sense, fostered the more intense product integration strategy, because such cross-marketing partnerships that develop and product programming fall under the radar gun. In film, product placement disclosure is not regulated, and as a result, inconsistent. Here too, disclosures tend to come at the end of credits when many in the audience have already filtered out of the theater (cf. Avery and Ferraro, 2000).

It seems quite clear that an ambiguous disclosure alluding to "promotional consideration" coming "after the fact" in end-credits does not sufficiently mitigate the deception issues that plague product placements.

Placing accurate acknowledgements up front would much more forthrightly alert the audience of what to expect. After all, a warning is not buried in the bottom of a pack of cigarettes. If they were done truly above-board, such disclosure would reveal fees paid, advertising subsidies, cross-marketing agreements, and the like to the audience. Mandating this positioning and level of disclosure would surely be met with considerable resistance by entertainment producers and their corporate partners. In today's climate of lobbying for a "free marketplace," such attempts would likely fail. Given this, RTMark, a media advocacy group, "has proposed adding a new rating system that would rank movies from one to five on the amount of product placement" (Merrill, 2001, p. 1D). This would follow the logic of the MPAA advisory movie rating system, and at least provide some guidance for those consumers most concerned with commercial saturation. Obviously, just like the MPAA system, the placement rating could provide useful guidance to parents. This issue of children being able to successfully negotiate product placement may indeed lead the way in any regulation leading to fuller, and more up front, disclosure. A "mother's code" proposed at a recent Consumer Kids Conference has suggested minimum standards that would allow "no product placement in movies and media programs targeted at children and adolescents" (Lewis, 2001, p. 10).

While there is evidence that the public is miffed at rising commercialism buried in its entertainment products, there is just as much evidence of a willingness to accept this "as the way things are," especially by young adults (DeLorme and Reid, 1999). As a result, it appears unlikely that a coherent push for disclosures will in short order lead to a policy shift or regulatory imposition. Even mounting an effective rating advisory system is a considerable task. Recent evidence from the "voluntary" television rating system suggests that the public is more confused than guided by the "alphabet soup" that appears fleetingly at the start of programs. The trump card, one unlikely to actually be played, is the reclassification of product placement-saturated media entertainment as "commercial speech." The present legal climate does not appear likely to adjudicate media entertainment as "commercial speech" because it is "mixed speech" with the primary intent to "entertain" rather than "sell" (Avery and Ferraro, 2000; Lackey, 1993; Snyder, 1992). However, if the role that product placement plays in media entertainment continues to advance at a blistering pace, media producers and marketers may find themselves in a very different legal climate. The threat of that hot water may provide the greatest impetus for "voluntary" up-front disclosure of product placements in media entertainment.

REFERENCES

Avery, R. J. and Ferraro, R. (2000). Verisimilitude or advertising? Brand appearances on primetime television. *Journal of Consumer Affairs, 34*(2), 217-244.

Berger, R. (1999, April 5). Digital technology virtually blurs reality: That Coke can you saw on UPN? It wasn't really there. *Electronic Media, 18*(14), 14-15.

Berkowitz, H. (1994, August 11). Product makers pay for film role. *Houston Chronicle,* 1D, 3D.

Bok, S. (1999). *Lying: Moral Choice in Public and Private Life,* 2d edition. New York: Vintage.

Branswell, B. (2002, May 13). Subliminal advertising: C-4 Communications places products on Quebec TV shows in exchange for services. *Montreal Gazette, Monthly Business Magazine,* E3.

Brown, C. (2002, January 15). Advertisers seek a bigger role in TV programming. *Los Angeles Times,* A1.

Buss, D. D. (1998, December). Making your mark in movies and TV. *Nation's Business,* 28-32.

Carroll, N. (2000). Art and ethical criticism: An overview of recent directions in research. *Ethics, 110,* 350-387.

Chabria, A. (2002, May 6). Getting a good product in front of the cameras: Placing a product on a TV show or in a film involves finding a good fit with the material: But getting an expert's help first is critical. *PR Week,* 18.

Cowlett, M. (2000, August 17). Public relations: Make it into he movies–Once a dirty word, now product placement in major films is big business. *Europe Intelligence Wire,* 29.

Crisafulli, C. (1995, September 3). It's a wrap (but not plain): From Budweiser to Butterfinger, brand names are popping up more and more on screen, and it's usually not by chance, it's big business. *Los Angeles Times,* Calendar section, 4.

D'Astous, A., and Chartier, F. (2000). A study of factors affecting consumer evaluations and memory of product placements in movies. *Journal of Current Issues and Research in Advertising, 22*(2), 31-40.

Davidson, K. (1996). When does creativity become deception? *Marketing News, 30*(20), 2.

Day, L.A. (2003). *Ethics in Media communications: Cases and Controversies,* 4th edition. Belmont, CA: Wadsworth.

DeLorme, D. E., and Reid, L. N. (1999). Moviegoers' experiences and interpretations in films revisited. *Journal of Advertising, 28*(2), 71-95.

Ebenkamp, B. (2001, June 4). Return to Peyton placement: Advertisers have long been partners in TV's development, but have they crossed into dangerous territory to stand out among their peers? *Brandweek, 42*(23), S10-19.

Elliott, S. (1999, March 29). A video process allows the insertion of brand-name references in TV shows already on film. *New York Times,* C11.

Elliott, S. (1999, October 1). Digital sleight of hand can put ads almost anywhere. *New York Times,* C1.

Elliott, S. (2001, May 23). Reruns may become a testing ground for digital insertion of sponsor's products and images. *New York Times,* C6.

Entertainment Resources and Marketing Association (n.d.). Product placement 101 (pamphlet).

Friedman, W., and Neff, J. (2001, January 22). Eagle-eye marketers find right spot, right time. *Advertising Age*, *72*(4), 4c (special section).

Goddard, P. (2000, February 12). The new ad fad. *Toronto Star*, Entertainment section. [Lexis-Nexis Academic Universe].

Govani, S. (1999, February 10). Product placement in movies–is it really so bad? *Christian Science Monitor*, 11.

Gould, S. J., Gupta, P. B., and Grabner-Krauter, S. (2000). Product placements in movies: A cross-cultural analysis of Austrian, French, and American consumers' attitudes toward this emerging, international promotional medium. *Journal of Advertising*, *29*(4), 41-58.

Gupta, P. B., Balasubramanian, S. K., and Klassen, M. L. (2000). Viewer's evaluations of product placements in movies: Public policy issues and managerial implications. *Journal of Current Issues and Research in Advertising*, *22*(2), 41-52.

Gupta, P. B., and Gould, S. J. (1997). Consumers' perception of the ethics and acceptability of product placements in movies: Product category and individual differences. *Journal of Current Issues and Research in Advertising*, *19*(1), 37-50.

Harrison, E. (1999, August 29). Cashing in: *E.T.* led the way. *Los Angeles Times*, Calendar section, 25.

Jhally, S. (2000). *Behind the Screens: Hollywood goes Hypercommercial*. Amherst, MA: Media Education Foundation [videotape].

Kern, T. (2001, June). Commercial television. *Snack Food & Wholesale Bakery*, *90*(6), 166.

Kinight. S. (2001, February). Tobacco use is still prevalent in films. *Student BMJ*, *9*, 7.

Klayman, B. (1998, May 23). Driven to stardom: Product placement in TV and film extends to cars and trucks. *Toronto Star*, G1.

Lackey, W.B. (1993). Can Lois Lane smoke Marlboros? An examination of the constitutionality of regulating product placement in movies. *University of Chicago Legal Forum*. Chicago: University of Chicago Press.

Leith, S. (2000, October 29). Coke leads push to place products in movies, TV. *Atlanta Constitution*, Business section, 1P.

Lewis, K. (2000, September/October). Advertisers be warned. *Sam*, 10.

Littlefield, K. (2000, March 27). Virtual advertising poised for a ceaseless pitch. *Denver Post*, C-10.

Lovell, G. (1998, January 4). Product placement, proper and improper. *Pittsburgh Post-Gazette*, G-4.

McCarthy, M. (2001, July 23). Advertisers pepper reality shows with product placements: Deals can be dicey, though. *USA Today*, Money section, 5B.

McCarthy, M. (2001, June 19). Ads are here, there, everywhere: Agencies seek creative ways to expand product placement. *USA Today*, Money section, 1B.

McCarthy, P. (1998, January 17). Ad ventures in tinsel town. *Sydney Morning Herald*, Spectrum section, 8.

Merrill, A. (2001, April 27). Advertiser 'driven': For companies large and small, getting their product or logos featured in films or TV shows has become another way to gain exposure and build up brand names. *Minneapolis Star Tribune*, Business section, 1D.

Movies may carry a hidden pitch. (1999, December). *USA Today Magazine*, 11-12.

Mueller, A. (2001, July 14). The brand played on: The movie world's $1 billion sideline in product placement is becoming a post-modern joke. *The Irish Times*, Weekend section, 61.

Neff, J. (2001, January 22). Sponsors behind camera: Content more critical, so marketers again turn producer. *Advertising Age, 72*(4), ps3 (special section).

Paul, N. C. (2002, April 16). What you see is what they want you to get: Ever since *E.T.* landed, advertisers have been hungry to have their products "placed" in films. *Christian Science Monitor*, 22.

Poniewozik, J. (2001, June 18). This plug's for you: Thanks to ever more stealthy product placements, ads are becoming the latest stars of the show. *Time*, 76.

Pressure mounts to make virtual advertising a reality (2000, November 6). *Sports Marketing*, p. VI.

Ross, C. (1999, May 5). Warner Bros. to test "virtual" ad concept: TV group would be first big syndicator to use technology. *Advertising Age, 70*(21), preceding p. 1 (not numbered).

Rothenberg, R. (2001). Marketing's 'borders' blurred by product placement revival. *Advertising Age, 72*(37), 24.

Ryle, S. (2001, August 12). When is a prop not a prop? When it's a plug: The soaps are awash with brands amid anomalies over product placement. *The Observer*, Business section, 5.

Shaw, J. (2001, April). Now starring at a cinema near you. *NZ Marketing Magazine, 20*(3), 35-38.

Smith, B. (1985, March). Casting product for special effect. *Beverage World, 104*, 83-91.

Snyder, S. L. (1992). Movies and product placement: Is Hollywood turning films into commercial speech? *University of Illinois Law Review*, 301-329.

Stanley, T. L. (2002, April 29). The hard sell. *Electronic Media*, 12-14.

Stanley, T. L. (2002, May 13). Prime time for sale. *Mediaweek*, 32-36.

Thompson, G. (1997, July 8). Product placement becomes more prominent in blockbusters. *Tampa Tribune*, Baylife section, 5.

Vagnoni, A., Halliday, J., and Taylor, C. (2001, June 23). Behind the wheel. *Advertising Age, 72*(30), 10-11.

Wells, M. (2001, October 29). Who really needs Madison Avenue? *Forbes, 168*(11), 131-132.

When is a prop not a prop? The advantages of product placement. (2001, September 19). *Sports Marketing*, 14.

The Role and Ethics
of Community Building
for Consumer Products and Services

Dean Kruckeberg
Kenneth Starck

SUMMARY. Kruckeberg and Starck (1988) argue that public relations
is the active attempt to restore and maintain the sense of community that
has been lost in contemporary society. Many manufacturers and service
providers seek "communities" of consumers. However, what is the social ethic of such consumer communities? Do they provide an authentic
"sense of community" as advocated by Kruckeberg and Starck? This article examines these and related questions and offers suggestions regarding the creation and maintenance of consumer "communities." Consumer
communities–when appropriately formed and nurtured–can have impact
on individuals and society at large that are best considered from a public
relations, not marketing, viewpoint. *[Article copies available for a fee from
The Haworth Document Delivery Service: 1-800-HAWORTH. E-mail address:*

Dean Kruckeberg (PhD, University of Iowa; APR and Fellow, Public Relations So-
ciety of America) is Professor and Coordinator, Mass Communication Division, 351
Lang Hall, Department of Communication Studies, University of Northern Iowa, 1801
West 31st Street, Cedar Falls, IA 50614-0139 (E-mail: kruckeberg@uni.edu). Kenneth
Starck (PhD, Southern Illinois University-Carbondale) is Professor, School of Journal-
ism and Mass Communication, W323 Seashore Hall, University of Iowa, Iowa City,
IA 52242 (E-mail: kenneth-starck@uiowa.edu).

[Haworth co-indexing entry note]: "The Role and Ethics of Community Building for Consumer Products
and Services." Kruckeberg, Dean, and Kenneth Starck. Co-published simultaneously in *Journal of Promotion
Management* (Best Business Books, an imprint of The Haworth Press, Inc.) Vol. 10, No. 1/2, 2004, pp. 133-146;
and: *Handbook of Product Placement in the Mass Media: New Strategies in Marketing Theory, Practice,
Trends, and Ethics* (ed: Mary-Lou Galician) Best Business Books, an imprint of The Haworth Press, Inc.,
2004, pp. 133-146. Single or multiple copies of this article are available for a fee from The Haworth Document
Delivery Service [1-800-HAWORTH, 9:00 a.m. - 5:00 p.m. (EST). E-mail address: docdelivery@haworthpress.
com].

Digital Object Identifier: 10.1300/J057v10n01_09   *133*

KEYWORDS. Chicago School of Social Thought, communitarian, community, community-building, consumer community, culture, ethics norms, public relations, social capital, social ethic, society, values

INTRODUCTION

And there were created many communities of consumers. (Boorstin, 1973, p. 90)

The meaning of "community" has been devalued, defaced, disfigured–mugged, if you will–to the point that the word, itself, has been rendered almost useless. Of course, the concept remains functional if only because–like a Rorschach inkblot–it enables us to project our own sense of meaning onto the term.

Much of the time the word appears as part of a modified phrase, e.g., "international community" or "Islamic community" or "broader community" or "financial community" or "local community," or, yes, "community of scholars." Increasingly, the notion of commercialism has invaded the domain of this concept. It is common today to come across references to "business" or "consumer" communities. A Lexis-Nexis search (2000, Oct. 25) of the phrase "business or consumer community" yielded more than 1,000 news entries for the preceding 90 days. That day alone (at 3 p.m. CST) revealed 25 such news stories. (For comparison, a search for the single word "community" disclosed 799 news items for the same 15-hour period.)

Of course, linking commercialism to consumption is nothing new. Historian Daniel J. Boorstin devoted a considerable portion of the final work of his expansive trilogy, *The Americans*, to the evolution of community in the post-Civil War United States. "Americans," he wrote, "were now held together less by their hopes than by their wants, by what they made and what they bought, and by how they learned about everything" (1973, p. 1). He continued:

Invisible new communities were created and preserved by how and what men consumed. . . . As never before, men used similar, and similarly branded, objects. The fellowship of skill was displaced by the democracy of cash. . . . No American transformation was more remarkable than these new American ways of changing things from objects of possession and envy into vehicles of community. . . . Now men were affiliated less by what they believed than by what they consumed. (1973, pp. 89-90)

Boorstin (1973, p. 89) emphasized the pervasiveness of consumption by pointing to the innocent question asked by the youngster in a Carl Sandburg poem, "Pappa, what is the moon supposed to advertise?"

FOCUS OF THE STUDY

Drawing on some of our previous work involving public relations and community (Kruckeberg and Starck, 1988; Starck and Kruckeberg, 2001), this article extends our investigation to the role and ethics of community-building when it comes to consumer groups, products and services. Our concern is with manufacturers and service providers who seek to create "communities" of consumers (e.g., Saturn, Jeep, Corvette and Harley Davidson, as well as such temporary and transient communities formed by Airstream Trailers and Winnebago motor home enthusiasts). Among questions guiding our inquiry are: What is the social ethic of such consumer communities? Do they promote elitism and exclusivity? If so, does this make any difference? Are such consumer communities exploitative? Again, what difference does it make? Finally, do such efforts provide an authentic "community" and what role does–or should–public relations play in this "community-building" process?

This inquiry should be considered more of a probe than a full-scale investigation. That is, we regard our present effort to be tentative and exploratory. We hope to reveal avenues for more focused and in-depth research. Our method will be to review and critically examine literature that we deem pertinent to understanding the relationship between business and consumer communities. Despite these caveats, we hope to be able to offer some suggestions regarding the creation and maintenance of consumer communities.

Specifically, we argue that consumer communities may be beneficial on occasion, perhaps benignly innocuous more often and definitely have the potential to be deleterious when abused. Such communities should not be taken at face value and uncritically by society, but should be viewed critically to assure that these consumer communities are functional both for society at large and for their individual members who can–without doubt–be harmed greatly by inappropriate participation in consumer communities. Finally, we argue that the public relations practitioner should be primarily responsible within the corporation for the development and nurture of such communities that are formed around that corporation's products or services. The implications of consumer communities extend far beyond marketing objectives. Consumer communities–when appropriately formed and nurtured–can have an impact on individuals and society at large that are best considered from a public relations, not marketing, viewpoint.

RELEVANCE OF COMMUNITY

In *Public Relations and Community: A Reconstructed Theory,* Kruckeberg and Starck (1988) submitted the thesis that public relations is best defined and practiced as the active attempt to restore and maintain a sense of community. They go on:

> Only with this goal as a primary objective can public relations become a full partner in the information and communication milieu that forms the lifeblood of U.S. society and, to a growing extent, the world. (p. xi)

They envisioned the public relations practitioner's role primarily as a community-builder, maintaining that this function was of critical importance in contemporary society:

> The public relations practitioner's role as a communicator, and more specifically as a communication facilitator, should be his or her highest calling. Being a facilitator of communication in the traditional sense–that is, seeking out and promoting discourse along all avenues–is a role of critical importance today, which can help to build a sense of community among organizations and their geographic publics. (1988, p. 112)

The fundamental reason public relations practice exists today is the loss of a sense of "community" in the contemporary world (Kruckeberg and Starck, 1988). New means of communication and transportation have destroyed the sense of geographic *community* that had existed earlier among proximate peoples. Thus, Kruckeberg and Starck (1988) argued that community-building must be regarded as the highest calling of public relations practice. Early attempts to influence public opinion often met with failure. Advocacy had its limitations both cognitively and ethically, and, while relationship-building might be noble and ethical, the authors argued that it was through community-building that public relations best served society as well as its organizations.

Many others have lamented the loss of community and pointed to the value of "community" as essential for the health of society-at-large as well as for its individual members. They range from the early perceptiveness of scholars associated with the Chicago School of Social Thought to contemporary scholars in nearly ever social-scientific discipline, e.g., John Dewey, Harold A. Innis, Daniel J. Boorstin and James W. Carey.

Examples

To take one example, Stephen (1995, p. 10) cites the link between bureaucratized, high-speed mass society and the consciousness of those who live within its domain–noting that there are few non-self-referential sources of meaning in modern society. The result? A sort of "permanent identity crisis."

In his penetrating examination of the evolution of community, Putnam (2000, pp. 283-284) points to similar factors contributing to the decline of the sense of community in the United States. He suggests generational change as one–perhaps the main–culprit. During the last third of the Twentieth Century, according to his data, the children and grandchildren of that era have become less involved in community life. But, as he notes, other factors contribute to this disengagement. These include pressures of time and money (e.g., pressure on two-career families), suburbanization (including commuting and sprawl) and, importantly, electronic entertainment, especially television. One response Putnam suggests is the creation or, maybe appropriately, cultivation of "social capital," a concept related to community that will be discussed later in this article.

In calling for a renewed "sense of community" or its equivalency, some social scientists and societal leaders call for more extreme measures than do others. Much of the discourse the past decade has been generated by the communitarian movement. Led by the work of its founder, Amitai Etzioni (1993), communitarianism seeks to place community at the core of social responsibility (p. 267).

Leeper (2001), in a thoughtful quest for a metatheory of public relations, explored the dueling concepts of communitarianism and libertarianism. From the communitarian perspective, values encompass "social cohesion, citizen empowerment and acceptance of responsibility" (p. 104). Libertarianism, on the other hand, espouses competition for the purpose of fulfilling self-interest. The key, it would seem, is a matter of articulating one's own philosophy, recognizing its inherent assumptions and then basing actions upon that perspective. Assuming harmony represents a desirable public relations goal, Leeper concludes that communitarianism serves as an appropriate guide for public relations practice and education.

Merrill (1997) argues for an opposing view. Although writing about journalism, he offers arguments questioning the fundamental tenets of communitarianism. He observes that the "antiliberals" consider values to be absolute and criticize liberalism for its "moral relativism and secularism" (p. 4). He warns that communitarians tend to endorse universal ethics as established by the community, using social pressures to enforce these community ethics. Carrying this outlook to an extreme, Merrill warns, can result in a major cultural shift.

ISSUES

A host of issues crop up in any discussion of contemporary community-building, particularly as engaged in by public relations practitioners for what are often perceived to be vested interests of the practitioner's corporation. The notion of "consumer communities" introduces additional elements.

Defining Concepts

As noted earlier, many concepts important to our discussion–including that of community, itself–are subject to diverse interpretations. While we do not want to give the impression that we possess the pure meaning or only definition of these terms, we do want to indicate how we view the concepts that are pertinent to this inquiry. Some of these concepts may, in fact, be peripheral or seem irrelevant to our discussion, but may help in understanding our approach and analysis.

Bell (1988, pp. 21-22) regards *mass society* as bringing people into closer contact with one another and bound in new ways because of revolutions in transportation and communication. Division of labor makes individuals more interdependent while, conversely, they grow more estranged from one another. Primary group ties of family and local community collapse, parochial faiths come into question, and few unifying values take their place. Critical standards of an educated *elite* no longer shape opinions and taste, resulting in uncertainty about mores and morals. Relations between individuals become tangential or compartmentalized, rather than organic. Meanwhile, greater mobility–spatially and socially–intensifies concern over status. People assume multiple roles and must constantly prove themselves in a succession of new situations that arise. Thus, the individual loses a coherent sense of self. Anxieties accompanied by an ensuing search for "new faiths" increase. This concept of mass society is important because it relates to the loss of the sense of community decried by Kruckeberg and Starck (1988). Acknowledging the variety of uses of the concept of *elite*, Bell (1988, p. 51) tends to agree with Mills, who defines *elite* primarily on the basis of "institutional position," although elite can have broader dimensions in a consumer community.

Goodstein et al. (1993, p. 60) regard *culture* as a pattern of beliefs and expectations deeply held in common by members of an organization (or society in another usage). These beliefs, in turn, give rise to *values* that are cherished by the organization and its members. These values, then, give rise to *situational norms* ("the way we do things around here") that are evidenced in observable behavior. *Normative behavior* becomes the basis for the validation of the beliefs and values from which the *norms* originated.

Useful in our discussion is the work of Dicken Garcia (1989, p. 15). She notes that the term *values* refers to the broad dominant social attributes, behaviors and larger goals that are advocated, promoted and defended by a society. She accepts John Finnegan Jr.'s definition of *culture* as "shared ideation behind social behavior among groups"; *society* as a "group of people in social and behavioral interdependence"; *social structure* as the manifestation of "the nature of social and behavioral independence"; and *values* as "ideals"–"desirable, preferable ends that . . . correspond to a pattern of choices or actions."

All of these concepts have importance when examining community, including the consumer communities under consideration in this article.

Of course, the most important concept is *community*, itself. In examining the writings of the Chicago School of Social Thought, Kruckeberg and Starck (1988, p. 56) identified six elements prevalent in the Chicago School's usage of this term:

1. An individual ordinarily belongs primarily to one community.
2. The individual participates in the common life of the community, is aware of and interested in common ends, and regulates activity in view of those ends. For this, communication is required.

3. Functional differentiation occurs to some extent because people have diverse occupations and activities.
4. People in a community occupy a definable geographic area.
5. Institutions spring up and become prerequisites to community formation.
6. A community develops particular cultural characteristics.

Finally, we define **consumer community**. Our definition is: a group of enthusiasts who believe in the superiority of a product or service whose members individually and as a group publicly identify with this product or service. Of course, individual members of these consumer communities remain a part of **mass society**; however, membership in consumer communities will–in most instances–be elitist and exclusionary because members distinguish themselves from others in mass society through their use of the product or service. Membership in a consumer community also requires a shared **culture, values** and **normative behavior** in relation to the product or service–even though members may be highly diverse in other areas of their lives. Furthermore, while participating in the consumer community, members may distance themselves from their other identities, i.e., it might be considered "bad manners" for a community member to make known his occupation or other social identification. Community members assume an identity as related to the product or service.

What are some characteristics of a consumer community? Such a community has to be created, although this could be done by its members or by the corporation providing the product or service. For example, geographically proximate enthusiasts of the Corvette automobile might form a "club" that exists primarily to perform communal activities around this particular product. They might reach out to similar clubs statewide and nationwide. Magazine publishers (and, increasingly, Web sites) are quick to provide a mass medium forum for these communities, e.g., the magazine *Corvette Fever.* General Motors, particularly GM units responsible for the Corvette badge, has been quick to support in a variety of ways such communal activities, especially at the national and regional levels. However, such consumer communities could equally as well be formed by the corporation providing the product or service, e.g., Saturn's pro-active attempts at owners' community-building and "relationship-marketing," not only with the manufacturer, but with other owners. However, the reason the consumer community exists is because of the existence of a product or service and its members' belief in the merits of this product or service. The community encompasses a belief in the superiority of and a loyalty to that product or service.

Finally, while marketing objectives might well be a primary reason the corporation nurtures the consumer community, the concept of consumer community extends beyond the usual consideration of "mission marketing." Duncan and Moriarty (1997), for example, weave together brand relationships and mission marketing. The latter, they say, "adds value and trust to brand relationships" (p. 127). The intent is certainly commendable, but the bottom line mentality still prevails and serves as the basis for any actions. Corporations must regard consumer communities as being something greater than a marketing consideration.

CREATING COMMUNITY

Kruckeberg and Starck (1988, pp. 112-117) identified eight ways in which public relations practitioners could restore and maintain a sense of community in their organizations and among stakeholders/publics:

1. Practitioners can help community members and the organizations they represent become conscious of common interests that are the basis for both their contentions and their solutions;
2. Practitioners can help individuals in the community to overcome alienation in its several forms;
3. Practitioners can help their organizations assume the role that Dewey reserved for the public schools, that is, in helping to create a sense of community;
4. Public relations practitioners should encourage leisure-time activities of citizens to enhance their sense of community;
5. Practitioners who are concerned with persuasion and advocacy should encourage consummately communication, that is, self-fulfilling communication;
6. Practitioners can help individuals find security and protection through association with others;
7. Practitioners can address interest in community welfare, social order, and progress; and
8. Practitioners can help foster personal friendships.

Putnam's discussion of "social capital" (2000, pp. 18-26) also deserves attention because it provides theoretical insight into identifying reasons behind the formation of "communities." (Putnam calls social capital a "conceptual cousin" of community [p. 21].) Increasingly, social scientists have been pointing to social capital in trying to understand the changing character of American society.

What is social capital? The theory of social capital, which, as Putnam notes, has surfaced independently several times during the Twentieth Century, can perhaps be best understood in relation to other forms of capital that interact in a mutually productive way. Physical capital, referring to tools, technology, resources, etc., and human capital, that is, skills, education, etc., both have obvious value. Interacting with one another, these two forms of capital have the potential to enhance productivity, both individually and collectively. However, social capital, or networks of people, has the same capability. Putnam defines social capital as referring "to connections among individuals–social networks and the norms of reciprocity and trustworthiness that arise from them" (p. 19). Social capital may be equated with "civic virtue," and the power of civic virtue, as Putnam points out, rests in "a dense network of reciprocal social relations" (p. 19).

The idea of social capital provides a theoretical underpinning in our examination of consumer communities. Social capital, in and of itself, is neither good nor bad. It can be directed toward antisocial acts just as with any other form of capital. We believe consumer communities are part of the larger social capital concept that manifests itself in the form of a social community. A consumer community then emerges as a subset of social community.

Kruckeberg and Starck (1988) observed the demise of community in contemporary society. They noted the Chicago School of Social Thought's attempt to regain community through the very means that had destroyed it and suggested that organizations could help restore and maintain this sense of community. Dewey, for example, regarded the local school as an "embryonic community" that puts a premium on personal contact and exchange within a setting of cooperative work and inquiry as well as being a social center for the neighborhood, unifying the community (in Quandt, 1970, pp. 48-49).

IMPLICATIONS FOR PUBLIC RELATIONS

In a type of any-community-is-better-than-no-community mindset, Kruckeberg and Starck (1988) noted that corporations could contribute to community-building in a way that is functional and beneficial for society-at-large as well as for individual members of society (see the eight ways of doing so earlier in this article). We are now extending the idea, albeit with several caveats, to consumer communities based on a product or service. Maximum benefits will only result, however, if the consumer communities are nurtured in a way that extends beyond a marketing relationship. Such consumer communities should not be dealt with lightly, however, because the implications are many.

What is the social ethic of consumer communities? One could ponder the apparent emptiness of the lives of those who center their whole identity around a consumer product or service. There is nothing inherently wrong about enthusiasts' fervor for a product or service to extend toward the desire for a consumer community based on that product or service. However, the corporation must bear some responsibility here, i.e., General Motors would be advised not to encourage irresponsible driving, nor should Harley Davidson promote an "outlaw biker" lifestyle. Jeep would be well-advised to minimize ecological damage in promoting its Jeep Jamborees. Certainly, the potential for harm to individual consumer community members as well as society-at-large and the physical environment of the world exists and must be resolutely minimized, if not eliminated.

Another moral issue is whether the individual member's time might be put to better use in other pursuits. That is, does membership in such a consumer community detract from membership in a community that might be considered more beneficial to the individual as well as to society? The question of elitism also must be addressed, i.e., such communities have a we/they exclusivity–those who ride Harleys vs. those who don't; those who own Corvettes and all other motorists. Such consumer communities are elitist and exclusionary because their membership is predicated on the enthusiastic consumption of a specific product or service. The person whose identity is primarily or exclusively based on a consumer product or service might ponder the comparative value of other communities having greater benefit to society.

Are consumer communities exploitative? They could be. Does this make any difference? Philosophically, probably not within a capitalistic, free-marketplace economic system.

Do consumer communities provide an authentic "sense of community?" Both normatively and positively, one must answer yes. However, again, this could be a functional or dysfunctional community, and one must question the social and psychological benefits of a dysfunctional community.

Finally, and most importantly for this article, what role does the public relations practitioner have in fostering and nurturing consumer communities? We argue for a primary role that encourages ethical motives and ethical communal activities and promotes the pursuit of activities beneficial to the community at large.

CONCLUSION

Consumer communities have existed and undoubtedly will continue to exist, both because of the fervor of those who belong to such communities and because of the marketing objectives of those corporations providing products and services that encourage such consumer communities. We argue that the public relations practitioner should be primarily responsible in the corporation for fostering and nurturing these communities, making every attempt to encourage the positive benefits of such communities while minimizing or hopefully eliminating the potential negative outcomes, i.e., to the individuals within the community, to society at large and to other elements of our environment.

Most certainly, consumer communities deserve increasingly scholarly inquiry in the public relations practitioner and educator community. Such inquiry should examine what consumer communities exist, what their impact is on society and what they ethically could and should be encouraging. There appears to be a dearth of literature, certainly in public relations, related to such consumer communities. A comprehensive search of the literature is called for, including in marketing and advertising. Case studies should be assembled and studied, and a range of empirical research carried out.

This article has not dealt with the impact of technology in the creation of consumer communities, though that topic too is ripe for investigation. Many of the public relations considerations that we have cited in the fostering consumer communities would seem applicable to e-commerce and virtual communities. There are differences between virtual and real communities, however, that merit special attention.

Etzioni (2000), for example, writes that while all communities tend to be self-policing, real communities minimize the role of official authorities, such as police and the courts, by relying on interpersonal communication or, as he says, "gossip." Online consumer communities need to develop similar reliable avenues of communication. The strength of virtual consumer communities, he writes, is breadth, while real communities boast depth. How can public relations practitioners best fulfill their role in supporting consumer communities arising out of new technologies?

Relatedly, what practices are available to public relations in dealing with groups organized by others? For example, consumer communities are being built online which enable members to comment freely about products and services they have experienced. One configuration of such a virtual consumer community brings together news and online service organizations. Thus, *The Denver Post* and *Minneapolis Star Tribune* join Word of Mouth to offer what Robins (2000) refers to as the first business-to-consumer-to-business-and-consumer (B2C2BC) service. (Their respective Web sites are *http://www.wordofmouth.com/dpo* and *http://www.startribune.com/wordofmouth.*) What should be the role of public relations in dealing with such services? Should it be to counteract false accusations? To investigate and respond to legitimate complaints?

In our consideration of consumer communities as related to a product or service, we have focused our attention on the private sector, essentially for-profit corporations. Should the same public relations principles apply among consumer communities involving nonprofit corporations, e.g., educational institutions and charities? This is another question awaiting further inquiry.

REFERENCES

Bell, D. (1988). *The End of Ideology.* Cambridge, MA: Harvard University Press.
Boorstin, D. J. (1973). *The Americans: The Democratic Experience.* New York: Vintage Books.
Dicken Garcia, H. (1989). *Journalistic Standards in Nineteenth-Century America.* Madison: University of Wisconsin Press.
Duncan, T., and Moriarty, S. (1997). *Driving Brand Value: Using Integrated Marketing to Manage Profitable Stakeholder Relationships.* New York: McGraw-Hill.
Etzioni, A. (2000, February 10). E-Communities build new ties, but ties that bind. *The New York Times,* D7.
Etzioni, A. (1993). *The Spirit of Community: The Reinvention of American Society.* New York: Touchstone.
Goodstein, L., Nolan, T., and Pfeiffer, J. W. (1993). *Applied Strategic Planning: A Comprehensive Guide.* New York: McGraw-Hill, Inc.
Kruckeberg, D., and Starck, K. (1988). *Public Relations and Community: A Reconstructed Theory.* New York: Praeger.
Leeper, R. (2001). In Search of a Metatheory for Public Relations: An Argument for Communitarianism. In R. L. Heath, editor, *Handbook of Public Relations.* Thousand Oaks, CA: Sage, 93-104.
Lexis-Nexis (2000, October 25).
Merrill, J. C. (1997). *Journalism Ethics: Philosophical Foundations for News Media.* New York: St. Martin's Press.

Putnam, R. D. (2000). *Bowling Alone: The Collapse and Revival of American Community.* New York: Simon & Schuster.

Quandt, J. B. (1970). *From the Small Town to the Great Community: The Social Thought of Progressive Intellectuals.* New Brunswick, NJ: Rutgers University Press.

Robins, W. (2000, October 2). Worst oil change ever: Now online. *Editor & Publisher,* 36.

Starck, K., and Kruckeberg, D. (2001). Public relations and community: A reconstructed theory revisited. In R. L. Heath, editor, *Handbook of Public Relations.* Thousand Oaks, CA: Sage, 51-59.

Stephen, T. (1995). Interpersonal communication, history, and intercultural coherence. In F. L. Casmir, editor, *Communication in Eastern Europe: The Role of History, Culture, and Media in Contemporary Conflicts.* Mahwah, NJ: Lawrence Erlbaum Associates, 5-25.

CASE STUDIES
OF PRODUCT PLACEMENT

A Comparison of Product Placements
in Movies and Television Programs:
An Online Research Study

Beng Soo Ong

SUMMARY. Product placement has expanded as a promotional tactic, aided by technological innovations which present new openings for, and challenges to, branded messages via television. Product placements in television shows differ from placements in movies in terms of (1) federal regulations, (2) greater vehicle choices, and (3) ability to embed brands into TV shows that have proven to be successful. In light of these differ-

Beng Soo Ong (PhD, University of Arkansas) is Professor, Marketing and E-Business Department, Craig School of Business, Fresno State University, Peters Business Building, Room 508, M/S PB7, 5245 North Backer, Fresno, CA 93740-8001 (E-mail: bengo@csufresno.edu).

[Haworth co-indexing entry note]: "A Comparison of Product Placements in Movies and Television Programs: An Online Research Study." Ong, Beng Soo. Co-published simultaneously in *Journal of Promotion Management* (Best Business Books, an imprint of The Haworth Press, Inc.) Vol. 10, No. 1/2, 2004, pp. 147-158; and: *Handbook of Product Placement in the Mass Media: New Strategies in Marketing Theory, Practice, Trends, and Ethics* (ed: Mary-Lou Galician) Best Business Books, an imprint of The Haworth Press, Inc., 2004, pp. 147-158. Single or multiple copies of this article are available for a fee from The Haworth Document Delivery Service [1-800-HAWORTH, 9:00 a.m. - 5:00 p.m. (EST). E-mail address: docdelivery@haworthpress.com].

http://www.haworthpress.com/web/JPM
Digital Object Identifier: 10.1300/J057v10n01_10

ences, an online survey was conducted with the purpose of examining attitudinal differences, if any, between product placement in movies and in TV programs. The study found that although three-fourths of the sample were aware of product placements in both media, respondents appeared to have less exposure to brand placements in television shows than in movies. That may have led to a weak impact of television placements on respondents' brand attitudes. *[Article copies available for a fee from The Haworth Document Delivery Service: 1-800-HAWORTH. E-mail address: <docdelivery@haworthpress.com> Website: <http://www.HaworthPress.com>* © 2004 by The Haworth Press, Inc. All rights reserved.]

KEYWORDS. Brand, films, movies, product placements, television

INTRODUCTION

While product placement is not a new marketing concept, the tactic has gained in popularity as technological innovations in the past several years such as DVDs, in-home theater systems, and TiVo sets pose new opportunities for and threats to brand communications. TiVo will continue to replace the video cassette player/recorder (VCR) as the consumers' tool for recording missed television program segments, and for zapping television commercials. The growth in DVD rentals and sales at both brick-and-mortar stores and over the internet (e.g., via Amazon and Netflix), sales of digital TV sets, as well as the proliferation of pay-per-view channels also present openings for brand communications through television.

Recognizing the fact that consumers are inundated with a vast number of TV channel choices (and subsequently turning some of us into channel surfers), having a brand featured or embedded into a popular TV program would likely gain more attention or exposure than having the brand advertised between program breaks.

PURPOSE OF STUDY

While films continue to draw audiences to theaters/cinemas, the secondary outlets of these films through television runs, re-runs, video and DVD rentals/sales cannot be overlooked. In light of the trends alluded to earlier, it would be timely to investigate the impact of product placements in movies where the movies were subsequently shown on TV. Furthermore, comparisons of consumer perceptions of product placement practices in films versus TV programs could shed additional knowledge of different impacts, if any, of this important brand promotion tool. Hence, this study seeks to ascertain awareness of, and attitudinal differences between, product placement in movies and in television.

BACKGROUND

Regulations of Product Placements in TV Programs

Avery and Ferraro (2000) explained that placements in television programs are usually unpaid because the Federal Communications Commission (FCC) has sponsorship identification rules governing paid placements in this medium. Placements in movies, on the other hand, are unregulated. The above FCC rule, however, does not apply to movies airing on television. To work around this "payment" restriction for television program placements, companies could (and often do) simply supply products free of charge to the syndicates or producers of the particular television program of interest. Staff and actors on the production set could be given the free product to consume, use, wear, or in turn, give away to others.

Products that are furnished as backdrops for a TV program scene do not have to be disclosed as long as they are not portrayed in an unreasonable manner that implies "commercial intent." Hence, we could argue that placements in TV programs are likely to be more subtle than placements in movies to avoid violations of the FCC rule. This subtlety could work in the favor of placements on TV as unrestricted placements in movies may tend toward overly obvious plugs for the brand. In their qualitative research, DeLorme and Reid (1999) found that their subjects were very aware of excessive showing of the brand and placements in unnatural or inappropriate settings including over-emphasis through camera techniques (e.g., close-ups on the brand name). Their subjects noted that such actions cheapen the movie-going experience and insult the audience.

Placements in Successful TV Series

Brand placement in a television series may have an advantage over that in a movie as placements may be made after ample opportunities to gauge the size of the viewership. With movies, the placement decision would have to be made on the basis of forecast(s) of the success of the movie. Even if the movie were subsequently aired on television, brand placements are unlikely to be developed and inserted into the movie at that point due to costs and time.

Many studies have noted that the impact of a placement is influenced by the position or scene in the program or movie (e.g., DeLorme and Reid, 1999; Russell, 2002; Ong and Meri, 1994). A television series may earn a loyal audience following where there would be more opportunity to build personalities of the characters in the series, and to design a script or scene to fit the brand placement in a very appropriate setting.

Choices of TV Program Formats for Placements

TV programs can be classified into situation comedy, documentary, drama series, feature magazine (e.g., NBC's *Dateline*; ABC's *20/20*, etc.), game-show, sports, made-for-TV movie, news program, and other types (Avery and Ferraro, 2000). Because of the wide choice of formats, brand placements in a TV program enjoy greater flexibilities than those in a movie. Due to restrictions on violence, nudity, and language (profanity) in program content offered by major US networks (i.e., ABC, NBC, CBS, and FOX), finding appropriate brand placements may also be less challenging here than in movies. From the author/researcher's experience, scouring for potential brand starring roles to recommend to an advertising agency handling a major studio's account, the prospect was greatly curtailed by the presence of violence and by the place/setting (e.g., mid-1800s, in the City of Birmingham) evident in the movie script. The brand in mind (to be potentially placed) may not have existed at that time, or may no longer be around today. TV programs, particularly situational comedies, tend to have more contemporary settings. Hence, the availability of greater choices and flexibilities in TV program placements may lead to more natural or appropriate placements.

However, the contemporary settings of many TV series could also increase the pressure on show producers to feature real brands in program scenes even if these would not be "paying" brands. DeLorme and Reid (1999) found that consumers felt irritated and insulted by generic product props. These props were judged to interfere with movie realism and to interrupt the movie viewing experience. Hence, the use of generic props and fictitious brands would not be ideal if there were no suitors for the brand role.

Measuring Effectiveness of Product Placements

Research in the early 1990s tended to measure effectiveness of product placements by aided and unaided recalls of brands mentioned or shown in the movie (Gupta and Lord, 1998). Since then, more researchers have opted for attitudinal measures and purchase intentions. For example, Gould, Gupta, and Grabner-Krauter (2000) compared consumer attitudes across their three-country samples on dimensions such as attitude toward product placement in general, perceived realism (e.g., Strongly Agree to Strongly Disagree for a statement "Placement of brand name products adds to the realism of movies"), attitude toward restricting product placements, and attitude toward television advertising in general. Purchase behavior, in their study, was assessed via a Likert-scale item "I buy brands I see movie stars using or holding in movies."

One might argue that the above attitudinal items would not be good correlates of purchase intentions and brand choice since product placements are subtle and consumers' brand decisions are influenced by a host of other marketing factors such as a brand's unique selling proposition (USP) and specific qualities. However, DeLorme and Reid (1999) noted that moviegoers are active interpreters, not passive receptors of encountered brands in movies. Subtle cues via placements are not likely to go unnoticed by the audience. The researchers further argued that because attitudes toward brands develop over time, brand placement can strengthen brand name recognition and positioning, and thus contribute towards long-term influence. Brand placement can create associations that are important in building a brand's image, which in turn, could be a part of the grand marketing plan.

Psychographic and demographic factors may significantly impact the effectiveness of product placements and, hence, their inclusion in product placement research would be prudent. In a study of moviegoers' experiences and interpretations of brands in films, DeLorme and Reid (1999) found older moviegoers to be receptive to "old brands" in the movie and related nostalgia associations. To the younger moviegoers in the study, brands in movies symbolized belonging and security.

Gould, Gupta, and Grabner-Krauter (2000) employed psychographic measures such as the total number of movies rented or watched in theaters in a typical month when studying product placement effects. However, they did not find the total number of movies rented/watched to be significant on purchase behavior. In the context of product placements in TV programs, it may be worthwhile to explore attributes such as whether research participants typically watch television alone or with another person, subscribe to cable, or when they typically watch television. In a multi-audience setting, there are likely to be more interactions among the audience members while watching television than while viewing a movie in a theater. Greater interaction among the people in the room may also lead to different reactions to a brand placement than when watching a program alone.

While academicians and scholars are striving for stronger measures of effectiveness of product placement, advertisers and practitioners are seeking to justify their expenditures in product placement. A new company, Brand Advisors, has come up with a pricing model that takes into account the size of the audience the movie may attract throughout its life cycle (at the box office, home video, pay-per-view, and television), and the starring role the brand is offered in the movie (Graser, 2003). Brand Advisors' financial assessment of product placement project states the audience size projections can be reforecast and repriced once the movie hits the theaters or airs on TV, allowing partners to alter their arrangement based on actual results as the movie moves into other distribution windows.

In regards to brand starring role, a car placement would be of greater marketing value if it is driven by the lead characters and the automaker's tie-in sponsorship is included in the movie's DVD release than a placement where the car appeared briefly in the movie. However, Ong and Meri (1994) questioned whether tie-in sponsorship undermines the positive impact of product placement. They argued the audience may be sensitized to the point of viewing the brand placement as tacky, too deliberate, or "not natural." Their contention of tie-in sponsorships impacting product placement values unfortunately has yet to be explored in a research study.

METHODOLOGY

An online survey to assess consumers' attitudes toward product placement in movies and in TV programs was developed at a professional survey builder website (i.e., *Formsite.com*). The survey was also hosted there. Following an introduction of the researchers conducting the survey, and an explanation of the purpose of the survey, respondents were provided with a brief description of product/brand placements in a movie or TV show. Respondents were told that the camera would focus on the brand or logo for a few seconds if the placement was intentional. They would also likely see the characters in the movie/program using or holding the product with the real brand/packaging featured rather than a fictitious brand or generic label such as "pizza" on the package. The brand may also be intentionally featured in the background of a scene.

Early in the online questionnaire, respondents were asked to list the name of the show/movie/program or series in which they have seen/heard a product/brand placement embedded within that show/program. Two open-ended questions were employed to probe the specific product/ brand seen/heard, and nature/scene of the placement (i.e., was the place- ment subtle or an "in-your-face" type; was the placement verbal or visual or both).

When answering the above questions, respondents were asked to think of TV shows or episodes in which they have watched the entire program/show on any of the major networks (i.e., ABC, NBC, CBS, and FOX) during the prime time hours of 7 p.m. to 11 p.m. during a par- ticular week. The data collection was confined to a seven-day period, but the researchers also tape recorded one week earlier as well in case respondents referred to a placement in a prior program. So television programs on all four major networks during the hours of 7 p.m. to 11 p.m. were recorded for a 14-day block, with the first recording day being one week before the starting date of the data collection. The recorded pro- grams provided the researchers a way to validate the product place- ments respondents said they recalled seeing/hearing on TV. The validation will be conducted and reported in a future article.

Respondents were solicited via e-mail survey invitations. Several students in an undergraduate marketing class were involved in the data collection. They e-mailed the survey invitations (containing a hyperlink to the survey hosted at *formsite.com*) to their friends, relatives, family members, and colleagues at work.

A total of 117 people responded to the survey but only 99 of these re- spondents fully completed the rather lengthy online questionnaire. Of the 91 respondents who indicated their gender, approximately 58% were fe- males, and 42% were males. Approximately 65% of the respondents were between the ages of "18 to 35." Another 15% were in the "36 to 49" age bracket while the remaining 20% were in the "50+" age group.

FINDINGS AND DISCUSSION

On the first question, "Were you aware of product placement before reading the introduction to this survey?" almost three-fourths of the 117 respondents indicated that they were aware of product/brand placement in both movies and TV programs. Approximately 12% were not aware of this promotional practice in movies or in TV programs. Comparing the awareness of product placements in movies and TV programs, 10% reported being aware of placements in movies only. Even fewer (i.e., 3%) indicated such awareness for TV programs only. From a public policy standpoint, it is evident that product placement is not a stealth marketing tactic that works at consumers' subconscious levels as some critics of product placement may claim. The practice of embedding brands within a program/movie (even in television programs) is widely known by the public.

On the next question, 77% of the 117 respondents indicated that they had watched at least one whole TV episode or show on a major network during prime time that week. Among the 53 people that indicated which shows they did watch or products they recalled (or didn't recall) seeing, seven people noted a specific brand appearance/scene in a specific TV show, and six respondents named a few brands they recalled seeing in movies aired on TV. While these responses have yet to be validated via the recorded programs, it appears that television placement brand recall ability was not as good as those reported for movie placements in other studies (e.g., DeLorme and Reid, 1999; Ong and Meri, 1994). Perhaps, there are not as many placements in TV programs as in movies. It may be more difficult for respondents to recall a placement from a number of TV programs they have watched during the week than to recall brands seen in a specific movie. Interestingly, 64% of the respondents who do rent/purchase movies to watch at home indicated that they do recall seeing product placements in the movies.

To ascertain attitudinal differences, if any, between product placements in TV programs and in movies, paired t-tests were performed on the following items (see Table 1) as the mean ratings comparisons were within-subjects. As can be seen from Table 1, none of the five-paired item comparisons yielded findings of significant differences. It is important to point out here that similar questionnaire items pertaining to TV product placement and to movie placement were spaced far apart in the online questionnaire so as to minimize sensitizing subjects to the intents of the similar questions. For some of these paired items, the questions appeared on different screens (pages). It appears that subjects in this study do not perceive product placements differently depending on the medium of delivery (i.e., movies versus TV programs).

As to why only an $N = 77$ to 78 is reported in this table, the numerous Likert items were grouped in blocks of 4 or 5 items arranged in a grid format online. These grid questions usually appear to be "labor inten-

TABLE 1. Attitudes Toward Product Placement in Movies and in TV Programs

Attitudinal Items	Mean
From the product placements I have been exposed to on TV, brands were cast in a positive image.	2.15
From the product placements I have been exposed to in the movies, brands were cast in a positive image.	2.14
Product placement is an unethical form of advertising in TV programs/shows.	3.68
Product placement in movies is an unethical form of advertising.	3.65
Product placement enhances the reality of a scene in a TV program/show.	2.62
Product placement enhances the reality of a movie.	2.62
Brands that appear in TV product placement are usually the well-known brands.	2.12
Brands that appear in movie product placement are usually the well-known brands.	2.05
If there were product placements in a show, I would be aware of them.	2.58
If there were product placements in a movie, I would be quick to notice them.	2.64
Note: 1 = Strongly Agree; 5 = Strongly Disagree. N ranges from 77 to 78. None of the paired t-test results were significant at the 0.05 level.	

sive" for respondents. Hence, my decision not to make the items required questions. That way, respondents can skip to the later questions that they wish to answer. From my experience, making grid questions compulsory tends to result in "less committed" respondents clicking the X on their browser and dropping out of the survey completely.

Unlike the qualitative results observed in the DeLorme and Reid (1999) study, the survey results here seemed to suggest that the impact of product placements was weak. Respondents tend to disagree that they can usually remember the product/brand placement(s) a few weeks after they have seen the placements (mean rating = 3.71 where 1 = Strongly Agree and 5 = Strongly Disagree). Similarly, subjects disagreed that they do usually remember the brand or company that sponsored a particular TV program or show after a few weeks (mean = 3.59). Again, respondents tend to disagree that when they see a particular brand at a store or supermarket that had appeared in a TV show or movie, they would usually think of that placement scene in the show/movie (mean = 3.44). These findings were somewhat surprising as subjects in the study agreed that they are usually focused on the story/content when watching TV (mean = 1.58 where 1 = Strongly Agree and 5 = Strongly Disagree), and disagreed that they usually engage in TV channel surfing and hardly watch full episodes of any program (mean = 3.53).

Consumers in the study tend to agree that product placements do not belong in educational and news programming (mean = 2.34). While they were not too opposed to product placements, respondents, as a whole, were neutral in how they generally feel about companies who use product placement in television programming. Perhaps, consumers may not be very positive about companies that engaged in TV program product placements because they (consumers) respect the persuasive power of such a product placement and sees advertisers engaged in product placements as manipulative. Interestingly, respondents tend to agree that people would be influenced in their purchase selections by the product/brand placements in movies or TV programs. However, in reference to the earlier finding that respondents usually do not think about the brands that have appeared in a movie or television show while shopping, it may be the consumers' ego at work. Many consumers like to think that promotional gimmicks work on others but not on them.

There were 33 respondents in the sample that indicated "typically watch TV alone." Forty respondents reported watching TV typically with another person. Independent t-tests did not reveal any significant differences in attitudes toward television product placements between respondents who watch TV alone and those who watch with a companion.

As for age differences, the "18 to 35" age group was significantly more agreeable that "brands that appear in TV product placement are usually the well known brands" than their cohorts in the "36 to 49" age group (means of 1.98 and 2.50 respectively, where 1 = Strongly Agree and 5 = Strongly Disagree). These two age groups also differed significantly on the item "When I see a particular brand at a store or supermarket that had appeared in a TV show or a movie, I would usually think of that placement scene in the show/movie." The "36 to 49" age group more strongly disagreed with the above statement than their "18 to 35" counterpart (means of 4.25 and 3.17 respectively). The older respondents (36 and above) tend not to watch commercials during program breaks and agree that product placements are intrusive compared to the "18 to 35" age group. Finally, comparisons of attitudes and perceptions of product placements in TV programs did not yield any significant differences between male and female respondent groups.

CONCLUSIONS

Respondents did not appear to differ in their attitudes toward product placements in TV programs and in movies. Perhaps audiences do not make a distinction by medium. This lack of differences could also be due to the small sample size or the specific characteristics of the sample. The predominantly younger respondents (18 to 35 age group) in the sample were found to be more tolerable of product placements in general than the older respondents. Perhaps, the younger respondents were quite indifferent to the medium (TV or movies) of the product/brand placement.

The lack of findings of different perceptions of movie versus television placements may also be due to subjects' infrequent encounters with placements in television. Product placements may be more concentrated in movies than in television programs considering the multiple television channel choices and 24/7 programming. Television is also a more cluttered medium than movies in terms of advertisements. Hence, respondents' lack of exposures to television product placements may have resulted in their drawing upon their movie placement exposures in projecting their attitudes toward product placement in television programs. Consequently, no significant attitudinal differences were detected.

So it would be premature at this point to conclude that product placements in television programs are likely to be less effective than those in movies. As noted in the literature on product placements, many factors could contribute to the effectiveness of a product placement, regardless of whether the brand is highlighted in a movie or TV show. For example, the amount of brand starring role has been shown to have an impact on the effectiveness of product placements in television shows (Russell, 2003).

In closing, the proliferation of placements in television programs will continue as advertisers seek more cost effective visual promotions. Further research on product placements, particularly in television programs, would be timely and beneficial to marketing practitioners.

REFERENCES

Avery, Rosemary J., and Ferraro, Rosellina (2000, Winter). Verisimilitude or advertising? Brand appearances on prime-time television. *Journal of Consumer Affairs*, *34*(2), 217-244.

DeLorme, Denise E., and Reid, Leonard N. (1999, Summer). Moviegoers' experiences and interpretations of brands in films revisited. *Journal of Advertising*, *28*(2), 71-95.

Gould, Stephen J., Gupta, Pola B., and Grabner-Krauter, Sonja (2000, Winter). Product placements in movies: A cross-cultural analysis of Austrian, French, and American consumers' attitudes toward this emerging international medium. *Journal of Advertising, 29*(4), 41-58.

Gupta, Pola B., and Lord, Kenneth R. (1998). Product placement in movies: The effect of prominence and mode on audience recall. *Journal of Current Issues and Research in Advertising, 20*(1), 47-59.

Graser, Marc (2003, June 9). Brand recognition: Entity to evaluate worth of product placement. *Daily Variety, 279*(44), 5.

Ong, Beng Soo, and Meri, David (1994). Should product placement in movies be banned? *Journal of Promotion Management, 2*(3/4), 159-175.

Russell, Cristel Antonia (2002, December). Investigating the effectiveness of product placements in television shows: The role of modality and plot connection congruence on brand memory and attitude. *Journal of Consumer Research, 29*(3), 306-318.

Product Placement of Medical Products: Issues and Concerns

Christopher R. Turner

SUMMARY. Product placement is a well-established marketing technique that nevertheless continues to provoke considerable criticism and debate. Likewise, direct-to-patient marketing of pharmaceuticals is legally acceptable but is controversial among ethicists and medical professionals. Little has been published regarding the ethical challenges and pitfalls involved in medical marketing, including the issues of whether medical products should be treated differently from consumer products and whether pharmaceuticals are distinct from medical devices. Discussed are examples of pharmaceutical marketing as well as an episode from the *Chicago Hope* television program in which a medical device was touted as a solution for a problem for which the Food and Drug Administration (FDA) has not approved the use of the device. Legal and ethical considerations for product placement of medical products as they influence patient demand are also analyzed, as well as some of the pitfalls that may accompany direct marketing of medical products. *[Article copies available for a fee from The Haworth Document Delivery Service: 1-800-HAWORTH. E-mail address: <docdelivery@haworthpress.com> Website: <http://www.HaworthPress.com> © 2004 by The Haworth Press, Inc. All rights reserved.]*

Christopher R. Turner (MD, Uniformed Services University of the Health Sciences, PhD, University of Wisconsin, and MBA) is Clinical Assistant Professor, Department of Anesthesiology, University of Michigan Medical System, 1500 East Medical Center Drive, Ann Arbor, MI 48109-0048 (E-mail: turchris@med.umich.edu).

[Haworth co-indexing entry note]: "Product Placement of Medical Products: Issues and Concerns." Turner, Christopher R. Co-published simultaneously in *Journal of Promotion Management* (Best Business Books, an imprint of The Haworth Press, Inc.) Vol. 10, No. 1/2, 2004, pp. 159-170; and: *Handbook of Product Placement in the Mass Media: New Strategies in Marketing Theory, Practice, Trends, and Ethics* (ed: Mary-Lou Galician) Best Business Books, an imprint of The Haworth Press, Inc., 2004, pp. 159-170. Single or multiple copies of this article are available for a fee from The Haworth Document Delivery Service [1-800-HAWORTH, 9:00 a.m. - 5:00 p.m. (EST). E-mail address: docdelivery@haworthpress.com].

KEYWORDS. Ethics, medical products, product placement

INTRODUCTION

Direct to consumer marketing of prescription pharmaceuticals is a phenomenon of approximately the last 20 years, coinciding with the period of time that physicians and lawyers have been allowed to advertise. This marketing has in the last five or ten years become not only very common but indeed pervasive and almost inescapable. In any current magazine such as *Time* or *Newsweek* within the first few pages are advertisements for Vioxx® and other COX-2 inhibitors, various gastric reflux remedies such as Nexium®, or for various psychiatric medications such as Paxil®. These are just a few of the prescription pharmaceuticals being marketed directly to patients. Another notable example of direct to consumer pharmaceutical marketing is the Claritin® antihistamine campaign which featured Joan Lunden, because this caused a great deal of controversy over the potential conflict between her roles as journalist and as spokeswoman. Claritin is still very aggressively marketed to consumers but Ms. Lunden is no longer their spokesperson. More recently, Viagra® has been widely marketed in advertisements featuring Bob Dole or stock car drivers.

WHY IS MEDICAL MARKETING DIFFERENT?

The furor over the American Medical Association's endorsement deal with Sunbeam Corporation clearly shows that a significant proportion of the American public feels that medical marketing is distinct from other commercial marketing. Why is medical marketing different? In one respect, it is because medical marketing plays for higher stakes: the patient's health and well-being. In addition, there are higher standards for the basis of medical advertising, because medical advertising falls under the purview of the FDA. The FDA has more stringent regulatory standards for the support of advertising claims than does the Federal Trade Commission (for example, see Adams, 2001), although there is regulatory overlap in the areas of nonprescription pharmaceuticals. Another difference is that the physician has prescription control of the purchase decision for these medications, despite the fact that there is increasing interest in patient autonomy. Direct to patient marketing must allow for the fact that it only indirectly influences the purchase decision. Another difference is that the Code of Ethics of The International Federation of

Pharmaceutical Manufacturers' Associations requires that marketing should be based upon an appeal to data or information (IFPMA, 1998). Decisions concerning medical care ideally should be rational and evidence-based. While it may be appropriate to mount an emotional appeal to someone who may be interested in buying a luxury automobile, it is not appropriate to appeal to his or her emotions when selling Nexium as opposed to Prilosec®. Last but not least, the issue of whether a patient has a right to medical care plays into medical marketing as well. The more a patient feels entitled to medical care as a right the less credence they may give to economic considerations which limit their access to the newest or most expensive treatments.

The non-sedating antihistamines provide good examples of the conflicts that patients and health organizations find themselves in when patient demand may run up against medical economics. These drugs have been widely marketed directly to consumers in large part because payors such as Health Maintenance Organizations (HMOs) are loath to pay the considerable extra money for these non-sedating antihistamines as opposed to the more traditional ones. These drugs are not markedly more effective than the traditional antihistamines and are much more expensive. However, the side effect profiles are more favorable for many patients primarily because these patients feel less drowsy when taking these antihistamines. Because of this, patients often prefer the newer antihistamines to the older ones. Thus, patients' demand for these medications may conflict with the prescribing practices of physicians who are working with an organization with a restricted formulary and pharmaceutical budget that only provides the older, equally effective antihistamines. Someone else's money, be it the government or the insurance company or the HMO's, is always worth less than yours, and these non-sedating antihistamines might be less attractive if the patients were paying for them directly as opposed to having them paid for under their health care benefits.

Purpose of Direct-to-Consumer Advertising

What is the intent of advertising these prescription-only pharmaceuticals directly to consumers? The advocates for the industry say that consumer education is a major goal. They point to anti-cholesterol advertising campaigns as examples of this. Consumers are taught about their risks for disease (such as the risk for cardiovascular disease posed by the presence of hypercholesterolemia) and the potential for medical intervention through commercials, magazine advertisements, and mailings.

Consumer information is also touted as a benefit to direct to consumer marketing of pharmaceuticals. In this case the advertisers not only educate the consumer but also specifically point them to the remedies that are available from particular companies. This serves to generate brand recognition. The intent in either case is to motivate patients to discuss these diseases and agents with their physician where they might not otherwise be likely to (Direct to Consumer Advertising, 2000). The most direct intent is to increase patients' demand for these medications in order to influence the prescribing practices of the physicians in the face of restrictive formularies and pharmaceutical budgets.

Reaction of Physicians

A rational prescriber prescribes the right drug for the right reason at the right dose with the right timing. What happens when a consumer presents to a physician with a medical problem or information they have garnered from direct to consumer marketing of prescription pharmaceuticals? There are several possibilities. In one case, the physician may say that this is reasonable medication for their particular illness and may prescribe the medication, even given the availability of other medications that may be cheaper or may be more appropriate but are not specifically requested by the patient. Counterbalancing this would be financial or formulary pressures intended by medical administrators to limit the availability of newer, more expensive medications. Another alternative is that the physician may tell the patient they are not clear this is a good idea but it might be, and in such a case, the physician is willing to let the patient try the particular medication. Only in the final case, where a physician feels that the medication is inappropriate for the patient or strongly feels that other medications are more appropriate for the patient, will the physician deny the request of the consumer for a particular agent that they have seen on television. In two out of three possibilities, the pharmaceutical company gains a patient who is taking their medication, at least for a time.

What are the motivations of the physician during these encounters? The physician may very well prescribe the agent without good indication because of the psychological comfort of the patient: the patient feels better when they know they are participating in their medical care and they are trying something that they think might be useful. Alternatively, the physician may be motivated by a desire to keep the patient coming back to them. Physicians who routinely deny patient requests for medical care may find themselves losing patients to other physicians who are more accommodating. Finally, in many busy clinics, the physician may simply prescribe the medication requested to get the patient out of the clinic within the limited amount of time available for each visit.

Nonprescription Product Placement

There are multiple examples of product placement of nonprescription pharmaceuticals such as the placement of the over-the-counter analgesic drugs Tylenol® in the Sally Field movie *Murphy's Romance* and Nuprin® in the movie *Wayne's World*. It is also worth noting parenthetically the *Chicago Hope* television episode in which a breast-fed baby was brought in suffering from malnutrition and ultimately died (Hall, 1998). This episode received considerable criticism from breast-feeding advocates because companies that manufacture infant formula underwrote that season of *Chicago Hope*. This may be an example of the increasingly blurry line between artistic content and product placement (such as in the novel *The Bulgari Connection* by Fay Weldon or the movie *You've Got Mail*). The only product placement for prescription pharmaceuticals that I am aware of is the placement of the antidepressant drug Zoloft® in the movie *The Sixth Sense*. This could be because placement of prescription pharmaceuticals isn't common yet or, more likely, because many of these placement deals are kept confidential and unpublicized.

Product placement offers for pharmaceuticals some of the same advantages as it does for consumer products: it allows advertisers to cut through the clutter facing today's consumers and to get their message through to consumers who have become increasingly skilled at tuning out commercial messages. In addition, product placement allows marketers to work in a regulatory gray area. Because the placements are not strictly speaking advertisements, the marketers are not obligated to follow regulations designed for overt advertisements such as the requirement that a summary of side effects and contraindications accompany advertising. Placement also allows marketers to create favorable emotional associations with their products, which is also contrary to some guidelines for advertising pharmaceuticals such as those published by the IFPMA.

Medical Devices

I do not know of any documented example of marketing direct to consumers of purely medical devices as opposed to pharmaceuticals. There are exceptions in the area of fitness equipment and pain relief equipment such as external electrical muscle stimulators marketed as exercise machines. There are also many examples of the marketing of companies as opposed to devices. For example, the Medtronic Company markets the company but doesn't advertise their specific pumps or pacemakers. There may also be unpublicized examples of marketing or placement of medical devices for internal marketing. A company might pay to place their device in a movie or television show, not for advertising to consumers but for internal marketing within the company. They could use these placements for morale boosting or education for their own or supplier employees.

A major reason why we have not seen much advertising or placement of medical devices as opposed to pharmaceuticals or consumer products is that in the case of medical devices, the medical system is completely in charge of the purchase decision (Fleisher et al., 1998). While physicians are the primary movers in the acquisition of medical equipment, these decisions are usually greatly influenced by regulators, payors, administrators, physicians' groups, and practice guidelines. Thus, the purchase decision for medical equipment comes from within the medical system, and patients rarely understand or care about the differences among various types of medical equipment.

One medical device which might have been placed in a television show is an intraoperative monitor that has been touted as a monitor of the depth of anesthesia. What is "depth of anesthesia"? Depth is an easy concept to think about that is very difficult to define. Increasing depth comes from a complex interaction of the components of anesthesia, namely analgesia, unconsciousness, amnesia, and appropriate surgical conditions. Anesthesiologists have classically assessed depth by physiologic changes and patient movement. The reason this has been successful is that the anesthetic required for analgesia is generally much greater than that required for unconsciousness. Current practice, however, is to use medications that will improve surgical conditions or control cardiorespiratory changes independently of anesthetic depth, so the picture has become more clouded and the classic indicators of anesthetic depth are not as useful as they used to be.

Intraoperative recall (an episode of memory in the middle of a general anesthetic) is one consequence of inadequate depth (Drummond, 2000). It has been called "one of the best-kept secrets" of anesthesiology (Weihrer, 2001). There are a variety of causes of recall including patient variation or the inability to provide an adequate anesthetic depth. The incidence of recall is reported as 0.2% for non-obstetric and non-cardiac surgery (Liu et al., 1991), yet most practitioners feel that this reported incidence is far greater than that seen in clinical practice.

Of those who are reported to have intraoperative recall, approximately 5% report having pain while they were aware of their surgery (Jones, 1994) and it is in these patients that debilitating psychiatric sequelae are most likely to occur. These psychiatric disturbances from intraoperative recall may range from nonspecific restlessness and anxiety to sleep disturbances to post-traumatic stress disorder.

The Aspect A2000 BIS Monitor® from Aspect Medical Systems (Natick, MA) is marketed as an anesthesia depth monitor. It uses mathematically processed brain waves to yield a single number that is supposed to represent the depth of anesthesia. According to the company, at BIS levels above 70 the patient is inadequately anesthetized. If the BIS level is below 60, the patient is adequately anesthetized. The marketing of this monitor has focused on minimizing anesthetics thus saving drug, facility, and personnel costs. In the past, it has also been marketed as a way to prevent intraoperative recall. However, this is not an FDA-approved claim and within the last few years the company has had to withdraw this claim from their marketing material. It is not a perfect monitor, as the multiple cases show that recall can occur at BIS numbers below 60 (Dushane, 2000).

This monitor has generated a great deal of controversy within the anesthesia community over whether this monitor should be a standard of care for anesthetic practice. The company has actively pursued the adoption of this monitor as standard of care because such a designation would require that this monitor accompany all general anesthetics. This would increase sales of both the monitors and the (higher margin) disposable electroencephalography electrodes.

The direct marketing of this monitor to anesthesiologists, nurse anesthetists, and hospitals has been typical for medical marketing to professionals. Promotional materials have included booklets, newsletters, and publications supplied to hospitals and anesthesia providers. Opinion leaders from academic anesthesia have been recruited and included on videotapes touting the benefits of this monitor. There has been a very aggressive sales force for this company selling the monitor. Selling points are cost savings and that hospitals may gain a competitive edge over other local institutions. The marketing materials include recommended press releases that emphasize that the monitor ensures that patients get "not too little or too much" anesthesia, thus dancing around the issue of recall. The monitor has been positioned in marketing material as a standard of care even though fewer than 15% of American hospitals currently use this monitor. It has been aggressively marketed by some members of Aspect's sales force for malpractice suit prevention, and this marketing has at times included overt threats to practitioners stating, "If you have a case of intraoperative recall, have not used this monitor, and are sued, you will lose."

The BIS Monitor has appeared in the popular press as well in the last couple of years. Articles have appeared in *Time* magazine, *USA Today* and other consumer periodicals such as *Popular Science*, *Men's Health*, and *Redbook*, and segments on this monitor have aired on the television shows *20/20* and *Dateline NBC*. There have also been multiple local news features describing the problem of intraoperative recall and touting the ability of this monitor to prevent it.

This monitor has now shown up in medical marketing such as the Midwest Physicians Service website that advertises the 20 BIS monitors at their hospital and describes these monitors as "a good tool to prevent awareness" (Islat, 1999). Many hospitals have acquired these monitors and then used them in their own marketing efforts. For instance, an operating room supervisor at St. John's Hospital (Springfield, IL) is quoted as saying, "No patient wants to receive too little anesthesia and wake up during surgery or on the other hand get more anesthetic than they need" (Innovative anesthesia, 1999). This sentence is almost word for word from the marketing material that Aspect has supplied to hospitals and anesthesia providers.

To add into this mix, there are now two patient-based foundations that attempt to address the problem of intraoperative recall. One is the Anesthesia Awareness Foundation, which was set up by a woman who had a horrific experience of eye surgery under inadequate anesthesia. The goal of this foundation is "to prevent, through education and empowerment, anyone else from becoming a victim of anesthesia awareness" (Weihrer, 2001). Anesthesia awareness is her term for intraoperative recall. Included in the material that she provides to patients and interested parties who contact her are some adhesive strips. One of these can be attached to a hospital chart noting that the patient is aware of the problem of intraoperative recall and wants to be sure that it does not happen to them. Another is supposed to be attached to the patient's forehead before they go into surgery to remind the anesthesia provider to attach the BIS Monitor to the patient.

Case in Point: "Chicago Hope"

This monitor has been featured prominently in an episode of *Chicago Hope* (1999). In the program, a patient was scheduled to undergo minimally invasive cardiac surgery. During the operation he was aware, felt excruciating pain, and heard disparaging comments made about his body by the surgeon. This episode featured the BIS Monitor prominently during the postoperative discussions among the Medical Staff as a solution to intraoperative recall. The story ended with the hospital acquiring BIS Monitors for every operating room to prevent a similar event from happening again. After the program aired, there have been anecdotal reports of patients appearing for their surgeries asking for "that monitor I saw on *Chicago Hope.*" Clearly some patients learned from this episode that the BIS monitor prevents intraoperative recall, even though the episode aired after the FDA had stopped the company from using recall prevention in their marketing. It should be noted that the company has vigorously denied that this episode was product placement, has denied trying to manipulate the popular press to publicize the monitor, and has denied strong-arm sales tactics.

There has been a backlash in the anesthesia community over this monitor and the way it has been marketed and publicized. This backlash was described in a *Wall Street Journal* article in August 2000 in which some members of the anesthesia community complained about the way that this monitor has been represented in the popular press (Rosenblatt, 2000). There have been letters to the journal *Anesthesiology* describing patient interactions after this media coverage in which patients come in and ask for this monitor (Katz, 1999; Todd, 1999). Aspect has responded to the backlash by modifying its marketing campaign and focusing its marketing efforts on cost aspects as opposed to depth aspects of the monitor.

Still an unanswered question is whether the company is a victim or beneficiary of the marketing buzz. Clearly, however, the company has altered its approach to marketing this product because of the backlash within the anesthesia community. They now have told the Anesthesia Awareness Foundation that they feel the Anesthesia Awareness story is negative marketing. It is worth noting also that she is attempting to get patients and patient advocates to write to the ABC television program, *The Practice*, to get them to run a story line featuring the BIS Monitor and intraoperative recall prominently. This may be a forerunner for more attempted product placement by parties with agendas distinct from those of the companies directly involved.

LEGAL AND ETHICAL ISSUES

What are the legal limits on the marketing of medical products? These come primarily from regulatory requirements for medical advertising. FDA regulations prohibit the promotion of any pharmaceutical or medical device for a purpose for which it is not FDA-approved, including "off-label" uses that are common medical practice (Selected provisions, 2001). This prohibition would almost certainly apply as well to medical product placement, although I do not know of any legal precedent addressing this issue. Thus, if the BIS episode on *Chicago Hope* were product placement, it stands a high likelihood of running afoul of the FDA. Medical marketers more than most tend to be extremely careful to stay within what is permissible by regulation, because the consequences of violating regulations can be publicly damaging as well as very expensive due to fines or required remedial action (Sweeny, 1992). However, attempting to covertly influence the publicity about a medical product is probably not illegal, although many consumers and professionals might find it offensive.

Aside from adherence to relevant laws and regulations, what other principles of ethical marketing apply to medical product promotion? Ideally, medical marketing would adhere to principles of rational as opposed to emotional argument, in keeping with the marketing standards already discussed. Beyond that, marketers are obligated to ensure that promotions are honest, supported by the available data without distortion, and not deceptive. Sales tactics should not be misleading, high pressure, or manipulative. Marketing efforts should do no harm and substantial risks associated with the product should be disclosed. Quite aside from issues of applying these ethical principles to standard marketing efforts, these principles are even more difficult to apply to product placements, because of the nature of the promotion. It is, for example, difficult to discuss the risks associated with a product that from the perspective of the movie is supposed to be a "prop," such as the Zoloft placement in *The Sixth Sense*. However, it is because of the difficulty of applying ethical principles to medical product placement that medical marketers should be extremely careful about how they place their products.

The marketing of pharmaceuticals to physicians has received some publicity recently over ethical issues (Relman, 2001; AMA Code of Medical Ethics, 2001). However, little attention has been paid to issues of how physicians respond to patients who bring issues raised by direct to patient marketing to their physician. The physician traditionally was the arbiter of what was best for the patient. Modern medicine, however, places increasing emphasis on patient autonomy. The AMA code of ethics addresses the rights of patients to direct their own healthcare, but specifically avoids the issue of patient motivation. Patients make their decisions for their own reasons, and part of patient autonomy requires that a patient's motivation not be an issue in their healthcare. Physicians must balance patient requests against medical advisability and the physicians' own ethics, as is shown most clearly by the debate surrounding physician-assisted suicide. This balance will generally tilt in favor of honoring the patient's request unless it is medically contraindicated or ethically unsupportable, even in cases where that request may be based upon an incomplete or inaccurate understanding of direct to consumer marketing materials.

CONCLUSIONS

So where does this leave us? The use of product placement is likely to increase in medical marketing for the same reasons that it is increasing for other marketing. The BIS example shows that publicity and placement (even if the company did not initiate the placement) can be as effective for generating patient interest in medical products as they are in other marketing areas. However, given the perceived differences between medical products and consumer products, it is essential for both ethical and business reasons that medical marketers adhere to the same kinds of standards for placement that the FDA requires for medical advertising. The BIS Monitor is a good example of what can happen when medical marketing goes astray.

How do we best address the issues raised by medical product placement? Existing ethical guidelines may be adequate if they are adhered to, although it is notable that the Pharmaceutical Research and Manufacturers of America does not publish a Code of Ethics independent of that of the IFPMA. Certainly vigorous FDA enforcement of reasonable regulation can help, as well as the promulgation of new guidelines as to what is permissible in the regulatory gray area of product placement for medical products. Physicians and patients both have responsibility to keep themselves abreast of direct to consumer marketing of medical products of relevance to them, as this can offer a fruitful area for physician-patient interaction both at the individual level and at the societal level. This interaction should not only deal with the medical aspects of the marketing effort but also, where appropriate, should educate the patients on the media aspects of the marketing. Only physicians and patients who are savvy to marketing and media will be in positions to influence medical marketing practices as they evolve.

REFERENCES

Adams, C. (2001, September 25). FDA warns Merck for misrepresenting its block-buster arthritis drug Vioxx. *Wall Street Journal.*

American Medical Association (2001). Code of Medical Ethics. Retrieved 26 December 2001 from *http://www.ama-assn.org/ama/pub/category/2512.html.*

Direct to Consumer Advertising (2000). Retrieved 26 December 2001 from *http://www.phrma.org/publications/backgrounders/other/dtc.phtml.*

Drummond, J. C. (2000). Monitoring depth of anesthesia. *Anesthesiology, 93,* 876-882.

Dushane, T. E. (2000). Con: Monitoring the amnestic state during general anesthesia should not be a standard of care. *American Journal of Anesthesiology, 27,* 509-512.

Fleisher, L. A.; Mantha, S.; and Roizen, M. F. (1998). Medical technology assessment: An overview. *Anesthesia and Analgesia, 87,* 1271-1282.

Hall, B. (1998). "The Breast and the Brightest" television episode (M. Mitchell, Director). In N. Yorkin (Producer), *Chicago Hope.* New York: CBS.

IFPMA Code of Pharmaceutical Marketing Practices (1998). Retrieved 26 December 2001, from *http://www.ifpma.org/.*

Innovative Anesthesia Technology at St. John's (1999). Retrieved 26 December 2001 from *http://www.st-johns.org/public_html/news/NG084.html.*

Islat, G. (1999). MPASOHIO FAQ. Retrieved 26 December 2001 from *http://www.mpasohio.com/faq.htm#where.*

Jones, J. G. (1994). Perception and memory during general anesthesia. *British Journal of Anaesthesia, 73,* 31-37.

Katz, S. M. (1999). The media and the BIS monitor. *Anesthesiology, 90*(6), 1796.

Kazdin, M. (1999). "From Here to Maternity" television episode (M. Harmon, Director). In N. Yorkin (Producer), *Chicago Hope.* New York: CBS.

Liu, W. H. D.; Thorp, T. A. S.; Graham, S. G.; and Aitkenhead, A. R. (1991). Incidence of awareness with recall during general anesthesia. *Anaesthesia, 46,* 435-437.

Relman, A. S. (2001). Separating continuing medical education from pharmaceutical marketing. *JAMA (Journal of the American Medical Association), 285,* 2009-2012.

Rosenblatt, J. (2000, August 2). Some doctors see scare tactics in marketing of "BIS" device. *Wall Street Journal.*

Selected Provisions of the Federal Food, Drug, and Cosmetic Act and Code of Federal Regulations for Prescription Drug Advertising and Labeling (2001). Retrieved 2 January 2002 from *http://www.fda.gov/cder/ddmac/SELECTED_PROVISIONS_2ND.HTM.*

Sweeny, T. M. (1992). The view and responsibility of the advertising agency toward advertising claims. *Journal of Public Health Dentistry, 52,* 401-402.

Todd, M. M. (1999). In Reply. *Anesthesiology, 90,* 1797.

Wiehrer, C. (2001). Anesthesia awareness. Retrieved 26 December 2001 from *http://anesthesiaawareness.com/.*

Cast Away and the Contradictions of Product Placement

Ted Friedman

SUMMARY. This essay looks at implications of product placement in *Cast Away*, the 2000 film in which Tom Hanks plays a Federal Express executive who is stranded on a desert island before making his way back home. It argues that *Cast Away* is a particularly valuable case study because of the conflict between its relentless product placement and its dark vision of contemporary global capitalism. The article investigates four aspects of global capitalism addressed by *Cast Away*: the compression of time, the compression of space, the rising influence of multinational corporations, and the dominance of consumer culture. *[Article copies available for a fee from The Haworth Document Delivery Service: 1-800-HAWORTH. E-mail address: <docdelivery@haworthpress.com> Website: <http://www.HaworthPress. com> © 2004 by The Haworth Press, Inc. All rights reserved.]*

KEYWORDS. Capitalism, *Cast Away*, Federal Express, globalism, motion pictures, movies, product placement, time, space

Ted Friedman (PhD, Duke University) is Assistant Professor, Department of Communication, Georgia State University, University Plaza, Atlanta, GA 30303 (E-mail: tedf@gsu.edu).

[Haworth co-indexing entry note]: "*Cast Away* and the Contradictions of Product Placement." Friedman, Ted. Co-published simultaneously in *Journal of Promotion Management* (Best Business Books, an imprint of The Haworth Press, Inc.) Vol. 10, No. 1/2, 2004, pp. 171-183; and: *Handbook of Product Placement in the Mass Media: New Strategies in Marketing Theory, Practice, Trends, and Ethics* (ed: Mary-Lou Galician) Best Business Books, an imprint of The Haworth Press, Inc., 2004, pp. 171-183. Single or multiple copies of this article are available for a fee from The Haworth Document Delivery Service [1-800-HAWORTH, 9:00 a.m. - 5:00 p.m. (EST). E-mail address: docdelivery@haworthpress.com].

Digital Object Identifier: 10.1300/J057v10n01_12

INTRODUCTION:
THE NEED FOR THE CLOSE ANALYSIS
OF PRODUCT PLACEMENT IN FILM

Most critical writing about product placement has taken a broad scope, surveying the history, economics, and ethics of the practice as a whole. This is understandable–given such a pervasive phenomenon, it's crucial to understand its full shape and context. But in addition to the broad view, it's equally important to get a close-up–to zoom from the forest to the trees, and understand in greater detail how product placement functions in individual films. How does product placement affect the narrative and texture of a film? What friction and tensions occur when real-world brands are inserted into fictional texts? How do films negotiate the competing demands of corporate sponsors and creative personnel? These are questions that can only be answered by looking in detail at how product placement works in specific films.

For this study, I have chosen to look at *Cast Away*, the 2000 film in which Tom Hanks plays a Federal Express executive who spends four years shipwrecked on a desert island before escaping back to civilization. *Cast Away* is a particularly fascinating case study because of the conflict between its relentless product placement and its dark vision of contemporary global capitalism. On the one hand, the prominence of FedEx in the film is striking: not only is the company the hero's employer, but the arrival of washed-ashore FedEx packages are major plot points in the movie. On the other hand, the film in many ways is a fantasy of escape from the "just in time" way of life FedEx represents. Getting shipwrecked frees Hanks' character, Chuck Noland, from the speeded-up pace of contemporary global capitalism and teaches him to live at a different pace. The film's conclusion highlights the rift between Chuck's newfound calm and the banal frenzy of contemporary American life, then struggles to offer some sort of resolution.

At first glance, the intersection of such blatant product placement with this critical perspective towards corporate culture suggests hypocrisy, a failure of nerve (and crass bottom-line decision making) on the part of the filmmakers. However, I'd like to suggest that in some ways the conflict makes the film a more richly ambivalent text. The prominence of FedEx makes the film's ultimate critique cut deeper–perhaps more deeply than the filmmakers (and FedEx) realized.

BEYOND PRODUCT PLACEMENT:
FedEx AS A CHARACTER

Cast Away was both a critically lauded and a commercially success-ful film. The Rotten Tomatoes film review database reports that 86% of national film critics gave it a favorable rating. Produced for a reported $90 million, it grossed $234 million in the US and another $175 million internationally (*www.worldwideboxoffice.com*). But amid the positive reviews, many critics did single the film out for what seemed like egre-gious FedEx product placement (Abramovich, 2000; Thomson, 2001; Schacher, 2000). As one reviewer wrote, "*Cast Away* is one big com-mercial for Federal Express; a connoisseur of product placement in films, I have never seen more egregious campaigning for one company in a film than I witnessed in this one" (Voigt, 2001).

The *Cast Away* producers' arrangement with FedEx, however, was not exactly the traditional form of product placement (the exchange of sponsors' money for product screen time). Director Robert Zemeckis, in fact, insists that it's not product placement at all. On the commentary track to the film's DVD, Zemeckis (2000) elaborates:

> There was absolutely no product placement. We weren't paid by anybody to place products in the movie. I did that in the past, and it wasn't worth the little bit of money that they give you, because then you end up with another creative partner, which you don't need. However, it just seemed to me that the whole integrity of the movie would be compromised if this was some phony trans-global letter delivery service, with some Hollywood fake logo and all that. It wouldn't seem like it would be real. So very simply, we asked Federal Express for their permission to use their logo, and they could've said no. And that was it.

Zemeckis, however, is not telling the whole story here. While no place-ment fee was paid, FedEx supplied extensive resources to the filmmak-ers, including airplanes, trucks, packages and uniforms (Barton, 2000). In addition, FedEx CEO Fred Smith was an investor in the film's pro-duction company (Abramovich, 2000).

The incorporation of FedEx into the story line of *Cast Away* appealed to the corporation precisely because it went beyond traditional product placement. Gail Christensen, FedEx's Managing Director of Global Brand Management, spent two years working with the producers of *Cast Away*. She told the *Sacramento Bee*, "As we stepped back and looked at it, we thought, 'It's not product placement, we're a character in this movie.' It's not just a FedEx product on the screen. It transcends product placement" (quoted in Barton, 2000).

This strategy is part of a trend of corporations attempting to move beyond advertising and other familiar marketing strategies to more firmly embed their brands into the culture. As journalist Naomi Klein writes in her scathing critique, *No Logo: Taking Aim at the Brand Bullies*:

> For these companies, branding was not just a matter of adding value to a product. It was about thirstily soaking up cultural ideas and iconography that their brands could reflect by projecting these ideas and images back on the culture as "extensions" of their brands. Culture, in other words, would add value to their brands. (Klein, 1999, p. 29)

The opening shots of *Cast Away* establish FedEx as a kind of character. For the movie's first few minutes, the camera follows the path of one package, from its pickup at an artists' studio in rural Texas, to its delivery in Moscow. At times, the camera even takes a package's-eye view of the action, imbuing the inanimate object with the kind of perspective normally reserved for the protagonists of a film. What's particularly striking about this scene is how it distinctly echoes a FedEx ad campaign of a few years ago: the "Golden Package" series, in which each commercial followed the trail of one package from pickup to destination, as narrator Linda Hunt described the process as if it were a modern-day fairy tale. The opening moments of *Cast Away* play eerily like *Golden Package: The Movie*.

CAST AWAY's *AMBIVALENT CRITIQUE OF GLOBAL CAPITALISM*

But if *Cast Away* starts like a big-screen commercial for FedEx, it soon evinces a much more ambivalent attitude toward the company and what it represents.

The movie is divided into three parts: the opening section establishing Chuck's life as a FedEx manager, the middle section chronicling his time on the island, and the concluding section back in the USA. The structure of the film, then, is a kind of double escape.

First, we see the pressures and frustrations of Chuck's "normal" life, after which crashing on a desert island seems like a blessed respite. The film, of course, presents the crash itself as a harrowing disaster, and life on the island as a grueling challenge. Nonetheless, it's also a thrilling adventure, a compelling fantasy of life outside the bounds of "civilization," in which a pudgy middle manager is transformed into a lean hunter and master outdoorsman. As Tom Hanks put it in an interview with Charlie Rose included on the *Cast Away* DVD, "The best thing that ever happened to this guy was his plane blowing up and getting stuck on an island for a very long time."

But the film also acknowledges the limitations of a life without companionship, without some form of social organization. And so Chuck escapes again–ending up back where he started, but with a new perspective. The final section of the film chronicles the culture shock between Chuck's old world and his new outlook, as he–and we–grope to find some common ground.

In the following sections, I want to look at four aspects of contemporary life under global capitalism addressed by *Cast Away*'s dialectic of double escape: the compression of time, the compression of space, the increasing power of multinational corporations, and the dominance of consumer culture. Please note that while I use the phrase "contemporary global capitalism," one could also refer, following David Harvey (1990), to "the condition of postmodernity," or, to use Michael Hardt and Antonio Negri's (2001) formulation, "Empire."

Compression of Time

First, let's look at how *Cast Away* addresses the compression of time under global capitalism. The sense that the pace of the world is continually speeding up has been brought about by new technologies of instantaneous communication, flexible production, and global transportation networks. FedEx, of course, is the perfect emblem of this phenomenon, delivering packages overnight around the world. The company, in fact, has been a prime mover in the quickening of the global economy, introducing to the business world the notion that any package could be "absolutely, positively" shipped anywhere overnight. The human toll of this speed-up, in the US, at least, has been to put more and more pressure on employees to keep up, resulting in a rise in average work hours, increased job stress, and the erosion of leisure time–the phenomena described by sociologist Juliet Schor (1992) in *The Overworked American.*

Chuck Noland in the first section of *Cast Away* is both victim of this speed up, and an enforcer of it upon others. We first meet him as that package we've been following arrives in Russia. Overweight, bleary, and bullying, Chuck is making a speech to the workers at a new FedEx outpost in Moscow:

> Time rules over us without mercy, not caring if we're healthy or ill, hungry or drunk, Russian, American, beings from Mars. It's like a fire. It could either destroy us or keep us warm. That's why every FedEx office has a clock. Because we live or die by the clock. We never turn our back on it. And we never, ever allow ourselves the sin of losing track of time. Locally, it's 1:56. That means we've got three hours and four minutes before the end of the day's package sort. That's how long we have. That's how much time we have before this pulsating, accursed, relentless taskmaster tries to put us out of business!

Back home in Memphis, Chuck remains preoccupied and rushed. Paged in the middle of a big family Christmas dinner, he's forced to rush off to catch a plane to Malaysia. In a comic moment before he departs, he and his girlfriend Kelly Frears (Helen Hunt) pull out their calendars and try to fit more time together into their hectic schedules. They end up hurriedly exchanging presents in the airport parking lot. At the last moment, Chuck pulls out one last gift–a box that clearly holds an engagement ring. He leaves it with Kelly, and asks her to wait to open it–it appears he'd planned to propose before being interrupted by that fateful page.

Once on the island, time operates in a completely different way. All the pressures of deadlines of the FedEx world no longer matter. Instead, Chuck's life is ruled by the inexorable cycles of nature: the rising and setting of the sun, the ebb and flow of the tide, the changing of the seasons. Chuck has to make an effort to keep track of linear time at all, marking the days on a cave wall in the time-honored shipwreck-movie tradition.

In place of the relentless rush of his life in the USA, Chuck on the island is faced with a different challenge: monotony. Chuck finally escapes back to our world, but a changed man. The film elegantly dramatizes the conflict between our hurried world and Chuck's new sense of time in a series of deliberately paced scenes in which Chuck is awkwardly welcomed back by his FedEx colleagues.

As the world rushes around him, Chuck appears to be moving in slow motion. In one shot, Chuck stands inside an empty office, while the FedEx welcome-home party continues outside the windows–complete with crowds, balloons, and even a brief glimpse (on a TV monitor) of FedEx

CEO Fred Smith. *Village Voice* critic J. Hoberman (2000) describes the scenes as "the least compromising, bleakest vision of the human condition in any Hollywood A-picture since Douglas Sirk's *Imitation of Life*." Hoberman goes on to take Zemeckis to task for the film's resolution, which, after conjuring up such a profound sense of alienation, "casts it away with pumped-up affirmation."

Compression of Space

The counterpart to global capitalism's compression of time is its compression of space. By reducing the time it takes for information, products and people to move from point A to point B, communications and transportation technologies effectively make the world a smaller place. FedEx is again both exemplar and prime mover here. The company operates in over 200 countries, enabling regions that would once have taken weeks to reach to receive product shipments from around the world overnight.

There are certainly potentially positive consequences to this transition, as the world is brought together into what McLuhan called a "global village." Much of how globalism has proceeded in practice, however, has led to worsening inequality and cultural domination (see, for starters, Hardt and Negri, 2000; Klein, 1999; Harvey, 1990). *Cast Away* does not deal with the worst of these excesses directly—it follows the travails of a white male American middle manager, someone of relatively great privilege in the global economy. And at moments, it seems to offer smug cheerleading for America's increased influence in the post-Cold War economy. As the camera follows that first package through the streets of Moscow, it happens to pan across a group of Russians in the process of taking down a bronze monument to Lenin. (The scene is set in the early 1990s.) It's a self-congratulatory moment, suggesting that FedEx has replaced the heroes of Communism in the hearts of Muscovites.

But the scene in Russia also demonstrates the ominous potential of globalization to level cultural differences, turning the world into a homogenous, US-dominated consumer culture. Chuck, in his speech to his Russian workers, is quite clearly the arrogant cultural imperialist, imposing his vision of time and efficiency on the natives—who in turn resist. As Chuck finishes his big speech about time, he realizes his translator has been taking some liberties. When Chuck asks what he's been saying, the translator replies, "I tell them what they want to hear. I say that this man, when his truck broke down, he stole a boy's bicycle to do his deliveries." Chuck in response can only protest, "I *borrowed* it!"

Globalism can be rough on white male American middle managers, too. Running a far-flung corporation means sending employees around the world at the drop of a hat, as the Willy Loman's of a previous generation become globe-trotting "road warriors." It's just such a trip which leads to the crash.

After the crash, Chuck's universe contracts to the size of one small island. He's escaped globalism by ending up on the one spot FedEx can't reach . . . except that, in the creepiest irony in the film, FedEx *can* reach the island–or its packages and logo can, at least, as the contents of the wrecked aircraft wash on shore. Even at the edge of civilization, apparently, you can't completely escape FedEx and its logo. As Hanks tells Charlie Rose on the DVD, "there will always be a FedEx . . . You can't imagine a world without FedEx." Hanks' quote recalls an observation of media scholar Susan Douglas (reported in Soar and Ericsson, 2000) about the use of product placement in films set in the past and future: by placing Perrier in the 1950s, or Taco Bell in the mid-21st Century, marketers *colonize time*, positing a universe in which their product is beyond history–it always has existed, and it always will. FedEx's placement in the middle of a deserted South Pacific island *colonizes space* in a similar way, suggesting that no corner of the globe could possibly be free from its influence. Given that FedEx didn't even pay outright for the privilege, the filmmakers' insistence on placing the logo so prominently on the desert island suggests something even more insidious than product placement: that the filmmakers' very imaginations have been colonized by the logic of global capitalism, so that it's impossible to think of a world without FedEx. To the film's credit, it doesn't seem so sure that's a good thing.

Role of Multinational Corporations

Next, let's look at how *Cast Away* addresses another central aspect of contemporary life: the increasing influence of multinational corporations. Critics of global capitalism observe today that multinational corporations have grown more powerful than nation-states. (See Hardt and Negri, 2000; Harvey, 1990.) FedEx is one of those corporations, with revenues in 2000 of $18.3 billion. At the start of *Cast Away*, Chuck is a company man–he's allowed FedEx to dominate his life. His loyalty to FedEx rises above that shown to his family or girlfriend, as we've seen.

On the island, Chuck maintains a perverse level of corporate loy-alty–especially for somebody whose corporate flight just crashed. (More than one critic has wondered why, when Chuck gets back home, he doesn't sue the hell out of FedEx.) When packages from the downed plane start to wash up, Chuck first refuses to open them, telling himself he'll deliver them once he gets home. By contrast, when the corpse of one of the other passengers on the crashed plane washes ashore, Chuck helps himself to the shoes and clothes without a second thought. Finally, though, necessity takes precedence over loyalty, and he opens the boxes–all except one, upon which he notices a drawing of a pair of wings. He leaves that one untouched, to deliver on his return.

Once back in our world, Chuck finds he can't rekindle his loyalty to FedEx. As we have seen, he remains alienated and apart amidst the cor-porate celebrations of his rescue. He does, however, deliver that final package–as I'll discuss below.

Consumer Culture

Before we get to the final package, though, let's look at one last aspect of global capitalism addressed by *Cast Away*: the dominance of consumer culture.

FedEx itself is not exactly a product, but rather a *service* which facili-tates the distribution of products. FedEx is also a critical cog in machine of consumer culture–the intermediary which ships products to stores, documents to managers, and catalog and Internet orders to customers. This mediating role makes branding FedEx particularly challenging, and helps explain why the company plasters its logos so relentlessly on boxes, trucks and planes–with no tangible product to sell, the logo must stand in for the product. This also explains why the company changed its name in 1994 from Federal Express to the shorter, more logo-friendly FedEx. As Bruce McGovert, implementation director for Landor Associates, the branding consultants who orchestrated the shift, told a trade publication, "Whereas Federal Express only permitted 58-inch letters on the side of a trailer, the letters spelling FedEx can stand six feet tall. Airplanes can be read across an entire airfield" (Corporate De-sign Foundation, 1995).

Consumer culture is the flip-side of the global capitalist system of production. The payoff for being an "overworked American" is supposed to be the chance to buy all those shiny consumer goods. One contradic-tion is immediately apparent, however: how are we supposed to enjoy those goods if we spend all our time and energy on work? This is Chuck

Noland's situation at the beginning of the film: so preoccupied with work that he hardly notices his material surroundings. Beyond this irony, however, the film doesn't push much of a critique of consumer culture in the early going, being more concerned with the work side of the equation.

The film gets much more interested in material culture once we reach the island. Here, as the packages wash ashore, Chuck begins to repurpose ordinary consumer goods into tools for survival. The blades on a pair of ice skates become knives. The netting from a dress crinoline becomes a sturdy fishnet. In a neat self-referential bit, reels of videotape, seemingly useless without a TV, VCR, and electricity, take on new function as the rope tying together Chuck's escape raft. And most famously, Chuck repurposes a volleyball to fulfill his need for companionship, fashioning a crude face on the sphere out of his own blood. Inspired by the manufacturer's name printed on the ball, Chuck dubs his new friend, "Wilson."

Many critics and viewers have spotlighted these feats of ingenuity as the high points of *Cast Away*. What makes this part of the movie so fun to watch is the way it defamiliarizes everyday consumer objects. In our own lives, consumer goods are *fetishized* objects–goods we purchase not just because they're useful, but because of the package of associations, values, and fantasies attached to them by advertising and marketing in our culture. The desert island strips away the layers of fetishization. All the shiny packaging and snappy commercials are incredibly beside the point when you're trapped on a desert island with no TV, no electricity, searching for the tools of survival. Price–the ultimate fetish, which converts use value into exchange value–is completely beside the point, as well. Stripped of their status as fetishized commodities, these objects are boiled down to their most basic use-value. *Cast Away*, then, provides a fantasy of escape from the blaring, obfuscating world of the commodity fetish, to a simpler world where we value objects simply for what we can do with them.

The irony–the fundamental, structuring irony of *Cast Away*–is that product placement is a quintessential form of commodity fetishization. Here, I think the film manages to negotiate this irony because FedEx, as I've already discussed, is more a *service* than a *product*. FedEx isn't defamiliarized and repurposed the way the ice skates and videotape are, since it was part of their delivery mechanism rather than their commercial packaging. In a way, FedEx, even on the island, continues to do exactly what it's supposed to do–deliver packages, albeit not to their intended recipient.

The one other prominent product placement on the island is the Wilson volleyball. Wilson Sporting Goods Co. didn't pay for the placement, but did provide the filmmakers with more than 60 volleyballs. Asked whether the film might cast his product in a negative light, Allen Davenport, business manager of volleyballs at Wilson, told the reporter, "I'm not sure how you portray a volleyball badly" (Silk, 2001).

RECONCILING CONTRADICTION

So, how can we make sense of the contradictions of *Cast Away*? How does the film ultimately reconcile the clash between its corporate backers and its cultural politics–or does it?

One interpretive strategy we could use to explain the resolution of this contradiction is to describe the result as "inoculation" (Barthes, 1957/1973). The marketer takes a small dose of self-criticism up front, and in return receives immunity from more damaging criticism. This analysis seems a useful way to describe the self-parodying product placement in films such as *Wayne's World 2* (for Reebok, Pizza Hut, and Pepsi) and *Demolition Man* (for Taco Bell). The advertiser winks at the audience, to let the viewers know it's in on the joke–then gets in its pitch all the same. But I think there's something deeper going on in *Cast Away*. The film doesn't just *tweak* FedEx–it demonstrates fundamental misgivings about everything FedEx stands for.

Alternately, we could describe the film as *subversive*–a subtle attack on FedEx and all it stands for. But this perspective fails us as well, I'd argue–would FedEx have gone along, if it suffered such clear damage? Would critics have attacked the film as a blatant commercial for FedEx, had the film been widely perceived as self-defeating?

I'd like to suggest a third option: that we see the contradictions in *Cast Away* as *dialectical*. Robert Ray (1985) in his landmark critical history of American film, *A Certain Tendency in the Hollywood Cinema, 1930-1980*, draws together Marxist and structuralist forms of film analysis to argue that Hollywood's most popular films succeed by offering their audiences *imaginary resolutions to ongoing social conflicts*. The quintessential version of this mythic reconciliation is the marriage plot, transcending class and gender divisions through the conventions of romance.

This is what the conclusion of *Cast Away* attempts to accomplish, as it struggles to reconcile its warring perspectives in a utopian synthesis. As we've already seen, after Chuck returns, we are first made aware of the yawning chasm between his new island-forged perspective, and that of his old friends and colleagues. His job no longer makes sense to him, and his girlfriend has married another man. But then the film tries to find a resolution–tries to reach the "happy ending" audiences expect out of a Hollywood movie, and tries to imagine a way to live in this world by a different set of rules. In the final scene, Chuck delivers the one package he never opened on the island, the one with the wings on the box. In a neat bit of narrative bookending, it belongs to the artist who we briefly met at the film's opening, shipping off the package that ended up in Moscow. She specializes in giant sculptures of wings. We see Chuck and the woman briefly flirt, with hints of a possible relationship to follow. The film ends on a shot of a rural crossroads, suggesting Chuck is free to choose his own path from here.

CONCLUSIONS

At film's end, then, *Cast Away* offers up the prospect of a new life for Chuck, one which will allow him to integrate his island-forged perspective with life in the USA. In place of our rushed experience of time, Chuck exhibits a Zen-like state of calm. In place of our crowded world of global commerce, we are left with the image of a blank rural crossroads. In place of consumer culture, we see the individualized craft of the artist. And even, in place of the FedEx logo, the artist's more personal visual signature, a stylized pair of wings.

Chuck does hold on to some sense of corporate loyalty at film's end, but it's a personally chosen, limited form of loyalty–he does deliver that final package. FedEx, then, still seems to have a place in the world after all the changes Chuck has gone through. But in an unhurried world where we could all live like Chuck, why would anyone bother to use it?

REFERENCES

Abramovich, A. (2000). Company Man. *Feed.* Available online at *http://www.feedmag.com/templates/search_all.php3?p_id=96.*
Barthes, R. (1957, Translated 1972). *Mythologies.* New York: Hill and Wang.
Barton, D. (2000, December 22). Packagetour. *The Sacramento Bee,* D1.
Cast Away (2000): Reviews and Preview (2001). *Rotten Tomatoes.* Available online at *http://www.rottentomatoes.com/movie-1103112/.*

Cast Away (2001). *WorldwideBoxoffice.com*. Available online at *http://www. worldwideboxoffice.com/index.cgi?order=worldwide&start=1900&finish=2002& keyword=cast+away&links=amazon.com*

Corporate Design Foundation. (1995). Why Federal Express Became FedEx. *@issue: The Journal of Business and Design*, 1(1) (special edition), 6-14.

Hardt, M., and Negri, A. (2000). *Empire*. Cambridge, MA: Harvard University Press.

Harvey, D. (1990). *The Condition of Postmodernity*. London: Basic Blackwell.

Hoberman, J. (2000, December 26). 100 Years of Solitude. *The Village Voice*. Available online at *http://www.villagevoice.com/issues/0051/hoberman.php*

Klein, N. (1999). *No Logo: Taking Aim at the Brand Bullies*. New York: Picador.

Ray, R. (1985). *A Certain Tendency of the Hollywood Cinema, 1930-1980*. Princeton, NJ: Princeton University Press.

Reed, J. (2001, January 4). The FedEx Movie Starring Tom Hanks. *Weep*. Available online at *http://www.weepmag.com/archive.asp?y=2001&m=01&d=04*

Schacher, Y. (2000, December 22). *Cast Away*. *Slate*. Available online at *http://slate. msn.com/?id=95479*

Schor, J. (1992). *The Overworked American*. New York: Basic Books.

Silk, Robin Kitzes (2001, February). From *E.T.* to *Cast Away*: Product Placement in Film. *International Trademark Association Bulletin*, 56(4). Available online at *http://www.inta.org/membersonly/bulletin/I.asp?I=11*.

Soar, M. & Ericsson, S. (Directors). (2000). *Behind the Screens: Hollywood Goes Hypercommercial*. Northampton, MA: Media Education Foundation.

Thomson, D. (2001, January 12). The *Castaway*. *Salon*. Available online at *http:// www.salon.com/ent/movies/feature/2001/01/12/hanks/index.html*

Voigt, J. (2001, February). *Cast Away* Redeemed. *The Cresset, 64*(4). Available online at *http://www.valpo.edu/cresset/len01voi.html*

Zemeckis, R. (Director) (2000). *Cast Away*. Twentieth Century Fox.

Brand Placement Recognition: The Influence of Presentation Mode and Brand Familiarity

Ian Brennan
Laurie A. Babin

SUMMARY. This study examines the impact of adding an audible reference to a visually prominent brand placement on recognition of the brand placed. Facilitated recognition scores were used to control for the effects of brand familiarity on brand placement recognition. Subjects exposed to one of two complete movies were asked to indicate recognition of brands that were or were not placed in their movie. Results indicate that brand placement recognition levels achieved by audio-visual prominent placements exceed the recognition rates achieved by visual-only prominent placements. Additionally, familiar brands achieve higher levels of recognition than unfamiliar brands, even when the recognition scores for familiar brands are adjusted for the guessing and constructive

Ian Brennan (PhD, University of Texas-Arlington) is Assistant Professor of Marketing, Hasan School of Business, Colorado State University-Pueblo, 2200 Bonforte Blvd., Pueblo, CO 81001 (E-mail: ian.brennan@colostate-pueblo.edu or ianbrennan@usa.net). Laurie A. Babin (PhD, Louisiana State University) is Associate Professor of Marketing, Department of Management and Marketing, University of Southern Mississippi, Box 5091, Hattiesburg, MS 39406 (E-mail: Laurie.Babin@usm.edu).

[Haworth co-indexing entry note]: "Brand Placement Recognition: The Influence of Presentation Mode and Brand Familiarity." Brennan, Ian, and Laurie A. Babin. Co-published simultaneously in *Journal of Promotion Management* (Best Business Books, an imprint of The Haworth Press, Inc.) Vol. 10, No. 1/2, 2004, pp. 185-202; and: *Handbook of Product Placement in the Mass Media: New Strategies in Marketing Theory, Practice, Trends, and Ethics* (ed: Mary-Lou Galician) Best Business Books, an imprint of The Haworth Press, Inc., 2004, pp. 185-202. Single or multiple copies of this article are available for a fee from The Haworth Document Delivery Service [1-800-HAWORTH, 9:00 a.m. - 5:00 p.m. (EST). E-mail address: docdelivery@haworthpress.com].

http://www.haworthpress.com/web/JPM
Digital Object Identifier: 10.1300/J057v10n01_13

recognition that may result from inferences associated with familiar brands. *[Article copies available for a fee from The Haworth Document Delivery Service: 1-800-HAWORTH. E-mail address: <docdelivery@haworthpress. com> Website: <http://www.HaworthPress.com> © 2004 by The Haworth Press, Inc. All rights reserved.]*

KEYWORDS. Audio cues, brand placement, movies, on-set placements, product placement, recognition

INTRODUCTION

Brand placement refers to the paid inclusion of branded products or brand identifiers, through audio and/or visual means, within mass media programming (Karrh, 1998). A number of studies suggest that brand placement recognition is more likely when a placement occupies a prominent rather than background position in a scene (Brennan, Dubas and Babin, 1999; d'Astous and Chartier, 2000; Gupta and Lord, 1998). In contrast, although the presence of an audible brand reference has become a factor in the establishment of brand-placement fees (Karrh, 1998), research addressing the effect on placement recognition of augmenting a prominent visual placement with an audible brand reference has produced conflicting results (Gupta and Lord, 1998; Law and Braun, 2000). Law and Braun's (2000) findings indicate that brand recognition is enhanced when an audible reference to a brand accompanies its visual placement. However, in their study, the audio-visual placement treatment condition was confounded with visual prominence. In contrast, research which has controlled for the effects of visual prominence has demonstrated only directional support for the notion that the audio-visual placement enhances the recognition achieved by its visual-only counterpart (Gupta and Lord, 1998). Given the conflicting results, we reexamine the impact that adding an audible reference to a visually prominent placement has upon recognition of the brand placed.

We also examine the practice of relying on facilitated scores to control for the effects of brand familiarity on brand-placement recognition (Babin and Carder, 1996a; Brennan et al., 1999; Law and Braun, 2000). Facilitated recognition scores reduce the recognition score for subjects exposed to a brand placement by the recognition scores reported by subjects exposed to a similar movie that did not feature the brand. Thus, facilitated recognition scores control for differences in constructive recognition that may occur when brands may be perceived to have different likelihoods of having appeared in a movie. Accordingly, a number of studies have used facilitated recognition scores to compare placement executions that involve inter-brand comparisons (Babin and Carder, 1996a; Brennan et al., 1999, Law and Braun, 2000). In the present study, we consider whether the use of facilitated recognition scores in inter-brand comparisons is sufficient to eliminate the effects on placement recognition of inter-brand differences in brand familiarity.

GROWTH OF THE BRAND PLACEMENT INDUSTRY

In the early days of filmmaking, brand owners typically donated or loaned the products that appeared in movies; indeed, in some instances branded goods were even purchased by filmmakers (DeLorme and Reid, 1999; Karrh, 1994; Volmers and Mizerski, 1994). By the mid-1940's, however, there is evidence, notably the Jack Daniels placement in the movie *Mildred Pierce*, that film-makers were inserting branded products into films in exchange for some form of consideration (Reed, 1989).

The practice of brand placement proliferated so that by the 1980s brand placement agencies had been established to wed marketers seeking brand placement opportunities with directors looking to add verisimilitude and/or reduce production costs. The growth of the brand placement industry was fueled by some well-publicized commercial successes. For example, Reese's Pieces candy enjoyed a 65% sales increase in the month following its placement in the 1982 movie *ET: The Extra Terrestrial* (Rosen, 1990). In a similar vein, in 1995, BMW supplied the makers of the move *Golden Eye* with prototypes of its Z3 roadster; within a month of the film's release, pre-booked product orders were almost twice as large as BMW's internal forecast (Fournier and Dolan, 1997). In the 1990's, researchers estimated that the transactions brokered by placement agencies were worth 100 million dollars (DeLorme and Reid, 1999). By the Millennium, the estimated value of placement transactions had soared to 360 million dollars per year (McNatt and Oleck, 2000).

A number of arguments support an increased role for brand placement in the promotional mix. First, audiences may ignore television advertising by switching channels (or even leaving the room) during a commercial break (Tse and Lee, 2001). In contrast, it is difficult to ignore brand placements that are integrated into movie scenes (Turcotte,

1995). Second, a brand used by a celebrity in a movie receives an implied celebrity endorsement. Such an endorsement may be particularly salient if the actor does not act as a spokesperson in traditional advertisements (Karrh, 1998). Third, in comparison to the fixed life span of the thirty-second advertising spot, successful movies have a virtually eternal after-life at video stores (Turcotte, 1995). Fourth, on a cost-per-contact basis, cinematic placement tends to be less expensive than traditional advertising (d'Astous and Chartier, 2000). Fifth, brand placement– a less obtrusive method of generating brand exposure than traditional advertising–may be less likely to spawn negative brand-related cognitions (Babin and Carder, 1996b), particularly when the visual placement is not used as a device to advance the plot (Russell, 2002).

In the following sections we examine the influence of placement mode (audio-visual versus visual-only) and brand familiarity on the rate of recognition achieved by prominent placements, but first we provide a rationale for our choice of dependent variable.

DOES BRAND PLACEMENT RECOGNITION MATTER?

A premise of classical conditioning theory is that affect may be transferred from a well-liked stimulus to an affectively neutral stimulus when the stimuli are jointly presented (Baker, 1999). Research on cinematic placements indicates that affect for a leading actor appears to transfer to a brand when the brand is jointly featured with the actor in a movie scene (d'Astous and Chartier, 2000). Studies have also found significant the effects for cinematic placement on both recall and recognition (Babin and Carder, 1996a, 1996b; Brennan et al., 1999; d'Astous and Chartier, 2000; Gupta and Lord, 1998; Karrh, 1994; Ong and Meri, 1994; Russell, 2002). In contrast, although two recent studies of brands placed on a television program found a significant effect for brand placement on brand choice (Law and Braun, 2000) and brand attitude (Russell, 2002), most research on cinematic placements has failed to demonstrate a significant placement effect on either brand attitude or purchase intentions (Babin and Carder, 1996b; Karrh, 1994; Ong and Meri, 1994; Vollmers and Mizerski, 1994).

Most brand placements feature well-known brands (Sopolosky and Kenny, 1994). Accordingly, since the stimuli for most brand placement research in movies are drawn from extant film stock, brand placement researchers have employed well-known (rather than fictitious) brands. As a consequence, subjects are likely to have been exposed to numerous advertising exposures and (possibly) consumption experiences for the featured brands, so it is hardly surprising that individual placements for well-known brands fail to influence brand attitudes and purchase intentions (Karrh, 1998). In contrast, it is noteworthy that the Reese's Pieces and the BMW Z3 brands were either new or not yet launched at the time of their movie placements in *ET: The Extra Terrestrial* and *Golden Eye*, respectively.

Despite the apparent inability of individual movie placements to have an immediate impact on brand attitude and choice, marketers are likely to continue to seek to understand the characteristics of a brand placement that enhances the likelihood of placement recognition. The rationale for such a statement is that individuals appear to possess an automatic frequency-counting mechanism that records the relative frequency of encounters with different stimuli (Hasher and Zacks, 1984). Accordingly, the relative frequency with which individuals perceive themselves to have encountered a brand may be used as a basis for making inferences about brand quality (Baker et al., 1986). As Hoyer and Brown (1990, p. 142) note: "if the automatic frequency-counting mechanism counts substantially more instances of communication about brand A than about brand X, then an inference may be made to the effect that brand A is better known, so it must be more popular and probably better." Indeed, Hoyer and Brown (1990) provide experimental evidence of the persuasiveness of the inferences invoked by a well-known brand. In their study, in spite of a product trial that revealed a well-known brand to be inferior in taste to an unknown brand, subjects selected the well-known brand of peanut butter over the unknown brand by almost a 3:1 margin.

AUDIO-VISUAL versus VISUAL-ONLY PLACEMENTS

When the Walt Disney Company made brand placement opportunities available in the movie *Mr. Destiny*, it doubled the asking price for an audible brand reference over the fee associated with a visual-only placement (Center tries to pull the plug, 1991). It is not clear, however, whether the strategy supporting a prominent visual placement with an audible brand reference elevates recognition over that achieved by the visual-only reference, since academic studies have produced conflicting results (Gupta and Lord, 1998; Law and Braun, 2000; Sabherwal, Pokrywczynski and Griffin, 1994).

In support of the hypothesis that recognition will be higher for audiovisual than for visual-only brand placements, Gupta and Lord (1998) cite the duel-coding model of advertising processing (Pavio, 1986; Unnava and Burnkrant, 1991). The duel-coding model suggests that advertising information that is encoded in audio-visual format is easier to retrieve from memory than advertising which presents information in the visual-only format. However, Gupta and Lord's results provide directional but not statistical support for their hypothesis. This result leaves the authors unsure as to whether (1) "marketers may enjoy essentially comparable results through the use of a prominent visual depiction as with a strategy which integrates audio and video presentation at a higher cost to the manufacturer" (Gupta and Lord, 1998, p. 57), or (2) whether the absence of an advantage (with respect to recognition) for a prominent audio-visual placement over a prominent visual placement may have resulted from ceiling effects. Consistent with the latter conclusion are the notions that (1) Gupta and Lord's test involved the manipulation of a single, and perhaps unusually memorable, placement stimulus–a Ferrari automobile and (2) Gupta and Lord's subjects were not exposed to the entire movie, instead they were exposed to the Ferrari placement within the less cluttered context of a movie excerpt.

In contrast, the results of studies by Law and Braun (2000) and Sabherwal et al. (1994) support the hypothesis that recognition will be higher for audio-visual than for visual product placements. Unfortunately, in the Law and Braun (2000) study, as the authors themselves acknowledge, the audio-visual versus visual-only manipulation was confounded with placement prominence: ". . . the audio-visual placements also happened to be the more prominent placements" (Law and Braun, 2000, p. 1065). Placement prominence has been conceptualized as a dichotomous variable (Murdock, 1992; Babin and Carder, 1996a) with the term *creative* placement describing those brands that appear in the background of a shot, and the term *on-set* placement describing those that are displayed more prominently. Gupta and Lord (1998) used the terms *subtle* and *prominent* to describe *creative* and *on-set* placements, respectively. *On-set* placements achieve higher levels of recognition than their creative counterparts (Brennan et al., 1999; d'Astous and Chartier, 2000; Gupta and Lord, 1998); thus, it is not clear from Law and Braun's (2000) study that audio-visual placements will enhance recognition when both audio-visual and visual-only placements are *on*-set.

Subjects in the Sabherwal et al. (1994) study were shown a ten-minute clip of the movie *Days of Thunder* in which the presence or absence of an audible reference to a visual placement for the Hardees fast-food chain served as the audio-visual versus visual-only manipulation. The authors report that unaided recall of the Hardees brand was significantly higher in the audio-visual condition. Unfortunately, the authors did not evaluate the relative prominence of the visual placement and so it is unclear as to whether their result extends to comparisons that involve *on-set* placements. Accordingly, we examine the incremental effect of placement mode on the recognition of *on-set* placements when subjects are exposed to an entire movie. Furthermore, our examination of the effect of the audio-visual versus visual-only placement on brand recognition also controls for the effects of exposure time, false recall and brand familiarity.

> *H1:* After controlling for the effects of placement exposure-time, false recall and brand familiarity, recognition will be higher for prominent, audio-visual brand placements than for prominent, visual brand placements.

While Russell (2002) developed and manipulated placements in three twenty-seven minute fictitious television programs, budget constraints prohibit researchers from producing full-length films to generate unconfounded tests of placement executions. Instead, brand placement researchers have measured responses to the real brand placements that have occurred within existing movies. As well as presenting difficulties in obtaining stimuli that differ on the treatment variable, the use of real-world stimuli usually necessitates inter-brand comparisons across treatment (i.e., placement execution) conditions (Babin and Carder, 1996a; Brennan et al., 1999; Law and Braun, 2000). In the following section, we consider the extent to which current research practice in brand placement adequately addresses the validity issues that result from inter-brand comparisons.

BRAND FAMILIARITY AND PLACEMENT RECOGNITION

Consumers use marketplace information to construct inferences about brand characteristics (Kirmani and Wright, 1989; Hoyer and Brown, 1990; Johar and Pham, 1999). For example, Johar and Pham (1999) note that differences in the perceived fit between various companies and an event may result in event-sponsor misidentification. Accordingly, when making a judgment as to whether a familiar brand appeared in a movie, respondents may infer that (1) a familiar brand is likely to be supported by a large promotional budget and (2) such a budget may increase the likelihood that it will appear in a movie. Furthermore, respondents who believe that brand appearances are governed by artistic considerations may infer that well-known brands are more likely to assist directors both in developing a character and in setting a scene. Consequently, whether motivated by commercial or artistic considerations, research suggests that most placements in films feature familiar brands (Sapolsky and Kinney, 1994).

Familiar brands tend to exhibit stronger associations with their product categories (Lee and Sternthal, 1999; Negunadi, 1990) making them more accessible in memory (Negunadi, 1990); however, Babin and Carder (1996b) note that early research in brand placement did not account for the fact that respondent inferences could inflate reported recognition. For example, Steortz (1987) measured the aided-recall of thirty placements spread across five movies; however, the absence of a control group (respondents not exposed to the placements) makes it impossible to assess the extent to which reported levels of aided-recall resulted from false recall. In contrast, recent research in brand placement has attempted to control for false recall through the use of facilitated recognition scores (Babin and Carder, 1996a; Brennan et al., 1999; Law and Braun, 2000). Facilitated recognition scores are obtained by examining two comparable movies (e.g., Brennan et al., 1999) or two episodes of a television program (e.g., Law and Braun, 2000) that feature different brands. Next, the proportion of respondents who recognize the brand after being exposed to the placement is reduced by the proportion falsely reporting having seen a brand in a stimulus in which it did not appear. Differences in the facilitated recognition scores across experimental conditions (placement executions) are then attributed to treatment induced memory effects rather than respondent inferences. The rationale is that the similarity in the program content viewed by treatment and control groups is assumed to produce equivalent levels of false recognition.

We contend that although the facilitated recognition scores may control for a difference in the likelihood that a familiar versus unfamiliar brand will be falsely associated with a movie, the use of facilitated scores does not control for all the effects of brand familiarity on placement recognition. Specifically, the procedure does not control for differences in brand recognition that may result from the effects of differences in brand familiarity on placement encoding. Our contention is supported by recent research in psychology which suggests that familiar words may enjoy an encoding advantage over words that are less familiar. In a series of experiments, Watkins, LeCompte and Kim

(2000) demonstrate that a list of words that occur more frequently in everyday language (e.g., letter, earth, captain, hotel and flower) are more recallable than a list of words which occur more rarely (e.g., proctor, kilt, mango, scooter and cobra), even when neither list shares an association with an underlying node that would facilitate retrieval. Thus, the placements of familiar brands are likely to benefit from encoding advantages when compared to their less familiar counterparts, so that the practice of adjusting recognition scores for false recall will not eliminate the effects of brand familiarity on brand recognition.

H2: Brand recognition will be higher for prominently-placed familiar brands than for prominently-placed unfamiliar brands.

H3: Adjusted for the effects of false recall, recognition will be higher for prominently-placed familiar brands than for prominently-placed unfamiliar brands.

METHOD

Research Design and Stimuli

Ninety-eight undergraduate business and communications students participated in the study by viewing a movie in its entirety. The sample was 40% male and at least 18 years old. Fully 95% of the sample was aged 18-25; 4% were between 26 and 35 years old. The use of a college sample is consistent with evidence suggesting that most filmgoers are aged 18-34, and that most have some college education (Johnson, 1981; *Motion Picture Almanac*, 1980). Moreover, attending movies is a common activity for the age range of the sample (Nebenzahl and Secunda, 1993).

Respondents were randomly assigned to one of two groups. One group viewed *Rocky III* (n = 54), and the other viewed *Rocky V* (n = 44). These two movies were chosen for several reasons. First, since coding of the placements prior to collecting data was necessary, we needed movies that were available on videotape. Five coders viewed the films several times to identify brands placed within them. Second, we needed films with several placements to increase our ability to find comparable placements to test our hypotheses. Both films had numerous brand placements (over 30 in each). Third, some brands appeared in both films. Fourth, the films were comparable. Finally, since both films were released several years ago, we avoided the potential confound of promotional tie-ins or announced sponsorships that could have drawn the audience's attention to the brand (Ong and Meri, 1994).

Both groups viewed their respective movies in a simulated theatrical experience in which the film was projected from behind the heads of the audience onto a 6 × 10 foot screen in a darkened classroom. While not entirely realistic of a movie-going experience, the goal was to have respondents view an entire film in a controlled setting to achieve a balance between internal and external validity. Viewing an entire film with several placements rather than a short film clip with only a few placements (cf. Gupta and Lord, 1998; Karrh, 1994; Law and Braun, 2000; Vollmers and Mizerski, 1994) simulates the real-world clutter currently found in films. For example, content analyses of product placement in films indicates an average of 11.6 (Sapolsky and Kinney, 1994) to 18.2 (Troupe, 1991) placement per film.

Immediately after viewing the movie, respondents were asked to write down what they thought was the purpose of the study, with none indicating the true purpose. Next, subjects were presented with a list of brands and asked to indicate those brand names that they recognized as having appeared in the movie. Details of the recognition test appear below.

Audio-Visual versus Visual Brand Placements

Initially, two judges (an audio-visual specialist and a marketing professor) coded all brands placed in both movies on two variables: placement category (*on-set* versus *creative*) and screen exposure time (cf. Brennan et al., 1999). Brands placed merely as background props were coded as *creative* placements, and any brand that was implicitly endorsed by a major actor or was the focus of the scene in which it was placed was coded as an *on-set* placement, which is in accordance with Murdock's (1992) conceptual definitions. To eliminate the potentially confounding effect of placement prominence, the brand placements employed in the current study were drawn from the pool of placements coded as on-set, resulting in a pool of thirty-nine brands as potential candidates to test our hypotheses. Next, exposure time was measured for these brands using professional editing equipment capable of slowing a film down to 30 frames per second. For each placement, exposure time was measured from the time at which the product's name, logo, advertising banner and/or shape was revealed, and total exposure time was measured for a brand receiving multiple placements. Exposure times ranged from 0.54 to 124.66 seconds for the on-set brand placements identified. Finally, two more judges blind to the research hypotheses also coded the pool of on-set placements into those that did provide/did not provide an audible brand reference (inter-judge agreement = 100%).

Consistent with Gupta and Lord's (1998) attempt to ensure an equivalency of exposure time in brand placement comparisons, we retained visual placements with an exposure time that was within one second of the exposure time attained by each of the audio-visual placements. In view of research indicating that the presence of the principal actor in a brand placement scene has a significant effect on placement recognition (d'Astous and Chartier, 2000), the judges matched each pair of brand placements employed in the test of the research hypotheses with respect to the presence or absence of the principal actor (all placements utilized in our hypotheses tests were associated with the principal actor, Sylvester Stallone). Finally, any pairs of audio-visual/visual placements that yielded significantly different brand familiarity scores (the pretest procedure is described below) were eliminated.

This procedure permitted two independent tests of H1 to be performed on *Rocky III* placements. First, we compared the recognition attained by the Wheaties audio-visual placement (screen-time 8.17 seconds) with that of the Caesar's Palace visual placement (9.00 seconds). Second, we compared the recognition attained by the Madison Square Garden audio-visual placement (5.17 seconds) with that of the Radio City Music Hall visual placement (5.00 seconds). To control for differences in the effects of false recall (whereby one brand is perceived to have been more likely than another to have been included in the movie) we performed two tests. For the Wheaties versus Caesar's Palace comparison we reduced the recognition scores of the Wheaties brand by the recognition rate attained by the brand from viewers of a similar film (*Rocky V*). Since Caesar's Palace appeared in both films we did not adjust its recognition rate in *Rocky III*. Clearly, a recognition advantage for the adjusted Wheaties rate of recognition versus unadjusted Caesar's Palace rate of recognition would provide strong evidence of the capacity of audio-visual execution to enhance recognition. Since the Madison Square Garden audio-visual placement appeared in both *Rocky III* and *Rocky V*, the adjusted recognition comparison was confined to Wheaties versus Caesar's Palace.

Brand Familiarity

To test H2, three pairs of brand placements were selected that: (1) received unobscured visual shots in the movie, (2) were classified as on-set placements, (3) had significant within-pair differences in brand familiarity when rated on the average of two seven-point items (familiar/unfamiliar, well known/not well known) by 30 subjects who did not take part in the recognition test, and (4) had within-pair on-screen exposure times that were similar (i.e., within one second of one another). All pairs meeting these criteria were English language publications, such as newspapers and magazines. This procedure yielded three independent tests of H2: *GQ* (exposure time = .61 seconds) versus *Press Herald* (exposure time = .54 seconds), *People* (exposure time = 1.0 second) versus *Ring Magazine* (exposure time = 1.0 second), and *Newsweek* (exposure time = 1.71 seconds) versus *London Examiner* (exposure time = 2.0 seconds). The brand familiarity scores were significantly different for each of the three pairs of brands: *GQ* versus *Press Herald* (t (29) = 6.01, p < .001, Ms = 4.62 vs. 1.98), *People* versus *Ring Magazine* (t (29) = 11.13, p < .001, Ms = 5.80 vs. 1.83), *Newsweek* versus *London Examiner* (t (29) = 11.72, p < .001, Ms = 5.92 vs. 2.15).

Recognition

The questionnaire listed seventy-four specific brands and asked respondents to circle "Yes," "No," or "Not sure" for each to the question, "Did you see or hear references to any of the following brands in the film you just saw?" The 74 brands consisted of all brands placed in each film as well as 10 brands not placed in either, with their order randomized on the questionnaire. Responses to these items were used to measure the dependent variable, recognition, for each specific brand tested in the hypothesis testing.

To test H3, we reduced the recognition rates attained by each familiar brand used in the test of H2 by the percentage of respondents who incorrectly reported recognizing the familiar brands after viewing *Rocky V*–a movie that did not feature any of the familiar brands employed in the test of H2. The adjusted recognition scores represent an attempt to isolate the subjects who directly retrieved the familiar brand from memory from those who falsely recalled (i.e., constructively inferred) the appearance of the brand in the movie (cf. Brennan et al., 1999).

RESULTS

The recognition data relevant for each of the two tests of H1 appears in Table 1. A McNemar test (for two related samples) was used for all tests of H1. Note that the McNemar test uses the Chi-square distribution only when the sample size minus ties (in this study the number of ties equals the number of subjects who recognized either both audio-visual and visual-only placements or the number who recognized neither) is large. In the small sample case the McNemar test is identical to the sign test with a binomial decision rule. The result of the McNemar test is significant for both the Wheaties versus Caesar's Palace comparison (recognition for Wheaties = 87% versus Caesar's Palace = 67%, Binomial, $p < .013$) and the Madison Square Garden versus Radio City Music Hall comparison (respondents only recognizing Madison Square Garden = 87% versus Radio City Music Hall = 35%, chi-square $[1] = 26.04$, $p < .01$). Thus, both tests support H1. A McNemar test indicates that H1 is also supported when the recognition obtained by the audio-visual execution only is reduced by the number of respondents who falsely recalled the brand in a similar movie: (adjusted recognition for Wheaties 83% versus unadjusted recognition for Caesar's Palace = 67%, Binomial, $p < .035$).

Table 2 contains the recognition data relevant for each of the three tests of H2. The result of the McNemar test is significant for each of the three tests: *GQ* versus *Press Herald* (chi-square $[1] = 18.27$, $p < .001$), *People* versus *Ring* (Binomial, $p < .001$), *Newsweek* versus *London Examiner* (chi-square $[1] = 14.82$, $p < .001$). Thus all three tests support H2.

The adjusted recognition data (i.e., recognition data adjusted for the effects of false recall) appear in Table 3. Consistent with H3, the result of the McNemar test is significant for each of the three tests: *GQ* versus

TABLE 1. The Effects of Audio-Visual versus Visual Placements on Placement Recognition

Placement Type		Recognition[a]			
Audio-Visual	Visual	Both	Audio-Video	Video	Neither
Wheaties	Caesar's Palace	33	14	3	4
MSG	RCMH	19	28	0	7

[a](n = 54), MSG = Madison Square Garden, RCMH = Radio City Music Hall.

TABLE 2. The Effects of Brand Familiarity on Placement Recognition

Placement Type			Recognition[a]		
Familiar	Unfamiliar	Both	F[b]	U[c]	Neither
GQ	Press Herald	7	32	5	10
People	Ring	13	21	2	18
Newsweek	London Examiner	3	24	3	24

[a](n = 54), [b]F = Familiar brand, [c]U = Unfamiliar brand.

TABLE 3. The Effects of Brand Familiarity on Adjusted Placement Recognition

Placement Type			Recognition[a]		
Familiar	Unfamiliar	Both	F[b]	U[c]	Neither
GQ	Press Herald	7	31	2	14
People	Ring[d]	13	15	2	24
Newsweek	London Examiner	3	19	3	29

[a](n = 54), [b]F = Familiar brand, [c]U = Unfamiliar brand, [d]Adjusted recognition score not available.

Press Herald (chi-square $[1] = 23.76, p < .001$), *People* versus *Ring* (Binomial, $p < .003$), *Newsweek* versus *London Examiner* (Binomial, $p < .001$).

DISCUSSION

The results indicate that brand placement recognition levels achieved by audio-visual, *on-set* placements exceed the recognition rates achieved by visual, *on-set* placements. The results also indicate that, for *on-set* placements, familiar brands achieve higher levels of recognition than unfamiliar brands. Moreover the *on-set* placements of familiar brands achieve greater recognition than those of unfamiliar brands even when the recognition scores of familiar brands are adjusted for the guessing and constructive recognition that may result from inferences associated with familiar brands. Thus, the results present compelling evidence that the superior encoding of familiar brand placements produces a recognition advantage over less familiar brands.

Our results are consistent with the notion that ceiling effects are likely to have been responsible for the absence of a statistically significant effect for the audio-visual versus visual-only placement in Gupta and

Lord's (1998) study. Future research might attempt to ascertain the characteristics of visually prominent placements that may propel recognition to a level that renders an audible reference superfluous. For example, the results of d'Astous and Chartier (2000) indicate that brand placements that are featured in scenes when the principal actor is present are better remembered than those that occur in the absence of the leading actor. Accordingly, future research might consider whether the audio-visual references associated with a protagonist have more impact on recognition than those associated with a minor character. Researchers should also consider whether recognition may be enhanced by the separation of an audible reference from its visual placement (in comparison with their simultaneous presentation). Given the financial premium that audio-visual placements command over visual-only placements (Karrh, 1998), such questions are likely to be of practical as well as theoretical interest.

With respect to the influence that brand familiarity has on the recognition of *on-set* brand placements, our results have important implications for the area of sponsorship research that addresses sponsor identification accuracy. Previous research by Johar and Pham (1999) suggests that event-sponsor recognition accuracy is not significantly affected by sponsor size (a surrogate for sponsor familiarity) when similarly-sized decoy firms are present both at encoding (in the media that disclosed the event-sponsor relationship) and during retrieval (as foils during sponsor recognition). Our results are consistent with the notion that sponsor familiarity may have a significant impact on the accuracy of sponsor identification when the task of encoding an event-sponsor relationship is rendered less challenging–specifically, when decoy brands are included in the choice set for the recognition test, but are absent at the time the event-sponsor relationship is encoded.

The influence that brand-familiarity has on recognition, beyond the effects of false recall, increases the research design challenges that confront brand placement researchers. Unfortunately our results suggest that inter-brand comparisons of visual differences need not only to control for potential placement execution confounds but must also account for differences in brand familiarity. Current practice of adjusting recognition scores for false recognition does not account for the effects of brand familiarity on placement encoding.

Clearly, there is a remote likelihood of utilizing existing movies to conduct intra-brand comparisons among placements that are equivalent on characteristics such as prominence, celebrity presence, exposure time and audio-visual presence. Given the practical problems inherent in conducting brand placement research with real products in real movies, Russell (2002) proposes a theater methodology whereby researchers would write scripts, hire actors and film performances. Control over the entire production process would enable researchers to conduct unconfounded tests of brand placement execution. While Russell (2002) did develop three versions of a fictitious television program, doing so for a full-length film would be difficult. For example, it is unlikely that academic budgets would permit the filming outdoor action sequences, the hiring of hiring celebrity actors, etc. Accordingly, we suggest that future researchers consider testing their hypotheses with virtual brand placements in existing programs or movies.

U.S. television networks have already experimented with virtual brand placements: for example, virtual products appeared on the NBC series *Law and Order* (Reed, 1991). Clearly, by utilizing virtual product placements a researcher could make intra-brand comparisons on a placement characteristic that could be added or manipulated by the researcher. Such a strategy would permit visual manipulations of the target and control executions to be examined in the same movie scene. Furthermore, it would also allow the researcher to test hypotheses about placement characteristics (e.g., extremely short or long exposure-times) that may not have occurred in the natural environment.

REFERENCES

Babin, Laurie A., and Carder, Sheri T. (1996a). Viewers' recognition of brands placed within a film. *International Journal of Advertising, 15*(2), 140-151.

Babin, Laurie A., and Carder, Sheri T. (1996b). Advertising via the box office: Is product placement effective? *Journal of Promotion Management, 3*(1/2), 31-51.

Baker, William E. (1999) When can affective conditioning and mere exposure directly influence brand choice? *Journal of Advertising, 28*, 31-46.

Baker, William E.; Hutchison, J. Wesley; Moore, Danny; and Nedungadi, Prakash (1986). Brand familiarity and advertising: Effects on the evoked set and brand preferences. *Advances in Consumer Research, 13*. Richard J. Lutz, editor, Provo, UT: Association for Consumer Research, 146-147.

Brennan, Ian; Dubas, Khalid, M.; and Babin, Laurie A. (1999). The effects of placement type and exposure time on product placement recognition. *International Journal of Advertising, 18*, 323-338.

d'Astous, Alain, and Chartier, Francis (2000, Fall). A study of factors affecting consumer evaluations and memories of product placements in movies. *Journal of Current Issues and Research in Advertising, 22*, 31-41.

DeLorme, Denise E., and Reid, Leonard (1999, Summer). Moviegoers' experiences and interpretations of brands placed in films revisited. *Journal of Advertising, 28*, 71-95.

Fournier, Susan, and Dolan, Robert J. (1997). Launching the BMW Z3 roadster. Boston, MA: Harvard Business School of Publishing.

Gupta, Paulo B., and Lord, Kenneth R. (1998, Spring). Product placement in movies: The effect of prominence and mode on audience recall. *Journal of Current Issues and Research in Advertising, 20*, 47-59.

Hasher, Lynn, and Zacks, Rose T. (1984, December). Automatic processing of fundamental information: The case of frequency of occurrence. *American Psychologist, 39*, 1372-1388.

Hoyer, Wayne D., and Brown, Steven P. (1990, September). Effects of brand awareness on choice for a common, repeat purchase product. *Journal of Consumer Research, 17*, 141-148.

Johar, Gita V., and Pham, M. Tuan (1999, August). Relatedness, prominence, and constructive sponsor identification. *Journal of Marketing Research, 36*, 299-312.

Johnson, Keith F. (1981, December). Cinema advertising. *Journal of Advertising, 10*, 11-19.

Karrh, James A. (1994). Effects of brand placement in motion pictures. In Karen W. King, editor, *Proceedings of the 1994 American Academy of Advertising Conference*. Athens, GA: American Academy of Advertising, 90-96.

Karrh, James A. (1998, Fall). Brand placement: A review. *Journal of Current Issues and Research in Advertising, 20*, 31-49.

Kirmani, Anna, and Wright, Peter (1989, December). Money talks: Perceived advertising expense and expected product quality. *Journal of Consumer Research, 16*, 344-53.

Law, Sharmistha, and Braun, Kathryn A. (2000, December). I'll have what she's having: Gauging the impact of product placement on viewers. *Psychology and Marketing, 17*, 1059-1075.

Lee, A. Y., and Sternthal, B. (1999). The effects of positive mood on memory. *Journal of Consumer Research, 26*, 115-127.

McNatt, Robert and Oleck, Joan (2000, November 6). The plot thickens, like Heinz Ketchup. *Business Week*, 14.

Motion Picture Almanac (1980). New York: Quigley Publishing Company.

Murdock, G. (1992, July). Branded images. *Sight and Sound, 2*(3), 18-19.

Nebenzahl, I. D., and Secunda, E. (1993). Consumers' attitudes toward product placement in movies. *International Journal of Advertising, 12*(2), 1-11.

Negunadi, P. (1990). Recall and consumer consideration sets: Influencing choice without altering brand evaluations. *Journal of Consumer Research, 17*, 263-276.

Ong, Beng Soo, and Meri, David (1994). Should product placement in movies be banned? *Journal of Promotion Management, 2*(3/4), 159-175.

Pavio, Alan (1986). *Mental Representations: A Duel Coding Approach*, New York: Oxford University Press.

Reed, Christopher (2001). Flakes on the box. *Bulletin with Newsweek, 119*, (6280) 52.

Reed, John D. (1989, 2 January). Plugging away in Hollywood. *Time*, 103.

Rosen, Daniel M. (1990, December). Big-time plugs on small-company budgets. *Sales and Marketing Management*, 142, 48-55.

Russell, Cristel Antonia (2002, December). Investigating the effectiveness of product placements in television shows: The role of modality and plot connection congruence on brand memory and attitude. *Journal of Consumer Research*, 29, 306-318.

Sabherwal, Shonall; Pokrywczynski, Jim; and Griffin, Robert (1994). Brand recall for product placements in motion pictures: A memory-based perspective. Paper presented at the Association for Education in Journalism and Mass Communication Conference, Atlanta, GA.

Sapolsky, Barry S., and Kinney, Lance (1994). You oughta be in pictures: Product placements in the top grossing films of 1991. In Karen W. King, editor, *Proceedings of the 1994 American Academy of Advertising Conference*. Athens, GA: American Academy of Advertising, 89.

Steortz, E. M. (1987). The cost efficiency and communication effects associated with brand name exposures within motion pictures. Unpublished master's thesis, West Virginia University.

Center tries to pull the plug on commercialism (1991, December 16). *The Toronto Star*, C1.

Troupe, M. L. (1991). The captive audience: A content of product placements in motion pictures. Unpublished master's thesis, Florida State University.

Tse, Alan C. B., and Lee, Ruby P. W. (2001, May/June). Zapping behavior during commercial breaks. *Journal of Advertising Research*, 41, 25-29.

Turcotte, Samuel (1995). Gimme a bud! The feature film product placement industry. Unpublished master's thesis, University of Texas at Austin.

Unnava, H. Rao, and Burnkrant, Robert E. (1991, May). An imagery-processing view of the role of pictures in print advertisements. *Journal of Marketing Research*, 28, 226-231.

Vollmers, Stacey, and Mizerski, Richard (1994). A review and investigation into the effectiveness of product placements in films. In Karen W. King, editor, *Proceedings of the 1994 American Academy of Advertising Conference*. Athens, GA: American Academy of Advertising, 97-102.

Watkins, M. J.; LeCompte, D. C.; and Kim, K. (2000). Role of study strategy in recall of mixed lists of common and rare words. *Journal of Experimental Psychology: Learning, Memory and Cognition*, 26, 239-245.

The Bulgari Connection:
A Novel Form of Product Placement

Richard Alan Nelson

SUMMARY. Product placement is the business process that seamlessly inserts an advertiser's commercial message into various entertainment and informational media vehicles (movies, videos, television programs, radio shows, newsletters, books, etc.) as an indigenous part of the story line. This paper presents an analysis of the controversy surrounding British novelist Fay Weldon's decision to accept financing from the famed Italian jewelry company Bulgari to prominently mention the firm and its products in her 2001 book, a fast-paced social comedy. The contract specified at least 12 mentions. However, in an interesting twist, Weldon decided to feature Bulgari prominently in the plot and incorporate the company name in the title. *The Bulgari Connection* (U.S. distributor, Grove/Atlantic) is believed by many to be "the first major novel containing paid product placement," although other books with commercial tie-ins predate it. *[Article copies available for a fee from The Haworth Document Delivery Service: 1-800-HAWORTH. E-mail address: <docdelivery@haworthpress. com> Website: <http://www.HaworthPress.com> © 2004 by The Haworth Press, Inc. All rights reserved.]*

Richard Alan Nelson (PhD, Florida State University; APR, Public Relations Society of America) is Professor and Public Relations Area Head in the Manship School of Mass Communication, Louisiana State University and A&M College, Baton Rouge, LA 70803-7202 USA (E-mail: Rnelson@LSU.edu).

[Haworth co-indexing entry note]: "*The Bulgari Connection*: A Novel Form of Product Placement." Nelson, Richard Alan. Co-published simultaneously in *Journal of Promotion Management* (Best Business Books, an imprint of The Haworth Press, Inc.) Vol. 10, No. 1/2, 2004, pp. 203-212; and: *Handbook of Product Placement in the Mass Media: New Strategies in Marketing Theory, Practice, Trends, and Ethics* (ed: Mary-Lou Galician) Best Business Books, an imprint of The Haworth Press, Inc., 2004, pp. 203-212. Single or multiple copies of this article are available for a fee from The Haworth Document Delivery Service [1-800-HAWORTH, 9:00 a.m. - 5:00 p.m. (EST). E-mail address: docdelivery@haworthpress.com].

KEYWORDS. Advertising, book industry, branding, credibility, product placement, promotions

INTRODUCTION

Weldon's 2001 novel *The Bulgari Connection* became the subject of debate after it was revealed that she was paid to write it. High-end Italian jewelers Bulgari contracted with the popular author to give Weldon an undisclosed sum for incorporating the company name 12 times in her novel. Weldon, however, irritated a number of literary purists when she featured the moniker even more than agreed to, and even included highlighted Bulgari in the title (Gleeson, 2001). For example, *New York Times* columnist Martin Arnold reports finding 34 mentions of Bulgari and about 15 other "rhapsodies of jewelry" (Arnold, 2001). As another leading journalist reported:

> The arrangement is believed to be a first for the book industry with a best-selling author, traditionally one of the few corners of the media free of sponsors' pitches and plugs. *The Bulgari Connection* is certainly the most highly visible episode yet in an ongoing courtship pairing authors and publishers desperate for marketing support with companies eager to capitalize on the power of a reader's immersion in a book, from organizing children's books around the names of well-known candy or cereals to holding literary readings in fancy boutiques. (Kirkpatrick, 2001)

Actually product placements in novels go back at least as far as Charles Dickens' *Pavilionstone* (1902). David Ogilvy's famed *Confessions of an Advertising Man* (1963) is a brilliant piece of prose, arguably the longest advertisement ever published. In addition, sponsored corporate histories and so-called "ghost writers" have been doing the actual writing of celebrity and political books for many years.

More recently, Maserati paid to be mentioned in *Power City* by Beth Ann Herman (1988). Maureen F. McHugh has stated that when the German rights for her science fiction novel *China Mountain Zhang* (1992) "were sold, her agent wondered whether all the characters would sit down to a nourishing bowl of Brand Something soup. When McHugh asked what he was talking about, he explained that in Germany, they sell product placements in books, so the characters might all stop their conversation to sit down to a bowl of their equivalent of Campbell's Soup, and then resume their discussion" (Leeper and Leeper, 1993). This apparently was also the experience with negotiations over the German edition of Kim Stanley Robinson's *Pacific Edge* (1990).

Another interesting example of an adult-oriented novel pre-dating *The Bulgari Connection* occurred in 2000. Writer Bill FitzHugh got Seagram's to pay him in whisky for mentions of their products within his "comic thriller" *Cross Dressing*. However, his purpose was to create interest in the book not publicize alcohol (see FitzHugh, To sell out, 2000). The strategy worked well, as FitzHugh got a mass market paperback contract with HarperTorch in 2002. Even the industry's leading journal, *Publisher's Weekly*, now is willing to market its cover to a paying advertiser.

A major growth industry has been in branded tie-ins with children's pre-school activity and math products typified by *The Cheerios Counting Book: 1, 2, 3* (Will McGrath et al., 2000) and *The Hershey's Milk Chocolate Multiplication Book* (Pallotta and Bolster, 2002). More than 40 such works have been published in recent years (see the *Amazon.com* guide "So you'd like to . . . Brand your children" by clevernickname2, nd). Unfortunately, the full history of these and other such incidences has not yet been written.

WHY A CONTROVERSY?

What made Weldon's venture so controversial is that she is such a "marquee" author, well-known in serious literary circles. According to Giles Gordon, Weldon's publishing agent, she "was approached by a 'very clever' product placement expert who had already secured exposure for Bulgari's products in several films" (BBC News, 2001). Gordon thought the idea so brilliant he indicated plans to work with other clients also interested in pursuing product placements "The current crop of 'chick lit' novels and memoirs about the lives of young women offers potential for touting vodka, cigarettes, clothing and other brands, he said. 'The sky is the limit' " (Kirkpatrick, 2001).

So does this development blending literature and marketing return us to the golden days of Renaissance patronage or symbolize a more modern crass grab for the gold? A valuable source of income for authors or blatant sell out? Novel form of financing art or new form of cultural debasement?

Put another way, is the work a harmless little experiment by a talented novelist; or harbinger of "the creep of product placement into the publishing industry that poses a threat to the cognitive commons and our ability to read and think without being bombarded by commercial messages"? (*Commercial Alert*, 2001).

FROM "FICTOMERCIAL" TO "LITERATISEMENT"

Britain may be more famous for Shakespeare, Jane Austen, *and* James Bond. But certainly the linkup of Weldon's word processor and Bulgari's finances has already resulted in some rather intriguing words and phrases to describe what is happening–as well as a new interpretation to the concept of "commercial fiction." The president of the Author's Guild, Letty Cottin Pogrebin, has labeled it the *"billboarding of the novel"* (Kirkpatrick, 2001). It has also been called a *fictomercial*, i.e., "a work of fiction in which a company pays the writer to incorporate the company's products into the story" (McFedries, 2002). Another critic dubbed the book part of an entirely new genre *"literatisement,"* or *"litad"* for short–*"bought books*, i.e., novels designed from the outline up to be vehicles for a company's marketing message" (Goodman, 2001; McFedries, 2002). Yet another emerging term is *publitizing* which can include utilizing "press releases to blatantly push products, rather than buying ad space" but here has the added meaning of product placement in books as in "He drove his Infiniti up to the Applebee's with aplomb, leaving his Starbuck's Frapuccino in the cup holder. Grabbing his Banana Republic jacket, he set the LoJack system and headed for the bar to order a Guinness" (Atkinson, 2002). Weldon herself prefers to see it as a *sponsored novel* (Associated Press, 2001).

Weldon has had a booming career with over 20 novels to her credit, including the earlier best-seller *The Life and Loves of a She-Devil*. She's also built credibility as a successful screenwriter, journalist, and advertising copywriter for Olgilvy & Mather. This career genealogy has influenced her approach to fiction. The author explains the origin of *The Bulgari Connection* this way:

> The intention was that once written, the novel would be limited to 750 beautifully bound copies commissioned and published by Bulgari. The idea was it was to give it away free, as part of a place setting, at a gala dinner to celebrate the opening of Bulgari's Sloane Street store. I'm commissioned to write many things but this was unusual, and I could see the charm of it so I said yes without much ado. *The Bulgari Connection* is not technically a product place-

ment novel, any more than Truman Capote's *Breakfast at Tiffany's*. I see it as a sponsored novel rather than a completed novel into which product names have been blithely dropped in return for a fee. (Gleeson, 2001)

Of course, Weldon and those she collaborated with on *The Bulgari Connection* failed to anticipate the firestorm of criticism (and a bit of praise) that soon emerged after the book's publication, especially since she already was an established international literary figure. So if the argument is true that any publicity is good (no matter how negative), then Weldon and Bulgari got more than they bargained for. A key concern–certainly a central issue for some–is that many readers may be unaware that Weldon was paid by the jewelry firm for the prominent placement Bulgari received. As noted above, numerous other writers, consumer groups, journalists, and publishing companies also interpreted her actions as having long-lasting impact, damaging to the credibility of all books and the integrity of all authors. Further examples of the reactions include:

Pro

"I think this is fantastic," said Jane Friedman, chief executive of HarperCollins Publishers, part of the News Corporation and the book's British publisher. "It gives me a lot of ideas–what better way to spread the word than to have a commissioned book? And if you are going to talk about jewelry you might as well talk about Bulgari." (cited in Kirkpatrick, 2001)

Such books are "part of the next wave of product placement," according to Michael Nyman, who works in product placement with the marketing firm Bragman Nyman Cafarelli, part of the Interpublic Group of Companies. Because consumers' involvement with books is greater than that for movies or television programs, he said, "It is a more personal relationship with a book; you can curl up on a chair with it, you read it before you go to sleep, it is very near and dear to people." (cited in Kirkpatrick, 2001)

Con

Jason Epstein, author of *Book Business–Publishing: Past, Present and Future* and former editorial director of Random House said,

"For a novelist to celebrate a corporation for a fee is a revolting idea." (cited in Rose, 2001)

Letty Cottin Pogrebin, the president of the Authors Guild mentioned earlier said, "I feel as if it erodes reader confidence in the authenticity of the narrative. It adds to the cynicism. Does this character really drive a Ford or did Ford pay for this?" (cited in Kirkpatrick, 2001)

A group of 20 authors sent letters to 85 book review editors asking them to "Treat Fay Weldon's New Work as an Ad, Not a Book." They argued that even though the story involves a chic jewelry business, that fact alone does not somehow transform the book into literary art. "Is it a novel to be reviewed, or is it an advertisement to be commented upon in the business pages?" they ask, arguing that when a company pays a writer to generate copy that features the corporation's product this is properly referred to as advertising. (Commercial Alert, 2001)

For the world's third largest jeweler firm, however, the book's publication has been an "altogether pleasant affair." Bulgari's CEO Francesco Trapani brainstormed the idea because: "When you take out an ad in a magazine, you only have a certain amount of space in which to speak . . . That is why product placement–whether you're talking about books, movies or Hollywood stars–is so important to us" (Fenton, 2001). According to a very informative business analysis in *The Times* (London):

The Bulgari Connection represents a step-change in the company's advertising campaign and has clearly stolen a march on the group's rivals. The number of newspaper column inches devoted to critiques of the book and its launch have surpassed the undisclosed–though presumably enormous–sum forwarded to Weldon. . . . For Trapani, simply placing the family jewels in Hollywood movies was becoming old hat in marketing terms. Clearly he needed something else. "It was my idea. If you want to shorten the distance between yourselves and the largest company you have to be more creative. You have to find a different way of communication," he said.

So Trapani embarked on a hunt for a writer who was famous and preferably English-ideally, the novel's launch was to coincide with the opening of a store. . . . "We started talking to Fay and she was intrigued with the idea," says Trapani. That Weldon, who justified her acceptance of the offer and the cash pile on the ground that she is never going to land a Booker Prize anyway, decided to use the Bulgari name in the title was a bonus. If the novel is made into a movie, that will be a bonus to end all bonuses, although that is out of Bulgari's control. But has Trapani read it? Well, no. But he does know the plot. (Patten, 2001)

THE NOVEL'S PLOT

Well what is the book about? Fay Weldon, who knows how to plot out stories of female revenge against those who wrong them, goes into action with what proves to be a pretty good, wryly comical, and quick-read novel. With the setting in today's stylish upscale London, we are introduced to the glitzy world of high art, charity auctions, corporate power and plenty of money to go round. As Kirkpatrick (2001) reports, one of the first scenes in the novel "takes place amid 'the peaches and cream décor' of the Bulgari jewelry store on Sloane Street. . . . There, attended to by 'charming girls, and men too,' the real estate mogul Barley Salt pays £18,000 to buy his scheming second wife 'a sleek modern piece, a necklace, stripes of white and yellow gold, but encasing three ancient coins, the mount following the irregular contours of the thin worn bronze'" (see also Elias et al., 2002, p. 3).

The storyline sounds rather common to other novels of sexual politics–a former wife pursues a comeuppance against her self-serving ex who has taken up with the trophy model (Doris Dubois, a pretty, but rather nasty, television personality who is the one lusting after a Bulgari necklace). But Weldon incorporates lots of envy and a wee bit of the supernatural along with some clever dialogue, and the reader is off on the adventure.

CONCLUSION

Frankly, trying to put a finger in the dike of product placement is not likely to work. Leaving aside US First Amendment free speech issues, a moral case can be made for possible regulation when children are involved. But for adults, the essence of freedom is choice. So what if Bulgari seems to be the only jeweler in town? No one is forced to read, let alone buy, the book. Weldon and her publishers were very open and above-board about Bulgari's sponsorship. Bulgari executives engaged in no censorship, approving the manuscript without change. In fact, if Weldon had abandoned storytelling simply to knock out a piece of schlock, sales would have dropped. In the end, give individuals some credit. *The Bulgari Connection* and future such sponsored "fictomercial literatisement" books will ultimately be judged by the marketplace in terms of their value to readers.

REFERENCES

Arnold, Martin (2001, September 13). Placed products, and their cost. *New York Times*, E3.

Associated Press (2001, September 3). Author writes commissioned book. Syndicated news story.

Atkinson, Roy (2002, January 7). Subject: Time again for Roy's wacky words. Available online at *http://packy.dardan.com/humor/archive/2002/20020107-0000.shtml.*

BBC News (2001, 4 September). Weldon's sparkling book deal. Available online at *http://news.bbc.co.uk/1/hi/entertainment/arts/1524437.stm.*

Books overview (2002). *Commercial Alert.* Available online at *http://www.commercialalert.org/books/index.html.*

clevernickname2 (nd, 2003). So you'd like to . . . Brand your children. Amazon.com reading guide for pre-school and youth books with corporate product placement tie-ins. Available online at *http://www.amazon.com/exec/obidos/tg/guides/guide-display/-/112DGJ3SRKX4W/ref=cm_bg_em_vg_htm_btm/.*

Commercial Alert (2001, October 1). Authors ask editors to treat Fay Weldon's new work as an ad, not a book. Press release. Portland, OR: Author. Available online at *http://www.commercialalert.org/index.php?category_id=1&subcategory_id= 17&article_id=29.*

Dickins, Charles (nd, 1902). *Pavilionstone.* With an introduction by Percy Fitzgerald, M.A., F.S.A. London: The Frederick Hotels Limited, 8 Bloomsbury Square. NOTE: Dickens visited Folkestone near Dover many times, utilizing the cross channel packet boat service to Boulogne. In 1853, he holidayed at the Pavilion Hotel with Folkestone described as Pavilionstone in this short work. However, this is the first appearance in book form of the sketch, originally published in the issue of *Household Words* for September 29, 1855, under the title "Out of Town." This version, produced as an advertisement for the Pavilion Hotel, is profusely illustrated with numerous half-tones, photographs and engravings.

Elias, Josh; Malani, Sajeel; Mikolinski, Michelle; and Santos, James (2002, June 5). Product placement in mass media vehicles. Student project, University of California-Davis, available online at *http://students.gsm.ucdavis.edu/sgmalani/projects/downloads/sajeel_malani_product_placement.pdf.*

Epstein, Jason (2001). *Book Business–Publishing: Past, Present and Future.* New York: W.W. Norton & Company.

Fenton, Ben (2001, September 4). Jeweller pays for Weldon's sparkling prose. *The Telegraph* (London). Available online at *http://www.telegraph.co.uk/news/ main.jhtml?xml=/news/2001/09/04/wfeld04.xml.*

FitzHugh, Bill (2000). *Cross Dressing.* New York: Avon. Republished (2002). New York: HarperTorch.

FitzHugh, Bill (2000, November 6). To sell out takes a lot of bottle. *The Guardian* (London). Available online at *http://www.absolutewrite.com/novels/product_placement. htm* and *http://books.guardian.co.uk/departments/generalfiction/story/0,6000,393973,00. html.* See also FitzHugh's website at *http://billfitzhugh.com.*

Gleeson, Sineád (2001, October 11). Fay accompli. *RTÉ Interactive Entertainment.* Available online at *http://wwa.rte.ie/arts/2001/1011/weldonf.html.*

Goodman, Ellen (2001, September 9). It's all becoming one giant commercial. *Boston Globe.* Reproduced online at *http://www.commondreams.org/views01/0909-05. htm.*

Grimshaw, Heather (2002). Review: *The Bulgari Connection. Bookreporter.com.* Available online at *http://www.bookreporter.com/reviews/0871137968.asp.*

Herman, Beth Ann (1988). *Power City.* New York: Bantam Books.

Hirsch, Arthur (2001, October 2). Writers call Weldon's new book an ad. *Baltimore Sun.*

Kennedy, Maev (2001, September 4). Jewellers sponsor Fay Weldon's latest literary gem. *The Guardian.* Available online at *http://media.guardian.co.uk/ marketingandpr/story/0,7494,546635,00.html.*

Kirkpatrick, David D. (2001, September 3). Now, many words from our sponsor; Fay Weldon produces a novel commissioned by a jeweler. *New York Times.* Available online at *http://www.nytimes.com/2001/09/03/business/media/03BOOK.html.*

Leeper, Evelyn C., and Leeper, Mark R. (1993). ConFrancisco 1993, Panel: Language: Barrier or bridge. Report online at *http://fanac.org/worldcon/ConFrancisco/w93-rpt.html.*

McFedries, Paul (2002, November 4). Fictomercial. *The Word Spy.* Available online at *http://www.wordspy.com/words/fictomercial.asp.*

McGrath, Will; Bolster, Rob (illustrator); McGrath, Barbara Barbieri; and Mazzola, Frank (illustrator) (2000). *The Cheerios Counting Book: 1, 2, 3.* New York: Cartwheel Books (Scholastic).

McHugh, Maureen F. (1992). *China Mountain Zhang.* New York: Tor Books.

Ogilvy, David (1963). *Confessions of an Advertising Man.* New York: Atheneum. NOTE: The book has subsequently been reprinted in several editions.

Pallotta, Jerry, and Bolster, Rob (illustrator) (2002). *The Hershey's Milk Chocolate Multiplication Book.* New York: Cartwheel Books (Scholastic).

Patten, Sally (2001, October 13). Bulgari steals a march with novel ploy; the Saturday business profile; Francesco Trapani. *The Times* (London), 51.

Product placement in books (2001, September 3). *Commercial Alert.* Available online at *http://lists.essential.org/pipermail/commercial-alert/2001/000092.html.*

Rall, Ted (2001, September 7). Selling out is easy to do. Bravely funding the new world. Available online at *http://www.commondreams.org/views01/0908-05.htm.*

Robinson, Kim Stanley (1990). *Pacific Edge*. New York: Tor Books.
Rose, M. J. (2001, September 5). Dismayed authors respond to the news that a fancy jeweler paid a noted novelist to put its products front and center in her new book. Salon.com. Available online at *http://archive.salon.com/books/feature/2001/09/05/bulgari/*.
Weldon, Fay (2001). *The Bulgari Connection*. London: Flamingo (HarperCollins). Published in the USA (2001). New York: Atlantic Monthly Press.

COMMENTARY

When Product Placement Is NOT Product Placement: Reflections of a Movie Junkie

David Natharius

SUMMARY. The development of product placement in films and television shows can be readily observed by anyone who has devoted a significant part of their lives going to the movies. The first product placements were generic and fictitious and were hardly noticed by the movie-going public. But, as the placement of real products became more prevalent, it became apparent to the serious film buff that the presence of a fictitious or clearly disguised product became more of a distraction

David Natharius (PhD, University of Southern California) is Professor Emeritus of Communication and Humanities, California State University, Fresno, and currently is Adjunct Professor, Walter Cronkite School of Journalism & Mass Communication, Arizona State University, Tempe, AZ 85287-1305 (E-mail: david.natharius@asu. edu).

[Haworth co-indexing entry note]: "When Product Placement Is NOT Product Placement: Reflections of a Movie Junkie." Natharius, David. Co-published simultaneously in *Journal of Promotion Management* (Best Business Books, an imprint of The Haworth Press, Inc.) Vol. 10, No. 1/2, 2004, pp. 213-218; and: *Handbook of Product Placement in the Mass Media: New Strategies in Marketing Theory, Practice, Trends, and Ethics* (ed: Mary-Lou Galician) Best Business Books, an imprint of The Haworth Press, Inc., 2004, pp. 213-218. Single or multiple copies of this article are available for a fee from The Haworth Document Delivery Service [1-800-HAWORTH, 9:00 a.m. - 5:00 p.m. (EST). E-mail address: docdelivery@haworthpress.com].

than the use of actual products. The attempt to make serious realistic films is sometimes sidetracked by a clearly fake product that strikes at the suspension of disbelief of movie goers, particularly when they have some familiarity with the product NOT being placed. *[Article copies available for a fee from The Haworth Document Delivery Service: 1-800-HAWORTH. E-mail address: <docdelivery@haworthpress.com> Website: <http://www.HaworthPress.com>* © 2004 by The Haworth Press, Inc. All rights reserved.]*

KEYWORDS. Cinema, films, logo, motion pictures, movies, product placement

REFLECTIONS ON EARLIER MOVIE EXPERIENCES

My first movie was either *Snow White and the Seven Dwarfs* (shouldn't that be "Dwarves?") or *Bambi*, depending on what my mother told me at various times while I was growing up. I really do not remember my first movie experience personally since I was only 3 or 4 at the time. I do remember that while I was still very young, my mother regularly took me to the movies and the movies were always Walt Disney feature-length animated cartoons. So, I can recall images of the singing dwarfs (dwarves?) as they go off to work, Bambi losing his mother, Dumbo's ears growing bigger, Mickey as the Sorcerer's Apprentice losing control of his broom (or is it a mop?). I can also recall some of the images of the early live-action films my mother exposed me to as I grew older: *Lassie Come Home, National Velvet* and *How Green Was My Valley*. I do not recall her taking me to see *Gone with the Wind* its first time around. It seems clear that my mother wanted me to experience a spectrum of movie magic but always on what would now be called G-rated films. As I grew older and I was allowed to venture to the movie palaces on my own, my image recall is filled with the Saturday morning serials and the seemingly endless films of Roy Rogers and Gene Autry.

I think I would have become a movie buff anyway, but my mother's willingness to support my regular venture into the world of cinema certainly created the desire that I have, to this day, to see most of the movies made. Regardless of how bad it might be, I hardly ever walk out of a film, or stop a rental DVD at home. The virtually endless supply of movies, from cable to satellite to rentals to DVDs, has made my mature and mostly retiring years a very full and enriching time.

They're Using Generics!

My reflections about product placement in films and television actually start in the late sixties when, as a doctoral student at the University of Southern California, I spent many end-of-paper-assignment celebrations by going to the all-night movie theatres in downtown Los Angeles. I saw literally hundreds of B, C, and D level films, sitting through all of them regardless of how poorly written, inadequately directed and acted, or awkwardly filmed. In these films I experienced the avalanche of generic milk cartons (MILK), beer bottles and cans (BEER), liquor bottles (WHISKEY, GIN, VODKA), soft drinks (SODA), and cigarettes (CIGARETTES). I also noticed the way in which even automobile logos and names were carefully obscured in the filming. I was smart enough to know that these generic labels existed because legal stuff like royalties and acknowledgements limited the use of actual name brands.

Reality Is More Real

So, when a product name occurred that I actually knew to be authentic, I was impressed with the "realism" of the scene. I would actually look for products in the movies that I could recognize as being real items like breakfast cereal and newspapers.

Of course, as other authors in this volume have indicated, product placement is now so prevalent in films and television that when we see a product that is obviously not a real name brand, we notice it. For me, there has been a complete reversal of my appreciation of films, particularly those that purport to be attempting to create a realistic visual experience. In films in which there have been product placements, I can readily identify them. Conversely, when I see an overt attempt to hide, or obscure, or disguise a recognizable product, I am disappointed in the filmmakers' failure to keep the authenticity consistent.

Most films today do not attempt to hide the make of automobile; that isn't necessarily a paid product placement unless the automobile plays an important part in the film, like an automobile chase, or escape, or race. The use of Ford Explorer in *Jurassic Park I* or Mercedes Benz in *Jurassic Park II* were clearly placements. The Aston Martins and BMWs used by James Bond were obviously placed by the producers of the 007 films. The attentive movie watcher recognizes in *The Truman Show* that product placement is spoofed by the insertion of fake commercials during the regular action of the film. The really sharp-eyed viewer also recognizes the placement of two real products–a Ford Taurus sedan and a Ford Ranger pickup truck.

I enjoy seeing an actual product being used or misused because it reinforces my suspension of disbelief, which becomes a bit harder to maintain when I see an obvious fictitious product in an otherwise realistic film.

I know that not everybody is bothered by these credible omissions. However, I am sure that many other film buffs like me become a bit disconcerted when a character in a movie or television show asks for a "beer" and is not asked "what kind" (Tom Cruise in *Eyes Wide Shut*), or hustles a stolen DVD player still in the box that looks like a Sony box but is labeled "SUNY" (Denzel Washington in *Training Day*), or uses a camera that is clearly a Canon but the name label is blacked out (Gil Bellows in a television episode of *The Agency*–curiously enough, in a later episode the camera logo is clearly identifiable. What's up with that?). Then there is the product that looks exactly like the real thing but, upon close scrutiny, is not (the bottle that looks like a J&B scotch bottle but the label name is something &D in *Memento*).

A recent film that, for me, had a glaring NON product placement was *Fifteen Minutes*, the thriller starring Robert DeNiro as a police detective who is also a media celebrity. In the film, DeNiro's character (Eddie Flemming) is kidnapped by two villainous murderers who videotape their murder of Eddie and then plan to sell the videotape to a local tabloid television news show. One of the villains has aspirations of becoming a movie director so, for almost all of his time in the film, he is using a camcorder to record the events that are occurring. The camcorder is so prominent in these scenes that it really is like an additional character. The camcorder being used in the film is a Sony DCRTV 900, a very distinctive model in the Sony lineup of digital camcorders. In the filmed scenes, the camcorder is very visible in close-up shots and its features are unmistakable. However, in the film, the Sony name on the camcorder is missing where it normally would be very visible: on the left side of the camera body and on the hand strap.

Now, if this were an academic research paper, I would report to you the specific reasons why this obscuration occurred. I have contacted Miramax, the studio that produced the film and the DVD, and the Sony Corporation to ask if they could tell me the reasons why this very identifiable object was not allowed (if, indeed, they did deny permission to use the name label) to be properly labeled. At the time of this writing, I have been unable to receive any response from either source. I am left with the following hunches or conjectures (in an academic paper these would be formatted as the research questions or hypotheses):

1. The producers did not actually ask Sony for placement approval (see also number 4 below);
2. The actual camera used was a "gray market" product with identifying marks removed;
3. The producers asked for product approval but Sony refused, given the graphic nature of violence in the film and the negative use to which the camcorder was put in the story;
4. The producers simply used the camcorder without any attempt to get product placement approval since the use of the camcorder in the film was within the general guideline of "being used in a way that the product is normally used." It was only used as a camcorder, not as a weapon with which to bash someone's head. (This thought makes me wonder if any ice-pick manufacturers were up in arms about the use of their products in *Basic Instinct*.);
5. The producers did not think that anyone in the audience would actually recognize the camcorder if it was not labeled.

This last hunch developed after I mentioned my concern to several of my friends who had seen the movie. Their response was simply, "Gee, I didn't even notice. I can't tell one camcorder from another."

Which brings me to my final reflection. Most of us who attend movies regularly are probably very familiar with at least a few products that are represented in film and television stories. I notice cameras and electronic equipment because part of my life has been spent as a professional and amateur photographer and videographer. My wife, because of her previous career as the national advertising manager for Maybelline, can immediately spot a fake tube of lipstick or a shade of color on a character who wouldn't actually use that color in real life. I'm sure many of you who are sophisticated electronics experts can spot the real thing from the fake boxes that look more like those cardboard replicas used in furniture displays. Or the generic box masquerading as a computer monitor that has a huge Apple logo sticker pasted on its side where no Apple logo is usually found (spotted in a recent re-run of *The Larry Sanders Show*). When I saw that, I wasn't sure what the intended purpose of the sticker was (perhaps to influence us to get a supply of Apple logo stickers?).

CONCLUDING THOUGHTS

To conclude, my guess is that, as product placement continues to proliferate in our mediated storytelling images, we audience members (at
least we who consider ourselves film junkies) will become even more
aware of when we are being given images of generic fictional products,
particularly in films that strive to create realistic scenes and images.

Will that distract us from enjoying the story? Probably not. But will it
motivate us to be even more conscious of how product placement has
become a ubiquitous part of our movie-going experiences, even when
we want to escape images of reality for a while? I'd bet a few matinee
admissions on that one!

INTERVIEWS

A Leading Cultural Critic
Argues Against Product Placement:
An Interview with Mark Crispin Miller

Mary-Lou Galician

Mark Crispin Miller, a nationally known media critic and activist for democratic media reform, is Professor of Media Ecology in New York University's Department of Culture and Communication, where he also directs the Project on Media Ownership (PROMO). Through the PROMO, Dr. Miller has worked to focus public attention on the growing problem of excessive concentration in the U.S. culture industries and on what he considers to be the "oligopolistic sway of the few media giants over television news, book publishing, popular music, and cable TV." His commentaries on film, television, advertising and rock music have appeared in numerous journals and newspapers, including *The Na-*

[Haworth co-indexing entry note]: "A Leading Cultural Critic Argues Against Product Placement: An Interview with Mark Crispin Miller." Galician, Mary-Lou. Co-published simultaneously in *Journal of Promotion Management* (Best Business Books, an imprint of The Haworth Press, Inc.) Vol. 10, No. 1/2, 2004, pp. 219-222; and: *Handbook of Product Placement in the Mass Media: New Strategies in Marketing Theory, Practice, Trends, and Ethics* (ed: Mary-Lou Galician) Best Business Books, an imprint of The Haworth Press, Inc., 2004, pp. 219-222. Single or multiple copies of this article are available for a fee from The Haworth Document Delivery Service [1-800-HAWORTH, 9:00 a.m. - 5:00 p.m. (EST). E-mail address: docdelivery@haworthpress.com].

http://www.haworthpress.com/web/JPM
Digital Object Identifier: 10.1300/J057v10n01_16

tion and *The New York Times.* He has written three books: *Boxed In: The Culture of TV, Seeing Through Movies,* and *The Bush Dyslexicon: Notes on a National Disorder.*

GALICIAN: You were one of the first critics to call attention to the growing trend of product placements in the increasingly conglomeratized media. In your April 1990 *Atlantic Monthly* article *Hollywood the Ad,* you argued that these plugs for products worked as "subliminal inducements because their context is ostensibly a movie, not an ad" and that their subliminal impact arises "not only from their cinematic camouflage but also from the pleasant welter of associations" that glamorize the placed products and stigmatize the competition. What's your current take on the practice?

MILLER: The practice is constant, and it has changed the movies. Cinema is worthwhile aesthetically because of its capacity to expose us to a kind of emotional experience we'd not otherwise have. Product placement is one way in which the forces of commercialization "domesticate" cinema, making it mundane, giving it a certain comfort. A touristic analogy works here: Going a long way to the same old thing equates to a deprivation. Likewise, going to the movies for commercial tableaux is a waste. For example, in *Cast Away* FedEx is a source of comfort, a savior, a way to protect us from the fearfulness of the void, a link of hope to the world of ads we know.

GALICIAN: Some media marketers argue that the current business model necessitates product placement. What about that?

MILLER: In the long run, the practice will only work against the interests of marketers as it worsens cinema. Everywhere we look we see promotions and stimuli to spend money. The more pervasive these are, the less effective they are. Marketing types are intrigued because the commercial is appearing outside the usual realm of obvious ads, where a blasé response usually follows network television spots and glossy magazine ads. But marketers are always looking for new venues and greener fields, so actually the increasingly pervasive practice is bad for business.

If movies were completely hospitable to placements, they'd be over as a viable art form.

GALICIAN: We see Harry Potter on the cover of *Time* magazine. What's the problem with cross-promotion of products owned by the same giant media conglomerate?

MILLER: Everyone covered the Harry Potter phenomenon, so maybe that's not so bad. The real question is: *Should major news magazines feature movies on the cover?* They never used to do that. Today we live in a celebrity culture. What's also new now are the huge promotions that make media culture one continuous ad.

GALICIAN: How did this happen? Aren't we as media consumers responsible, too?

MILLER: In the shadow of the culture cartel, all media have converged, so the news is completely continuous with entertainment. There's a smaller audience for real news, but real news is crucial to democracy. One problem is that media managers envision the audience as a huge mass, but we're not. There are many audiences out there, and many segments are deprived of what they'd enjoy. People who say, "We're giving the public what it wants," forget that people change frequently. Australian movies like *Shine* and *Babe* wouldn't be made in Hollywood.

GALICIAN: What's the larger danger? What should media consumers do?

MILLER: It's complicated–partly civic, partly existential. We lose touch with reality. These commercial forces would put people to sleep, in a trance. People have to protect themselves. If you're immersed in product placements and celebrity news, you won't know what's going on. That works against the best interests of democracy itself.

The larger consideration is that in the commercial culture it's important to be "happy." If you spend your whole life distracted and reassured that all's swell and the best thing to hope for is an endless shopping mall, you're living in a fantasy based on an unsupportable order of things. The subtext to the media spectacle is that it's not reassuring, because advertising makes you feel less than good. The subtext of advertising is, "You're a schmuck. You're powerless unless you have this product," which makes you an addict.

GALICIAN: Should product placement in media geared to children be more heavily restricted?

MILLER: It should be *illegal*–as should *any* advertising targeted to kids! Children don't have enough sophistication to sort through and deal with such messages.

GALICIAN: What do you say to those proponents who claim that placed products merely enhance realism?

MILLER: It does and it doesn't. Visually, placed products are never realistic. The director has to please the people who are paying for the brand to be displayed. In the real world, logos and labels don't jump out at us in vivid and attractive ways as they do in a movie or television scene. In real life, they fade into the background. We're not struck by the Rice Krispies in someone's kitchen or the Tylenol in someone's medicine cabinet. But product placement wraps the product in glamour and foregrounds it. It calls attention to itself.

It's true that generic products aren't realistic, but art isn't reality.

GALICIAN: But some product placement proponents argue that it reinforces character development. How do you respond to that argument?

MILLER: I think that demonstrates a pretty crude sense of what a person is. It's stereotyping at its worst to suggest, for example, that Dunkin' Donuts represents the working class (as in *Good Will Hunting*). I'm not a purist. I can tolerate some placements–for example on the *Sopranos*. But most are merely intrusive. The collusion of movies with mere advertising fantasy robs us of a great range of experience, which is what makes movies worthwhile.

A Rising Independent Filmmaker
Argues for Product Placement:
An Interview with Samuel A. Turcotte

Mary-Lou Galician

Samuel A. Turcotte is Senior Partner Manager of Internet Media at Sun Microsystems in the Silicon Valley. He has taught and consulted with top executives of many Fortune 500 companies including Time Warner, McGraw-Hill, and PricewaterhouseCoopers, and he personally trained President George Bush how to use the Internet. In addition to his technology savvy, he is an award-winning filmmaker (His short film *Kata* received the Bronze Medal at the Houston International Film Festival.), and a pop record album he produced–Baila's *Shall We Dance?* (distributed by Universal Music via Joan Jett's Blackheart Records label)–was favorably profiled in *Billboard* and its first three singles have been played on more than 150 radio stations across the United States and the Caribbean. Turcotte was awarded a Meritorious Achievement Medal while serving in the U.S. Air Force for his role in developing an interactive video production studio.

He earned a B.S. in Radio-Television-Film, an M.A. in Communication/Advertising, and an M.B.A. in Marketing from The University of Texas, where he was President of the Advertising Council. For his 1995 master's thesis, *Gimme a Bud! The Feature Film Product Placement Industry*, Turcotte conducted a series of in-depth interviews with industry

[Haworth co-indexing entry note]: "A Rising Independent Filmmaker Argues for Product Placement: An Interview with Samuel A. Turcotte." Galician, Mary-Lou. Co-published simultaneously in *Journal of Promotion Management* (Best Business Books, an imprint of The Haworth Press, Inc.) Vol. 10, No. 1/2, 2004, pp. 223-226; and: *Handbook of Product Placement in the Mass Media: New Strategies in Marketing Theory, Practice, Trends, and Ethics* (ed: Mary-Lou Galician) Best Business Books, an imprint of The Haworth Press, Inc., 2004, pp. 223-226. Single or multiple copies of this article are available for a fee from The Haworth Document Delivery Service [1-800-HAWORTH, 9:00 a.m. - 5:00 p.m. (EST). E-mail address: docdelivery@haworthpress.com].

http://www.haworthpress.com/web/JPM
Digital Object Identifier: 10.1300/J057v10n01_17   *223*

professionals at major studios, independent production companies, and top product placement agencies, as well as with corporate marketers whose goods and services are actually being placed in the movies. Turcotte is a proponent of product placement. His complete thesis, which includes a review of the product placement industry and offers "a blueprint for conducting the business of product placement, whereby the interests of both the filmmakers and the corporate marketers are maximized" (Turcotte, 1995), is on the web at *http://advertising.utexas.edu/research/papers/Turcotte/*. You can also view a sample studio product placement contract there (*http://advertising.utexas.edu/research/papers/Turcotte/samplecontract.html*).

When I interviewed him, he was completing the editing of his own feature film with one dozen product placements, *No Pain, No Gain* (*www.no-pain-no-gain.com*) which he produced, directed, and co-wrote for Zukor Entertainment, an independent feature film and record company founded by industry legend Sammy Zukor and managed by Turcotte (*www.zukor.com*).

GALICIAN: Before we talk about your movie, let's talk about your master's thesis. You called it "Gimme a Bud! The Feature Film Product Placement Industry." Where did that title come from?

TURCOTTE: In real life, no one says, "Gimme a *beer!*" It's ridiculous not to use a brand in such a case in a movie. Moviemakers used to think that using brand names undermined the artistry of the cinema, but today we know that it undermines reality *not* to use them when they would be in real life. There's a difference between reality and whoring to commercialism. Product placement isn't about sales; it's about brand awareness.

GALICIAN: At the end of your study of the industry, you offer some recommendations that you wrote were "intended to maximize the interests of the studios and the corporate marketers alike and thus raise the viability of the entire product placement industry" (see *http://advertising.utexas.edu/research/papers/Turcotte/recommendations.html*). Do you think they're applicable today?

TURCOTTE: Absolutely. Nothing's changed, except that product placement is even more acceptable today. But the rules haven't changed.

GALICIAN: O.K. Now I have to ask: Are there product placements in your film?

TURCOTTE: Of course! I sought placements that fit. The movie is a far-cical drama about a very bright body-builder who wants to be respected for his mind. The character is from a small town in Ohio, where no one takes him seriously. He's got very scientific views about physiology and anatomy, and in the midst of his intellectual pursuits he's let his body go. So he goes to California to get back in shape and make it big in a super competition, proving his ideas about the ultimate training regi-men via his own body. He's kind of a nerdy fish-out-of-water, which gives the movie its zaniness.

The wrestling world is filled with brand names and logos, especially at competitions, where they're all over the place. It wouldn't be realistic to do the movie without seeing them. I believe it's the obligation of film-makers to include only placements that fit the theme and the reality and the ethics of the situation.

GALICIAN: How did you go about connecting with the placed brands?

TURCOTTE: There were many related companies to choose from–equipment, T-shirts, banners at the wrestling competitions–and I looked for the best deals with good marketing partners. I collaborated with the actors, who really use the stuff. Of course, I avoided companies with ridiculous advertising campaigns, and I got some refusals from companies that didn't have the budget or didn't see the value or didn't like the movie.

GALICIAN: So what placements are in the movie?

TURCOTTE: We wound up with 12:

- Champion Nutrition
- World Gym
- Valeo
- Hyde Park Gym
- Science Stuff
- Iron Grip
- Balazs Boxing Gear
- Crown Labs
- M.D. Labs

- Charles Atlas Company
- Jagware
- Metabolic Innovations

All of these are listed in the closing credits.

GALICIAN: What do you see as the future of product placement in movies?

TURCOTTE: If too many movies carry too many unnecessary or unsuitable placements, it'll lead to over-exposure. Then it'll self-regulate. But audiences are sophisticated enough to understand the context. Most filmgoers don't really care.

Harry Potter, Coca-Cola, and the Center for Science in the Public Interest: An Interview with Michael F. Jacobson

Michael F. Jacobson is the Executive Director of The Center for Science in the Public Interest (CSPI), a nonprofit education and advocacy organization that focuses on "improving the safety and nutritional quality of our food supply and on reducing the carnage caused by alcoholic beverages." Founded in 1971 and supported almost entirely by the 800,000 subscribers to its newsletter, CSPI accepts no government or corporate funds. In 1996, Dr. Jacobson was awarded the U.S. Food and Drug Administration's highest public honor–the agency's Special Citation–at a dinner commemorating CSPI's 25th anniversary. In 1990, he co-founded the Center for the Study of Commercialism (CSC) to help "immunize citizens against advertising's siege," including product placements in movies. Its publications include *Marketing Madness* (1995) which he co-wrote.

GALICIAN: In the early 1990s, you denounced product placement as "the most insidious form of advertising," and as the representative of CSC you petitioned the Federal Trade Commission to ban it or at least

[Haworth co-indexing entry note]: "Harry Potter, Coca-Cola, and the Center for Science in the Public Interest: An Interview with Michael F. Jacobson." Galician, Mary-Lou. Co-published simultaneously in *Journal of Promotion Management* (Best Business Books, an imprint of The Haworth Press, Inc.) Vol. 10, No. 1/2, 2004, pp. 227-231; and: *Handbook of Product Placement in the Mass Media: New Strategies in Marketing Theory, Practice, Trends, and Ethics* (ed: Mary-Lou Galician) Best Business Books, an imprint of The Haworth Press, Inc., 2004, pp. 227-231. Single or multiple copies of this article are available for a fee from The Haworth Document Delivery Service [1-800-HAWORTH, 9:00 a.m. - 5:00 p.m. (EST). E-mail address: docdelivery@haworthpress.com].

http://www.haworthpress.com/web/JPM
© 2004 by The Haworth Press, Inc. All rights reserved.
Digital Object Identifier: 10.1300/J057v10n01_18

to require movies to list all product placements during the opening credits. Although you encountered a cool FTC reception, your advocacy garnered media attention and aroused anti-placement sentiments–and soon afterward the placement industry began to address its problems, including establishing the Entertainment Resources and Marketing Association (ERMA).

NOTE: Soon after Jacobson's 1991 FTC petition, the placement industry began to address its problems (Magiera & Colford, 1991). In the same year, the Entertainment Resources and Marketing Association (ERMA), a trade group, was founded by studio executives, marketing managers, and placement agents to further the placement industry's interests and to improve its image (Turcotte, 1995). By 1995, under ERMA's influence, the placement industry was showing signs of maturation and product placement was coming into its own as a marketing tool for corporate America ("Let Us Put," 1996). Backlot-style deals were replaced by officially sanctioned contracts tied to performance standards and professional guidelines (Karrh, 1995). (For a sample contract, visit the website noted in the Turcotte interview.) The relationship between studio executives and brand managers became so enmeshed that pre-production meetings to discuss possible placement promotions had become commonplace (Turcotte, 1995). (For more information about ERMA, visit www.ERMA.org.)

Do you think the industry has changed for the better–or for the worse–and what is your current position about product placement?

JACOBSON: I haven't changed my opinion, and I suspect that the practice, if anything, is more widespread and brazen in movies and television.

GALICIAN: Are media audiences more sophisticated these days, rendering the effects of product placements, merchandising tie-ins, and cross-promotions less insidious?

JACOBSON: I don't think so. Product placement is so subtle that it is probably generally perceived subconsciously or subliminally. Viewers just don't think about the possibility that they are being advertised to.

GALICIAN: CSPI was cited in the *Los Angeles Daily News* (in the Fall of 2001) as criticizing Warner Bros. for accepting a reported $150 million from Coca-Cola for exclusive global marketing rights to *Harry Potter and the Sorcerer's Stone.*

Would you comment further and provide any update to your point of view–as well as your thoughts about whether product placements aimed at children should be handled differently from those targeted at adults?

JACOBSON: That was Coca-Cola's advertising/packaging/pr effort to use *Harry Potter* imagery to attract young drinkers. Product placements should be forbidden from kiddie media. Please see our website on this issue: *www.saveharry.com.*

NOTE: The cleverly designed site–with translations in French, Spanish, Japanese, and "Magyarul"–features Potter-esque imagery and language to capture the attention and interest of fans. Links to other related sites include video of the protest at the Washington D.C. premiere of the movie. The centerpiece is an email template to send to Potter author J. K. Rowling.

On the page entitled, "What YOU can do: TAKE ACTION!" and under the statement, "It's time that we stood up to junk-food peddlers like Coca-Cola and told them that our health is more important than their profits!", these specific recommendations are offered:

First, send a message to author J. K. Rowling [a link to the suggested letter, which can be sent by clicking "on the Owl"] telling her how disappointed you are that "Harry Potter" is being used to sell junk food. (See end of this interview for a copy of the suggested letter.) Links next to the letter tell "What Other Wizards & Witches have written . . .," and a counter notes how many Witches and Wizards have sent letters.)

Use the Alert Your Friends! postcard [a link] to tell your friends, relatives, and colleagues–your entire address book–to go to www.Save-Harry.com and send an e-mail.

Distribute "Save Harry" leaflets in front of movie theaters, children's bookstores, Coca-Cola Co. offices, and anywhere that fans of "Harry Potter" can be found. Click here [link] to see the SaveHarry.com protest at the Washington D.C. premiere.

Write a letter to the editor [link] of your newspaper deploring the use of "Harry Potter" to sell junk food.

Are soft drinks and other junk foods sold in your local school, Boys and Girls Club, YMCA, religious school, or museum? To protect students' health, join with other parents and students to get rid of them! The Cen-

*ter for Commercial-Free Education [link] has suggestions on how you
can make a difference in your school.*

*Interested in improving your nutrition? Learn what you can do, from
your breakfast table to your community, on the Center for Science in the
Public Interest's [link] website. There's a special page for kids [link],
too, that talks all about how to think healthy at any age.*

GALICIAN: Incidentally, I asked Coca-Cola to contribute a piece to this
volume but, as you might suspect, they refused politely . . .

GALICIAN: Does digital enhancement of placements pose a new threat?

JACOBSON: That will make the practice more practical and widespread, but the underlying issue is the same.

GALICIAN: Might over-exposure render the practice less effective?

JACOBSON: I hope so!

REFERENCES

Karrh, J. A. (1995). Brand placements in feature film: The practitioner's view. Paper
     presented at the 1995 Conference of the Academy of Advertising, Waco, TX.
Let us put you in movies (1996, September 16). *Brandweek*, 37, 2-10.
Magiera, M., and Colford, S. (1991, June 10). Products in movies: How big a deal? *Ad-
     vertising Age*, 55, 4.
Mazur, Laurie, and Jacobson, Michael F. (1995). *Marketing Madness: A Survival
     Guide for a Consumer Society*. Boulder, CO: Westview Press.
Turcotte, S. (1995). Gimme a Bud! The Feature Film Product Placement Industry. Un-
     published master's thesis, University of Texas at Austin.

WWW.SAVEHARRY.COM FORM LETTER

Dear Ms. Rowling,

As a fan of "Harry Potter," I urge you to save Harry from the grasp of Coca-Cola. We love "Harry Potter" and hate to see your wonderful creation used by that giant corporation to sell soft drinks to children around the world.

Coke and other soft drinks are JUNK, and certainly not what Harry would want kids to drink. They are basically empty calories, thanks to the 10 teaspoons of sugar in a typical 12-ounce (360 mL) serving. The sugar promotes obesity, a worldwide problem, and the caffeine, a mildly addictive stimulant drug, encourages people to keep drinking this "liquid candy." Also, soft drinks may replace water, lowfat milk, fruit juice, and other more healthful drinks in the diet. The bottom line: Liquid candy is bad for health, both for Muggles and Wizards.

Please, Ms. Rowling, help us Save Harry–and protect children's health! Donate the royalties from the deal to fund nutrition campaigns, and stop all future sponsorship by Coca-Cola!

Sincerely,

[Boxes and drop-down menus enable a user to insert (Name), (Email), (City), (State/Province), (Country), (ZIP), and (Age).]

A Pulitzer Prize-Winning Media Critic Discusses Product Placement: An Interview with Howard Rosenberg

Mary-Lou Galician

Howard Rosenberg was the Pulitzer Prize-winning media critic of the *Los Angeles Times* for 25 years (until his retirement in 2003), during which time he worked at home, watching television news and entertainment programs on four TV sets. His thought-provoking, insightful columns were distributed nationally via the *L.A. Times/Washington Post* wire. He has also taught journalism and critical studies courses at the University of Southern California, UCLA, and California State University at Northridge. He holds a B.A. in history and an M.A. in political science. In addition to his 1985 Pulitzer for criticism, he has won several Los Angeles Press Club Awards for his entertainment reviews, the Anti-Defamation League Torch of Liberty Award, the Greater Los Angeles Press Club Joseph M. Quinn Memorial Award for "a career of distinction," and the *L.A. Times* Editorial Award for best column/commentary. In 1996, the nation's TV critics named him "Best TV Critic" in the United States in a poll conducted by *Electronic Media* magazine. (This interview was conducted prior to his retirement from the *Los Angeles Times*.)

GALICIAN: You watch a lot of television for a living. What's your opinion of product placement and cross-promotion on television?

[Haworth co-indexing entry note]: "A Pulitzer Prize-Winning Media Critic Discusses Product Placement: An Interview with Howard Rosenberg." Galician, Mary-Lou. Co-published simultaneously in *Journal of Promotion Management* (Best Business Books, an imprint of The Haworth Press, Inc.) Vol. 10, No. 1/2, 2004, pp. 233-235; and: *Handbook of Product Placement in the Mass Media: New Strategies in Marketing Theory, Practice, Trends, and Ethics* (ed: Mary-Lou Galician) Best Business Books, an imprint of The Haworth Press, Inc., 2004, pp. 233-235. Single or multiple copies of this article are available for a fee from The Haworth Document Delivery Service [1-800-HAWORTH, 9:00 a.m. - 5:00 p.m. (EST). E-mail address: docdelivery@haworthpress.com].

http://www.haworthpress.com/web/JPM
Digital Object Identifier: 10.1300/J057v10n01_19

ROSENBERG: These marketing strategies are extensions of the way TV can influence us. We're all subjected to so many messages. Some are O.K.; some are not. Consumers should be made aware when they're watching an unidentified commercial in a seemingly non-commercial context. For example, a recent excellent television production of the stage play *Wit* carried a product placement that was distracting. In the hospital room, a visitor brings a book to read to the dying cancer patient [played by Emma Thompson]. It's in a shopping bag clearly labeled *Barnes & Noble*. Why not *Borders*? Why no label at all?

GALICIAN: Some proponents claim that product placement enhances realism. What's your take on that?

ROSENBERG: It's simply not true. In some cases it sets the symbolic tone, so it's O.K. I don't believe in banning smoking, for example, if it fits the theme. But I do object to gratuitous placements, and we're seeing more and more of those.

Here's the problem: I think we become desensitized to these promotions. We don't even think about them. Even a professional critic like me who has been watching these programs for so long and see so much. We're all influenced, and at a later time some of us recall these promoted items.

GALICIAN: What about the ethics of such influential practices?

ROSENBERG: It's crass, and it's greedy. I used to love professional tennis on television. But now it's all patches and labels. The players are walking ads. It spoils the sport. At least at Wimbledon they don't allow it. These athletes make more than enough money without the brand promotion during the game. Football bowl games all have products as part of their title. I find it sad that the public is always being sold something.

What's worse is the use of fictional TV characters in ads–like *Law & Order's* Steven Hill, who appears unnamed in many commercials, as if he's really the lawyer he portrays. When Robert Young played the beloved fictional Dr. Marcus Welby, he was even invited to address a medical convention! It's absurd.

Worst of all, however, is cross-promotion and tie-ins in the *news*– creating a news story solely to promote something. That's the most unethical thing. It's done all the time with movie and television stars appearing on morning news shows, especially during sweeps [key ratings seasons]. It's an unholy double rub-off: The news show gets viewers who want to see the star, and the promoted program gets an audience it might not otherwise get. ABC's Diane Sawyer interviewed Rosie O'Donnell when she came out publicly, and then the local ABC stations carrying Rosie's show did tie-ins to promote the show.

It'd be O.K. if they did it for shows on other networks, but they rarely do. It's getting more and more flagrant every year. The worst part is that no one seems to care any more. It's what TV does relentlessly: sell, promote. Everything is about self-promotion–from athletes to movie stars to politicians, so it's no problem to promote products.

Perhaps the most disgusting example I've seen lately was a Los Angeles news station, KCBS, that interviewed the parents of a boy who had died. *The parents were wearing the T-shirts of the news station for the interview, and the TV news truck was in the background!*

MEDIA REVIEW

Screening MEF's *Behind the Screens: Hollywood Goes Hypercommercial* (2000)

Mary-Lou Galician

SUMMARY. This review offers a summary of a Media Education Foundation video about product placement and related media marketing practices and makes recommendations for using it with school and college-age audiences as well as at professional and academic meetings. University of Massachusetts Communication Professor Sut Jhally established The Media Education Foundation in 1991 "as an independent non-profit organization to produce and disseminate educational videotapes as well as conduct research on timely media issues" with a stellar Board of Advisors that today includes cultural critics Noam Chomsky, Susan Douglas, Susan Faludi, George Gerbner, Todd Gitlin, Stuart Hall, bell hooks, Robert W. McChesney, and Naomi Wolf. *[Article copies available for a fee from The Haworth Document Delivery Service: 1-800-HAWORTH. E-mail address: <docdelivery@haworthpress.com> Website: <http://www.HaworthPress. com> © 2004 by The Haworth Press, Inc. All rights reserved.]*

[Haworth co-indexing entry note]: "Screening MEF's *Behind the Screens: Hollywood Goes Hypercommercial* (2000)." Galician, Mary-Lou. Co-published simultaneously in *Journal of Promotion Management* (Best Business Books, an imprint of The Haworth Press, Inc.) Vol. 10, No. 1/2, 2004, pp. 237-240; and: *Handbook of Product Placement in the Mass Media: New Strategies in Marketing Theory, Practice, Trends, and Ethics* (ed: Mary-Lou Galician) Best Business Books, an imprint of The Haworth Press, Inc., 2004, pp. 237-240. Single or multiple copies of this article are available for a fee from The Haworth Document Delivery Service [1-800-HAWORTH, 9:00 a.m. - 5:00 p.m. (EST). E-mail address: docdelivery@ haworthpress.com].

http://www.haworthpress.com/web/JPM
© 2004 by The Haworth Press, Inc. All rights reserved.
Digital Object Identifier: 10.1300/J057v10n01_20

KEYWORDS. Product placement, media education, videotape, cross promotion, tie-ins, hypercommercialism, Hollywood film, media conglomerates, cultural criticism

Behind the Screens: Hollywood Goes Hypercommercial (2000; 37 minutes; $250/$125 for high schools; study guide and "other helpful resources" available). Videotape from Northampton, MA: Media Education Foundation/MEF; 1-800-897-0089; <*www.mediaed.org*>. Free preview copies available.

A WELL-DOCUMENTED CRITIQUE

The subtle impact of video images on unsuspecting but susceptible audiences is the theme of *Behind the Screens: Hollywood Goes Hypercommercial,* a video released at the end of 2000 by the Media Education Foundation. Using well-selected and highly relevant up-to-the-minute movie clips and commercials as evidence, *Behind the Screens* convincingly argues that mainstream, big-budget movies have become a major vehicle for advertising and marketing in an era of "hypercommercialization" marked by a phenomenal rise in product placements, tie-ins with fast-food chains, and mammoth toy merchandising deals and cross-promotions.

Its four sections cover the field admirably:

- Product Placement: Advertising Goes to the Movies
- Making Movies for Marketers: Cross Promotions, Merchandising, Tie-ins
- Hijacking the Movies: Hollywood in an Age of Conglomerates
- Limiting Stories: Making Movies in a Hypercommercial Age

The video presents both on-screen and voiceover commentary from six compelling experts: five well-known scholars (Susan Douglas, Mark Crispin Miller [see *"INTERVIEWS"* in this volume], Robert W. McChesney, Eileen Meehan, and Janet Wasko) and an independent filmmaker (Jeremy Pikser, Oscar®-nominated screenwriter of Warren Beatty's *Bulworth*).

MEF's videos make good use of illustrative film clips from such blockbusters as *Forest Gump, The Lion King, Summer of Sam, Toy Story, Good Will Hunting, You've Got Mail,* and the product placement satire *Wayne's World.*

Useful graphics also help convey the message that "the new media giants aim to turn our cultural environment into an 'echo chamber' for their latest film releases and that the imperative to foreground well-known products compromises our common reservoir of values and stories as it becomes increasingly colonized by the clutter of commercial messages."

CLASSROOM AND CONFERENCE USE

I have used this video in my Mass Media and Society class of 200 students as well as in a program on product placement I presented for colleagues at the National Communication Association's national convention in 2000. In both venues, this video was very well received and generated a great deal of valuable discussion.

Several factors should be considered. As noted above, the commentators in the video are all cultural critics, and their attack on the conglomeratization of media and global culture is decidedly anti-business. Nevertheless, although business students might be a bit uncomfortable viewing it, they could benefit from this appeal to more ethical advertising and marketing that challenges assumptions of the current models and invites self-reflection. For media students, it is a valuable instructional tool.

I've found that supplementing the presentation with clips of current examples is particularly effective. I usually precede the presentation of the MEF video with a 3-minute clip from *The Truman Show*–the scene in which Cristo (Ed Harris), the producer of the show, is talking to a TV news interviewer about the product placements and embedded commercials that make the show possible. It's an easy segue to demonstrating to students that the high satire of that scene is not just satire but reality, as documented by the MEF video.

I've also used clips from *SportsNight* (originally airing on ABC and now in reruns on the Comedy Channel), Aaron Sorkin's well-written and well acted half-hour comedy/drama that frequently included blatant unlabeled cross-promotions; for example, one story line had one of the fictional sports anchors appearing on ABC-TV's *The View*, and another had the sports show's producer raving about seeing Disney's stage show version of *The Lion King* just prior to its national tour. While the story lines made sense, the unacknowledged placements amount to ads. Students are shocked to see these. (I screen the clips first, and then ask if they know what's "wrong" with these mentions. Sometimes they immediately recognize the corporate incest; other times it takes a few hints.)

James Bond movies offer a wealth of product placements that are usually long and frequently multiple. It's almost impossible to find movies that don't include placements or tie-ins.

The MEF video and other examples help sharpen students' critical media skills and provide an ethical challenge to those going into the business.

These presentations are also highly effective with professional and academic groups. In such settings, the video works well to stimulate and focus discussion and debate.

ROUNDTABLE

Product Placement in the 21st Century

Edited by Mary-Lou Galician

This volume opened with Kathleen J. Turner's piece that took us back to the beginning of television and its product placement connections. We conclude with a "roundtable" of contributors' responses to questions about product placement in the present and in the future.

You will see that although they do not always agree, they always offer intriguing arguments about this controversial practice and related media marketing strategies. On one issue they are in total agreement: The need for consumer education about the mass media.

I have edited their commentaries, which are grouped by question to suggest avenues for readers' own contemplation and further study. (The resources in the final section–*Recommended Publications and Websites*– should also be helpful.)

The work of this group of collaborating contributors continues. If you would like to offer comments, please contact any or all of us. We would be delighted to hear from you.

[Haworth co-indexing entry note]: "Product Placement in the 21st Century." Galician, Mary-Lou. Co-published simultaneously in *Journal of Promotion Management* (Best Business Books, an imprint of The Haworth Press, Inc.) Vol. 10, No. 1/2, 2004, pp. 241-258; and: *Handbook of Product Placement in the Mass Media: New Strategies in Marketing Theory, Practice, Trends, and Ethics* (ed: Mary-Lou Galician) Best Business Books, an imprint of The Haworth Press, Inc., 2004, pp. 241-258. Single or multiple copies of this article are available for a fee from The Haworth Document Delivery Service [1-800-HAWORTH, 9:00 a.m. - 5:00 p.m. (EST). E-mail address: docdelivery@haworthpress.com].

http://www.haworthpress.com/web/JPM
Digital Object Identifier: 10.1300/J057v10n01_21

THE FIVE QUESTIONS

Each contributor responded independently to the five questions posed, so the term "roundtable" is used loosely. Here are the five questions:

1. *Does product placement have any negative social effects, and if so what are they?*
2. *Should the entertainment industry put any limits on the practice?*
3. *Should all placed products and all target audiences be considered the same? (For example, should product placement aimed at children be regarded and handled any differently?)*
4. *Does the sophistication of audiences stay a step ahead of the placement practice?*
5. *What does the digitalization of media imply for the future of product placement?*

THE CONTRIBUTORS

Besides myself, 10 of this volume's 17 other authors participated:

> Peter G. Bourdeau
> Ted Friedman
> Dean Kruckeberg
> Charles A. Lubbers
> David Natharius
> Richard Alan Nelson
> Scott Robert Olson
> Paul Siegel
> Christopher R. Turner
> Kathleen J. Turner

THE ROUNDTABLE

Q1: Does product placement have any negative social effects, and if so, what are they?

CHRISTOPHER R. TURNER: Only if you consider pervasive commercialism to be a bad effect on society.

RICHARD ALAN NELSON: Product placements reinforce the ideology of consumerism, that is purchasing products is the way to happiness. Yet we know from research that material things are not the key to a successful life, nor mental security.

SCOTT ROBERT OLSON: There are two main negative social effects to product placement: One effect is the propagation of a culture dedicated primarily to shopping, which brings with it the increasingly prevalent notion that identity is something that can be purchased, and the other effect is the increasing attitudes of skepticism and even cynicism with regard to veracity of information of any kind.

The culture of shopping is something I've written about elsewhere, but to summarize the concern, it is that so many aspects of American culture have been connected to advertising, marketing, and consumption that it becomes difficult to find any other form of discourse or ideas that are not connected to consumption or branding. We have a generation entering its twenties that has never known anything different: They have never known a culture that wasn't organized around marketing or one that was really of their own spontaneous creation, as had been youth culture for at least the two generations before them, as opposed to the mere appearance of spontaneity. For these young people, the way they think about who they are, the way they understand their very identity, is tied to their consumption patterns. Much of what they want to say to each other and to the rest of the world they communicate through the brands they wear, the beverages they drink, the fast food they prefer, the music they buy, and movies they see. In my personal experience, most of them don't seem aware of any other way to communicate who they are. Product placement bears a significant amount of the responsibility for this cultural effect because it propagates marketing in arenas that need not be associated with it–narrative and the visual arts.

But at the same time that we are shopping for our identity, we have become increasingly skeptical and in some cases even cynical about the possibilities for honest storytelling and other forms of communication. American audiences, especially young audiences, tend to assume that all forms of communication have hidden agendas and are therefore fundamentally deceptive, including news and information. Product placement is partly responsible for this, too. A culture that does not trust its own stories can be a dangerous one. 9-11-02 was a traumatic day in U.S. history, but one positive ancillary result seems to be a greater use and trust of media across the demographic spectrum. However, this may be short lived, and several advertisers have used patriotic imagery in an attempt to sell products, which can only contribute to future cynicism about the industry.

Of course, we need to remember that there is a version of the Third Person Effect at work here. One tends to attribute greater advertising susceptibility to other audience members than to oneself. Studies of the Third Person Effect and viewer perceptions of product placement are needed to see how it functions in that environment.

DAVID NATHARIUS: It certainly has at least one negative effect: We might be led to believe that the only soft drinks are Pepsi and Coke and the only beer is Budweiser.

Just as independent films are seen by far fewer people than those films distributed by the major studios, the opportunity for smaller market products to gain visibility is further reduced by the convergence of the major media conglomerates and their promotion of major brands with placement deals.

TED FRIEDMAN: I think product placement is more a symptom than a root cause of the problems with Hollywood.

If product placement were banned tomorrow, the range of American films would still be just as narrow, studios would be just as craven, and the barriers for entry just as high. What really needs to happen on a political level is a breakup of the concentration of power in the media industry, so that more voices can fairly compete with the brand bullies.

DEAN KRUCKEBERG: Yes, product placement is misleading and arguably unethical because it suggests a normative use of a specific brand by people who are positioned to be role models, e.g., "heroes," in a fantasy environment (movie, etc.) that is not perceived to be an advertisement, i.e., a movie is not obviously a persuasive message to sell products or services.

PETER G. BOURDEAU: When it comes to understanding the supposed negative social effects engendered by product placement, what must first be addressed is how can any determination be made of its effects that is not based on empirical analysis that does not reflect some kind of guesswork or personal prejudice?

In fact, the question itself presupposes that audiences are not even aware of what's happening on the screen and need to be protected from the obviously odious influences of product placements. I would argue that most of today's movie audiences, in particular the targeted 17- to 25-year-old group, have an intimate understanding of the presence of placed brands within motion pictures. They get the joke and don't mind it.

Q2: Should the entertainment industry put any limits on the practice?

SCOTT ROBERT OLSON: It's important to remember that U.S. case law precedents have determined that prior restraint of the media is unconstitutional, so there really is no ability to prohibit or restrict the practice of product placement through direct external controls.

The legal principle of subsequent punishment is always possible for instances when the law has been broken, but such instances are few and far between, and it's hard to imagine how that might apply to product placement except in instances of gross and negligent deception.

So that leaves self-censorship, which has been the way that the media typically manage complaints of an offensive practice. Self-censorship is the model that brought about the Motion Picture Association of America (MPAA) rating system for theatrical motion pictures, the Comics Code Authority, and the self-rating systems of the television, recorded music, and video game industries. All of these are administered by the industries themselves, not by some external political or legal authority, because that would be prior restraint. Self-censorship is always a possibility for controlling or restricting product placement. It is highly unlikely, though—at least at this point in its history. Every other instance of self-censorship emerged from a public outcry. It was outrage over the perceived negative effects of "horror" comic books like *Tales from the Crypt* that led to the congressional hearings of the Kefauver Commission, which in turn led to promises from the comic book industry to clean itself up, and then to the creation of the Comics Code Authority, which certifies wholesome content in the industry by others in the industry. The same basic story is true of the MPAA and other self-censorship groups.

But in the case of product placement, there is no public outcry. Those members of the audience who even manage to notice the practice may actually like it. Daniel Boorstin was one of the first to notice that American audiences generally *like* advertisements, and product placement has come to be seen as something like a game, a pleasant diversion. This means that industry-driven product placement self-censorship is just as unlikely as prior restraint. The likelihood of self-censorship is a separate question from whether the industry should limit the practice, but in the history of media no industry has ever limited itself in the absence of legal or political pressure, so the question of whether the industry *should* limit product placement is moot.

CHARLES A. LUBBERS: My inclination would be to say that the industry should stay out of regulating product placement.

I believe that artistic freedom and the free market system should make the rules. I feel that the creators of entertainment programming should have the freedom to create material to fit their vision. My belief in this system is further supported by the funding nature of media in America. If the use of product placement or any other element exceeds the sensibilities of the masses, they will vote with their box office purchases, as well as calls for industry and government control. Somewhere between complete creative chaos and complete government control, there is a happy medium developed through the use of the free market economy and political activism.

Having said the preceding, allow me to point out at least one argument for regulation. The broadcast industry has examples of similar practices that have led to industry and government regulation. The "payola" scandal in radio bears at least a little resemblance to the product placement controversy. After all, payola is about paying to have your music played on a radio station, and product placement often involves paying to have your products included in a motion picture. Also, broadcasters are clearly prevented from allowing advertisers to exercise editorial control, as advertisers did in the early days of television. That doesn't mean advertisers have no say. It simply means that they can't completely call the shots. The comparison of product placement in movies and these issues in the broadcast industry is clearly problematic because the issues are not exactly the same, and the regulation basis of the broadcast industry (because of the use of public airwaves) is very different. However, examination of similar issues in the broadcast industry at least warrants further investigation.

TED FRIEDMAN: Product placement is clearly a sleazy and unethical practice, akin to payola in the music industry.

A good start to cleaning the situation up would be to require all product placement agreements to be acknowledged in film credits and promotional materials, including the amount of money paid and the value of products and services "donated." Cases of intracorporate cross-promotion (AOL and CNN appearing in Warner movies, etc.) should also be acknowledged.

RICHARD ALAN NELSON: I am leery of direct government intervention. However, self-regulation is a proven method to avoid excesses.

It is not in the interest of entertainment firms to have their product be seen as only a commercial medium: It still has to pack entertainment value.

PETER G. BOURDEAU: While First Amendment considerations rule out any externally imposed limits on product placements being forced upon the entertainment industry by some government entity, perhaps a self-imposed set of guidelines would waylay any undue criticism from reactionary media critics.

DAVID NATHARIUS: I really do not see how the industry could develop a workable policy that would limit the practice of product placement, particularly since it has become a major source of revenue for the entertainment business.

There would be a great deal of resistance to any restrictions on how films and television shows are financed (although there are some restrictions concerning how actors can sell products on television as the character they portray in a television show).

CHRISTOPHER R. TURNER: I have so far been unimpressed with the entertainment industry's attempts to regulate themselves.

The limits on the practice (other than legal or regulatory) will probably come from consumers, who are likely to avoid entertainment where the placement messages overwhelm the entertainment value.

DEAN KRUCKEBERG: Just because something may not be ethical doesn't mean it should be legislated.

I think education concerning what product placement is remains the best antidote for any influence of product placement.

**Q3: Should all placed products and all target audiences
be considered the same? (For example, should marketing
aimed at children be treated differently?)**

DEAN KRUCKEBERG: My "free speech" argument against legislation
(in answer to Question # 2) doesn't transcend to policies regarding messages for children.

I think children's entertainment should be examined very closely to
discourage product placement.

PAUL SIEGEL: Wouldn't it be nice if we treated all advertising aimed
at kids entirely differently from those messages aimed at adults? But the
law has not been very accommodating on this point.

There have been limits imposed by the FCC on the total number of
commercial minutes in children's programming on TV, as well as a few
other regulations without much teeth. Certainly, the FTC is able to take
into account the likely audience for a message when considering if that
message is deceptive. Beyond that, there is little that can be done within
our legal system. Moreover, as I suggested in my essay, there is an excellent chance that courts would determine that most product placements
are not commercial speech at all, and thus much less subject to regulation.

CHARLES A. LUBBERS: There is clear regulatory and statutory precedent that messages targeted to children must be treated differently.

Current government regulation related to broadcasting makes a number of distinctions for the times of day when children will be watching. It
is only reasonable to assume that targeting children with product placement would be considered in a different category from adult targeting.
Additionally, the motion picture and television industry have established voluntary ratings systems ostensibly to "protect" children from
objectionable material and to warn parents that such material is contained within the entertainment. Surely the use of product placement
would have to be similarly differentiated.

RICHARD ALAN NELSON: There isn't much choice. Ever since
we've had regulators, they've always focused on more vulnerable populations–including younger children.

KATHLEEN J. TURNER: Legally, morally, and ethically, the differences in audiences should be considered.

Children are more susceptible because they generally have not had the opportunity to develop their critical faculties and their sense of self (and yes, I know some parents are chuckling at the latter!), and they are an increasingly popular target for marketers. "Caveat emptor" seems inappropriate for those too young to beware of those who wish to buy their attitudes and actions.

DAVID NATHARIUS: There already is a fine line between what we can see in a "family" show and the use to which products are handled, particularly by under-age characters.

All manufacturers who place products have clear guidelines about how their products are going to be portrayed in film and television. They rarely allow their placed products to be shown in a negative manner. The more troublesome issue is when a product is being used in a manner for which it is intended and, therefore, needs no manufacturer approval but is being used by someone not of an appropriate age to be using the product, such as under-age drivers who have been drinking.

CHRISTOPHER R. TURNER: I think that target audiences that might be considered more vulnerable than others (such as children or the ill) should receive more regulatory protection than others.

These audiences already do to some extent, and the largest debate will probably revolve around how much extra protection should be given to them. However, it will still end up being the primary responsibility of the family unit to monitor what vulnerable family members see and to educate them as to how to respond to placed messages.

PETER G. BOURDEAU: Perhaps establishing a self-regulating industry-prescribed set of guidelines might act as an early remedy against future criticism of the use of product placements in certain films, especially those aimed at juvenile audiences.

SCOTT ROBERT OLSON: There has been an evolution in the types of products and types of audiences to which product placement has been directed.

At first only consumer goods–things to buy–were placed and these were often products upon which swift consumer action could be anticipated: inexpensive consumables that in some cases were available for sale in the lobby of the theater. Over time, product placement came to include much more sophisticated and expensive products, products that would be of interest to only a limited segment of the audience, like automobiles. More recently, ideas, themes, and brands are placed, a scenario in which no specific product is pitched and no specific action is expected because these placements are designed to build image.

So, should all placed products be considered the same? Clearly not–they have different objectives, and that needs to be taken into account. Likewise, audiences are not the same, are not treated the same by those placing products, and should therefore not be considered the same. Product placements are differentiated by film selection and also by audience segments within a film. A placement like the Teenage Mutant Ninja Turtles eating Domino's Pizza clearly has a different target audience than a placement like James Bond driving a BMW: different age, different income level, different education level, and other differentiated demographics.

Because audiences are segmented and aligned to the product being placed, special consideration always needs to be given to audiences with reduced abilities to understand media content. Children are the most common example. In the absence of media literacy programs in the U.S. schools, the ability of children to interpret and contextualize media content is limited. Unfortunately, a huge amount of product placement is aimed directly at children. The blending of product, idea, theme, and brand within placements creates an overwhelming marketing blitz aimed at kids. The whole Pokemon concept, for example, is one big product placement: a television series that sells movie ticket sales, ticket sales that sell trading cards, trading cards that sell toys, toys that sell apparel, apparel that sells the television series, and so on. Children usually lack the ability to serve as reflective and analytical agents in the face of this blitz.

Happily, the law in most cases treats juveniles differently than the way it treats adults. This is proper; there ought to be more restraint for kids. Unfortunately, we already have a generation for whom youth culture was not spontaneous and emergent but designed and marketed directly to them. They equate their identity with things they buy. Also unfortunately, the law does not really apply to restrictions of product placement for reasons discussed elsewhere in this forum. There are exceptions, such as the practice of avoiding the advertising of a specific toy during a television show based on that toy, but then again the program is itself an advertisement for the toy. Should marketing aimed at children be different? Yes–but the only tool for *making* it different is political pressure derived from parental outrage, yet there seems to be no outrage.

Q4: Does the sophistication of audiences stay a step ahead of the product placement?

PAUL SIEGEL: Necessarily, this inquiry would be part of any adjudication of a claim that product placements are inherently deceptive.

I just do not think the claim would be accepted. Surely, advertisers would be able to proffer much survey data showing that audiences are highly aware of the practice of product placements. How could they not be after viewing such satiric treatments of the issue as seen in *Wayne's World* and in *The Truman Show*?

DEAN KRUCKEBERG: One cannot legislate against stupidity, of course; however, I think significant numbers of people are not sophisticated in their knowledge of product placement and what the practice intends to accomplish.

CHRISTOPHER R. TURNER: The sophistication of the audience lags a step or two behind that of the marketers.

Think of it in terms of offense and defense: The offense has the initiative because they are the ones acting first while the defense has to wait to react to the moves of the opposing force. As audiences gain sophistication in dealing with one form of marketing, marketers adapt their delivery methods in order to keep getting their message through.

RICHARD ALAN NELSON: I tend to have faith in audiences. They know what they like and don't like.

This means product placement firms have to take into account new and different ways to get their messages incorporated in media without reaching the saturation point of audience boredom, inattention, and active rejection.

DAVID NATHARIUS: More and more people are able to recognize when a generic, fictitious product is being displayed in a film or television show.

We know that in real life no one goes into a bar and asks for "a beer." We can see when the breakfast cereal being served or the milk being poured is coming from a fictitious container and when an automobile has clearly had its name labels removed or disguised. No doubt most audience members are becoming as aware of fake products as they are of the ubiquitous and silly use of "555-" for all telephone numbers–a practice that is particularly excruciating to the sensibilities and sophistication of regular viewers of shows that purport to be realistic.

PETER G. BOURDEAU: Academics must avoid looking down their collective noses in determining the relative gullibility of many of today's consumers of motion picture products.

These are a media-savvy lot, raised on commercial images of singing raisins and horses that kick field goals. Today's twenty-somethings get the jokes offered by advertisers but remain unswayed in their buying choices. They still prefer Gummi Bears over Raisinets and Micro-beers over Bud.

TED FRIEDMAN: Audiences are often more sophisticated than Hollywood presumes (or at least hopes).

For example, teens stayed away in droves from the phony, condescending *Josie and the Pussycats*, which tried to have it both ways by combining ubiquitous product placement with a clunky plot involving an evil corporation placing subliminal ads in pop music. I think fans could tell that the "satire" was just an excuse to squeeze every frame full of ads for McDonald's, Revlon, Target, Bounce, Tide, Kodak, Starbucks, Motorola, Evian, Advil, Krispy Kreme, Bloomingdales, Steve Madden, Puma, Adidas, Foot Locker, Pringles, Pizza Hut, Diet Coke, and more. However, the question isn't whether viewers can successfully "resist" individual promotions; the question is how this relentless corporatized culture affects the texture of our lives. Michael Schudson in *Advertising: The Uneasy Persuasion* describes advertising as "capitalist realism"– our society's ubiquitous, official culture, equivalent to "socialist realism" under communism. Movies, since they're not directly sponsored by advertisers, have a chance to get a little outside this culture and comment on it. (Likewise, think how much more independence HBO has compared to broadcast TV). Product placement narrows (and often obliterates) the gap between movies and the rest of our marketer-dominated culture.

KATHLEEN J. TURNER: On the one hand, my students often show a surprising sophistication about the practice. On the other hand, they also seem (at least at the beginning of a class on the analysis of media) to have given little thought to the economic and political processes leading to the placement or to the ramifications of such placement.

Here I'll mount my favorite soap box: We need more systematic and far-reaching education about the media. We live in an environment saturated by mediated messages, to which the educational system pays remarkably little attention. We need to help our students and members of the wider public understand that the media are businesses, that corporations own a diverse range of products and outlets that are interconnected, that economic choices shape creative decisions, that mediated messages can make elements seem "natural," that brand identity may come from a variety of choices–in short, to understand the structure and effects of contemporary media. Such awareness will help people become better consumers and critics of such practices as product placement.

SCOTT ROBERT OLSON: There are three different types of audiences within the United States, and their level of sophistication is proportional to their media use volumes and patterns.

Pre-modern audiences, for example those who grew up before the widespread diffusion of television or for other reasons were not extensively exposed to television, bring traditional values to their media use experiences and in most cases do not even notice product placements. This audience is not terribly sophisticated in its use of media, and would not be able to deconstruct and analyze instances of product placement nor be amused by them.

Modern audiences–baby boomers in most cases–are probably aware of the practice of product placement, would notice some instances of it, and generally feel it is in some way improper, deceptive, or immoral. The modern audience is probably the most susceptible to the Third Person effect: They worry about their children or others who they feel are being influenced by product placement, but they doubt the placements affect them.

Postmodern audiences–Gen X and Gen Y–are heavy and ironic users of media, know the conventions of film and television well, and are very good at spotting placements. In my purely anecdotal experience, I've come to believe that this audience enjoys product placements very much. For them, the placements are like one of Wittgenstein's language games.

Marketers can go on placing products as usual if the market segments they hope to reach are pre-modern or modern, but these groups tend not to be of primary interest. It is the postmodern audience, the most desirable demographic for many advertisers, who is and will remain the most sophisticated with regard to product placement. There is the strong possibility that for this audience, product placements may become part of the landscape, the way billboards are, noticed but disregarded, even irrelevant. For them, placements may cease to correlate to consumer behavior and would therefore lose their effectiveness from the marketing standpoint. This would presumably lead marketers to develop more clever and aggressive strategies to capture the fancies of the postmodern audience. Those other strategies will include the use of digital media technology to place advertising and products into settings it has not been before–in and around characters and settings in images new and old. Advertising tends to be a resourceful profession and will undoubtedly find alternative means of reaching the postmodern audience.

Q5: What does the digitalization of media imply for the future of product placement?

RICHARD ALAN NELSON: On one hand it will be easier to place product messages in current and pre-existing media.

Sporting events are a common usage today, with entirely digital messages appearing on football fields and baseball backdrops. We are also already beginning to see inserts into television reruns. Similarly, there will be opportunities for overt and covert product placements in everything from video games to music. This could also provide a backlash if not handled properly.

DEAN KRUCKEBERG: Maybe I'm missing something, but I don't think digitalization (except for lying or falsifying through digitalization) is a factor in considering policies regarding product placement.

PETER G. BOURDEAU: It is conceivable that digitalization can have an immense effect upon the future of product placements in cinema.

Imagine a bidding war for a beer placement within a crucial scene long after its filming as part of a huge blockbuster that has received the appropriate amount of buzz from industry insiders. The magic of computer imaging techniques within motion pictures means a virtually limitless array of placed product opportunities in any film ever made. Cinema purists would howl as they witnessed their favorite film classics re-released with modern day product placements. The only limit to all of this would be the relative cleverness of marketers and filmmakers in taking advantage of this technology.

CHRISTOPHER R. TURNER: One of the recent pushes in marketing is individualized targeted marketing, so one effect of digital placement, especially when combined with increasing broadband access in homes, is that the placements in entertainment downloaded by individuals will be tailored to those individuals.

For instance, an actor might drink a Coke in a movie downloaded by a teenager but a Diet Coke if an older individual downloads the same movie. The more data on individual consumers the marketers have the more accurately they will be able to target the messages to those individuals.

DAVID NATHARIUS: I think the paradox is that products will no longer need to be actually handled by the actors and, therefore, in a virtual world, couldn't manufacturers refuse to pay any placement fees since no REAL product is exhibited?

Products will no longer be actually on the set or in the hands of the actors. They will be digitally placed or the labels will be digitally generated. I can see a future where many films, hopefully not ALL films, will be completely digitalized, removing the need for real actors, stunt people, props, and sets. Personally, I'm in rapt anticipation about how the whole digital virtual reality universe will be manifested in movies and television.

SCOTT ROBERT OLSON: To answer this question, we would need to know what economic models will emerge as the dominant ones for digital media. That will make clear how money could actually be made from the media, and how product placement will fit in. Which model will emerge is not clear yet.

We do know that the digital media will use a different model than the print or broadcast media. At this point, we don't know yet what those models will be, and we don't know how the digital media will pay for themselves. But we do know that things will be different. The change is already happening thanks to digital devices that destroy broadcasting's business model: TiVo and Replay may finish the job started by the remote control and kill television advertising altogether. As motion pictures move toward digital distribution, and as more consumers build home theaters, that industry will be changed as well.

So digital media frees consumers from advertising, but those who live by the sword die by it, and it seems that the same digital technology that frees us from advertising is the same technology that will find new ways to market to us. Digital product placement may be one of the few ways for marketers to send advertising messages through visual narratives, and it is an avenue available through every business model currently being discussed for digital media:

- *Advertising.* This is the current funding model for broadcast television, and the model that largely failed on the Internet, leading to the dot-com crash. This model may be revived for future types of digital media, but straight advertising as the means for underwriting the production and distribution of digital media seems to be an unreliable model for digital media now. Digitalization provides new ways to advertise, however, such as the ability to place virtual backboard ads into baseball games or the insertion of products into old films in which they originally did not appear.
- *Subscription.* This is the model borrowed from the print media and HBO and adopted with limited success by some digital media content providers, such as the *WallStreetJournal.com, Bloomberg,* and the RealOne media player. These companies tend to know a great deal about their subscribers, and the digital media provide the ability for extensive customization of content, so it may be possible in this model to place different products in different ways based on the psychographic profiles of each subscriber.
- *Usage-based billing.* This model is more unique to the digital media and it relies on charging an amount proportional to the number of uses a consumer makes of a digital media product. Pay-per-view and the new digital Internet technology called Video On Demand (VOD) are examples. This environment provides an economic advantage to digital product placement because models and patterns of consumer use can be easily tracked.
- *Value-based billing.* In this scenario, prices for digital media products are tiered for desirability rather than use. Something highly

desirable, such as a Hollywood hit film in theatrical release, would have a higher usage price than something less desirable, such as a classic silent movie. *The Economist* Intelligence Unit has provided differential pricing for access to its data based on its sophistication and scarcity. As with usage-based pricing, this environment provides an economic advantage to digital product placement because it allows for easy tracking of models and patterns of consumer use of media.

• *Cross-selling.* This model, unique to the digital media, provides tools for encouraging a viewer to convert content-watching into product-purchasing. Canal+technology, for example, enables someone viewing a music video on television to call up a menu of interactive choices, including the immediate purchase of a CD of the music being heard with direct billing to a prescribed credit card. Linkage between the Disney Channel, *Disney.com*, and the Disney Store is another example. It is easy to see how this might empower product placement in new ways: What if a product seen in a movie or television program can be clicked and purchased while the narrative is being watched? Under such a scenario, the narrative is both product placer and online catalog.

• *Discounting.* In this scenario, the price of digital media content is variable contingent on the amount of advertising a user is willing to tolerate. Those who are willing to watch a lot of advertisements would get the content for free, but those unwilling to watch advertisements would be expected to pay for the content, perhaps on a sliding scale. Eudora is a pioneer in this revenue model. This might mean that those who do not object to product placement would see a movie filled with placements but would see it for free, and those willing to pay for the same film would see it free from placements.

• *Direct sales and physical format.* In the digital media environment, most large scale media events (for example, blockbuster films) will still be consumed through direct purchase of a physical object– a ticket to see it in a theater, or a DVD version of a movie or television program, or some other object. In this environment, product placement will operate as it has in the past. Digitalization in this scenario provides some interesting advantages, such as the ease of placement during the production process, whereby for example a Pepsi logo could be digitally added to a scene during the post-production process rather than during filming, and even the customization of placements in the narrative based on the preferences of particular consumers. ICONceptual makes a product capable of such instantaneous customization, including such variable placement as the insertion of a "Coke" or "Pepsi" logo on a soda can used in a video based on audience preferences. This technology also allows narratives to be changed instantaneously to suit audience preferences–different pacing, different music, and different imagery.

In most profitability scenarios for digital media, product placement has new and more aggressive opportunities. Steven Sheiner, the Chief Revenue Officer of Vivendi-Universal, said at the 2002 Digital Media Summit that "product placement is the ideal revenue model for digital media. Soon we'll see the band in a music video wearing T-shirts adapted to each individual viewer, coded to audience wants, and linked to the ability to click and buy the CD, the video, and even the T-Shirt." The band no longer wears real clothes, only virtual clothes, which are advertisements and products at the same time. The digitalization of media creates an environment in which Baudrillard is right: There is reality, only hyperreality, and one geared toward the commercialization of everything.

So, in a nutshell, what digitalization means for product placement is that content producers can place anything, anywhere, all the time. Narratives will be protean, able to change to suit the buying habits of the audience to maximize the notability of the products. These placements will provide consumers with opportunities to purchase the product with the click of a button. Only films on the protected safe list established by the United States Congress are immune from such manipulation. Digitalization means that all forms of media entertainment–from *Amelie* to *Zelig*–will be interactive infomercials.

TED FRIEDMAN: Digital technologies make it easier to insert logos into every spare inch of screen space.

However, they also have the potential to cut costs of production and distribution, giving more creators access to viewers, and viewers more options. Ultimately, what will kill product placement is viewer rebellion: If there's enough else to watch, why choose to watch an ad?

RESOURCE GUIDE

A Product Placement Resource Guide:
Recommended Publications and Websites

Richard Alan Nelson

In *The Truman Show* (1998), Jim Carrey plays a character who has no idea he is starring in a live pseudo-reality 24-hour a day television program where everyone surrounding him is acting a part, that everything he uses and consumes is an embedded brand captured by 5,000 cameras that run non-stop. To me the movie really hit the nail on the head, as the plot seems to be closer to reality than many thought (see the website at *http://www.transparencynow.com/truprod.htm*).

The purpose of this review is to provide a selective guide to useful resources for the person interested in doing more research on the product placement phenomenon. Constructing a total bibliography is beyond the scope intended here, but this should prove helpful.

[Haworth co-indexing entry note]: "A Product Placement Resource Guide: Recommended Publications and Websites." Nelson, Richard Alan. Co-published simultaneously in *Journal of Promotion Management* (Best Business Books, an imprint of The Haworth Press, Inc.) Vol. 10, No. 1/2, 2004, pp. 259-267; and: *Handbook of Product Placement in the Mass Media: New Strategies in Marketing Theory, Practice, Trends, and Ethics* (ed: Mary-Lou Galician) Best Business Books, an imprint of The Haworth Press, Inc., 2004, pp. 259-267. Single or multiple copies of this article are available for a fee from The Haworth Document Delivery Service [1-800-HAWORTH, 9:00 a.m. - 5:00 p.m. (EST). E-mail address: docdelivery@haworthpress. com].

Digital Object Identifier: 10.1300/J057v10n01_22   *259*

IDENTIFYING PRODUCT PLACEMENT FIRMS

Actually, there are now more than 100 companies practicing in the field of product placement internationally. Their trade group is called ERMA (Entertainment Resource Marketing Association), which has an excellent organizational website at *http://www.erma.org/* with useful links. There is even a product placement awards organization (see *http://www.productplacementawards.com/*).

Many individual product placement firms are doing especially cutting edge work that is interesting to learn more about and has global implications. Some examples include:

1. *First Fireworks Group (FFG), http://www.firstfireworksgroup. com/.* The company's proprietary process, the Biztainment Profile™, helps clients "discover and maximize the value of your brand's distinct entertainment identity. Then we can identify the right methods for leveraging, integrating or creating the right entertainment properties, providing the greatest return for your marketing investments."

2. *Creative Entertainment Services (CES), http://www.acreativegroup. com/ceshome/main.html.* With over 18 years of experience, CES defines product placement as "the art of locating and negotiating prominent placements for our client's Product, Name or Service in both feature films and television programs. Product Placement is an inexpensive way to build national recognition, enhance your corporate image and provide promotional opportunities with some of today's most successful films and television programs. The inherent benefits of the medium–exciting setting, implied celebrity endorsement, captive audience, uncluttered environment–make product placement an ideal medium to support an image building campaign."

3. *First Place Product Props Ltd., http://www.1stplaceprops.com/.* Since 1991, First Place has been proactively and successfully promoting its clients products to both TV and film productions. They "are now the UK's leading product placement agency and work with a list of clients including Kellogg's, Dyson, VW and Canon. We also have a close working relationship with some of the largest media agencies including MindShare, Initiative Media and MediaCom."

4. *MMI Product Placement, http://www.mmiproductplacement.com/.* "The leader in the Canadian product placement and entertainment marketing industry" describes product placement as "the process

that integrates an advertiser's product into movies and TV shows for clear brand exposure. Product Placement is an essential component of the rapidly expanding entertainment marketing industry, because of its ability to reach millions of people through movies, television, and video. Product Placement has an important role in the marketing mix and is a key tool in building brand awareness."

5. *Alt Terrain, Alternative Media and Customized Marketing, http:// www.altterrain.com/alternative_product_placemnt.htm.* This firm specializes in product placement "in magazine 'product feature' sections, in celebrity interview photos, and fashion spreads (online and offline), is a critical element in building awareness and authenticity for brands. Third-party endorsements communicate a higher brand credibility than that of paid advertisements. Custom product placement in magazine interview photos, magazine articles, and website content. A standing product placement program should be instituted for all consumer brands, particularly for brands in the clothing, consumer electronic equipment, video game, and food & beverage industry."

6. *iTVX, http://www.itvx.com/default.asp.* "iTVX is the leading provider of data, measuring the effectiveness of product placement in television and motion pictures. Through "Instant Access," clients can view TV product placements in real time with scientific valuations on their performance justifying your Return On Investment. The emerging interest of integrated programming in TV and film has fostered the need to help unify and quantify industry standards. iTVX was created by a team of experts encompassing the fields of product placement, media, psychology, statistical research and technology for the specific purpose of measuring and archiving accurate information. We can help solidify "embedded programming" deals between networks and marketers by objectively quantifying product placement performance and clarifying subjective interpretations." In addition to featuring their business, the site has useful links to industry news, data, and other resources.

NEWS SOURCES AND ITEMS

Commercial Alert asks FCC, FTC to require disclosure of product placement on TV (2003, September 30). Press release. Portland, OR: Commercial Alert. Available online at: *http://www.commercialalert.org/index.php/category_id/1/subcategory_ id/79/article_id/193. Short Summary*: Commercial Alert is requesting the Federal

Communications Commission and the Federal Trade Commission to require prominent disclosure of embedded advertising on television, including product placement, product integration, plot placement, title placement, paid spokespersons and virtual advertising. Increasingly, programs with these embedded ads resemble infomercials. Commercial Alert's petition to the FCC contains a request for a rule-making to require conspicuous and concurrent disclosure of embedded ads on TV, a complaint against TV networks for failure to comply with federal sponsorship identification requirements, and a request for investigation of current product placement practices on TV. Commercial Alert also asked the FTC to investigate TV product placement practices, and to issue new guidelines for disclosure of TV product placement. "Embedded advertising is the new reality of television, and it is time for the Commission to address it. TV networks and stations regularly send programs into American living rooms that are packed with product placements and other veiled commercial pitches. But they pretend that these are just ordinary programming rather than paid ads. This is an affront to basic honesty," wrote Commercial Alert in its petition to the FCC. "To prevent stealth advertising, and ensure that viewers are fully aware of the efforts of advertisers to embed ads in programming, the Commission should require TV networks and stations to prominently disclose to viewers that their product placements are ads. In addition, product placements should be identified when they occur." The FCC and FTC documents are available at: *http://www.commercialalert.org/index.php/category_id/1/subcategory_id/79/article_id/191.*

Culture, communication and control: Product placement and politics of advertising (1999). Critical resources website at: *http://www.bilderberg.org/product.htm*

Emery, Gene (2002, January 30). What's in a name: Product placement in games. *USA Today.* Available online at: *http://www.usatoday.com/tech/techreviews/games/2002/1/30/spotlight.htm.*

Fadner, Ross (2003, October 7). Agencies: Attack on product placement is misplaced, likely ineffective. *Media Post's Media Daily News.* Available online at: *http://www.mediapost.com/dtls_dsp_news.cfm?newsId=221486. Short Summary:* "Many in the ad business see it as a solution to ad-zapping technologies, but the so-called practice of product integration into TV programming came under official government scrutiny last week. In a complaint filed with the Federal Trade Commission, Commercial Alert, a public advocacy group backed by Ralph Nader, requested the federal government investigate the wave of product placements and other undisclosed product pitches that have begun infiltrating TV shows. The complaint singles out ABC, CBS, NBC, Fox, UPN, the WB and Walt Disney Co. for failure to comply with sponsorship identification requirements. Gary Ruskin, author of the complaint and executive director of Commercial Alert, asserted product placement and plugs are a deliberate ploy on the part of advertisers to mislead consumers into thinking such products are part of regularly scheduled programming. But agency executives contacted by MediaDailyNews counter the accusations are driven by wrong-headed logic and challenged Commercial Alert's fundamental assertion that advertising and commercialism are not in the public interest. More importantly, federal scrutiny notwithstanding, media buyers said the effort likely will fall on deaf ears."

Gaffney, John (2003, June 10). Exclusive *MDN* survey: Planners, TV viewers warm to product placements. *Media Post's Media Daily News.* Available online at: *http:// www.mediapost.com/dtls_dsp_news.cfm?newsID=208686. Short Summary*: Two recent studies report product placement ads are increasing and almost half (48%) of TV viewers are taking notice. Nearly 25% of viewers said that product placements influenced their buying decisions. Four out of five media planners surveyed also see product placements as an effective ad-buy. "Obviously, product placements are catching on because they are a more creative, less obtrusive way of getting a product in front of viewers," said Evan Fleischer, co-founder of The Michael Alan Group, a non-traditional marketing agency. "As an added bonus, product placement seems to rub viewers in the right way. I would expect that product placement would only increase in popularity as products like TiVo continue to threaten the reach and impact of traditional television commercials."

Kinney, Lance, and Sapolsky, Barry (nd, 1999). Product placement. Available online at: *http://comm2.fsu.edu/faculty/comm/Sapolsky/research/ProductPlacement.doc*

Mohabir, Nalini (1999, October 18; updated 2002, December 8). Product placement agencies. Available online at: *http://bodarky.www1.50megs.com/termpaper.html.*

Neer, Katherine (2003). How product placement works. Howstuffworks, Inc. Available online at: *http://howstuffworks.lycoszone.com/product-placement.htm.*

Park, Michael Y. (2002, August 09). Product placement hits the small screen. *Fox News Channel.* Available online at: *http://www.foxnews.com/story/0,2933,59743, 00.html.*

Product placement (regularly updated). Informative site with many links available at: *http://www.med.sc.edu:1081/prodplacement.htm.*

Product Placement News (current). Available online at *http://www.productplacement. biz/index.html.* They also offer a free email newsletter service with the latest industry updates.

Quit Victoria (1995). Smoking in Australia: Section 15.7 product placement. Available online at: *http://www.quit.org.au/quit/FandI/fandi/c15s7.htm.*

Reebok v. Tristar (1996, December). *Court TV* Online Legal Documents. Available online at: *http://www.courttv.com/archive/legaldocs/business/reebok.html.* In this complaint, "Reebok International claims Tristar Pictures broke a product placement deal to promote the athletic shoe manufacturer's products in the film, *Jerry Maguire.* An uplifting Reebok commercial was supposed to be part of the film's ending, the suit maintains. The filmmakers included a disparaging reference to Reebok."

Rössler, Patrick, and Bacher, Julia (2002). Transcultural effects of product placement in movies: A comparison of placement impact in Germany and the USA. *Zeitschrift für Medienpsychologie, 14*(N.F.2),3, 98-108. Available online at: *www.hogrefe. de/zmp/2002/zmp1403098.pdf.*

Smoke Free Movies (2003), available online at *http://www.smokefreemovies.ucsf.edu/ problem/index.html.* "Smoke Free Movies aims to sharply reduce the U.S. film industry's usefulness to Big Tobacco's domestic and global marketing–a leading cause of disability and premature death."

York, Anthony (2001, April 26). The product placement monster that E.T. spawned *Salon.com*. Available online at: *http://dir.salon.com/tech/feature/2001/04/26/ product_placement/index.html*.

Zazza, Frank (nd, 2003). From *E.T.* to itVX: The evolution of product placement. Available online at: *http://www.itvx.com/SpecialReport.asp*.

STUDENT PROJECTS, THESES AND DISSERTATIONS

Balfanz, Dirk; Finke, Matthias: Jung, Christoph; and Wichert, Reiner (2001). An interactive video system supporting e-commerce product placement. Student project, Zentrum für Graphische Datenverarbeitung (ZGDV) in Darmstadt, Germany. Available online at: *http://www.zgdv.de/zgdv/departments/z3/Z3Veroeffentlichungen/ An_interactive_Video_System/* and *http://www.igd.fhg.de/~rwichert/publications/ balfanz2001Interactive.pdf*. *Short Summary*: "Based on the technological progress within the Internet, content like digital video has become more and more popular for any kind of user. Because of these new technologies a merging process of different media types has been started which leads to new kinds of applications. Within this paper such a new application is presented based on an interactive video system for the area of E-commerce. In order to be competitive as an e-shop provider on the market it is highly important to supply the customers with an recognizable added value concerning the presentation of the product line. The embedding of such a system for using an interactive video in the context of E-commerce is the main focus of this work."

Kalinichenko, I. A. (1998). Brand props in prime-time television programs: A content analysis. Master's thesis, University of Georgia at Athens.

Ljungberg, Emma, and Rodrigo, Isabel (2002, January 17). Product placement–A way to communicate brand identity? Student thesis, Luleå Tekniska Universitet, Sweden. Available online at: *http://www.ep.liu.se/exjobb/eki/2002/iep/013/*. *Short Summary*: "The consumers of today have the possibility to choose from a wide range of products and services. Consequently, the ability to differentiate the products is essential for the brand owners. If a brand owner does not manage to differentiate its product, it can be difficult to make the consumers realise the benefits of the product and convince them to buy it. One way to differentiate the product is to create a distinguished brand identity. However, it is not enough to create a strong brand identity, the brand owner must also be capable of communicating the brand identity successfully. There are several ways to communicate a message and one is to use product placement. Purpose: The purpose of the thesis is to create an understanding for product placement's ability to communicate a brand identity, seen from the brand owners' point of view. Delimitation: We have chosen to limit our study to only treat product placement in Swedish film. Proceed of the study: We have conducted a qualitative study where the empirical material consists of four personal interviews. Three of the interviewees represented brand owners that have used product placement and one was a product placement agent. The theoretical frame of reference consists of three main theories; marketing communication theory, theories on brand identity and theories on consumer behaviour, where communication theories will be given strongest emphasis. Results: We observed that product placement has possibilities to communicate brand identity, under certain circumstances. The product placement must either be supported by a cross promotion-campaign or expose a product that has distinguished physical characteristics as part of the brand identity."

Spets, Erik, and Berglund, Niklas (2003, June 17). Product placement as communication tool: Role of the public relations firms–A case study of Hedberg & Co. Student thesis, Luleå Tekniska Universitet, Sweden. Available online at: *http://epubl.luth. se/1404-5508/2003/137/. Short Summary*: "The world of advertising is becoming more and more competitive, and to get messages through to the intended target audience it is important to try different means of communication. The purpose of this thesis is to gain a better understanding of an alternative mean of communicating messages, namely product placement, and especially public relations firms' role in this process. The thesis describes issues influencing public relations firms' recommendation on product placement to clients and also the selection of media to place products in. A case study was conducted at Hedberg & Co., using a qualitative research method. The study shows that product placement is inexpensive compared to traditional means of advertising. Consumers also view product placement with acceptance, mostly because the benefit of product placement is that products or brands is shown in the right context."

Steortz, Eva (1987). The cost efficiency and communication effects associated with brand name exposure within motion pictures. Master's thesis, School of Journalism, West Virginia University.

Turcotte, Samuel (1995). Gimme a Bud! The feature film product placement industry. Master's thesis, University of Texas at Austin. Available online at: *http://advertising. utexas.edu/research/papers/Turcotte/*. A key study of the field.

Vista Group (nd, 2002). Writing a thesis on product placement? Available online at: *http://www.vistagroupusa.com/thesishtm.htm*. A guide to useful links.

Weaver, Dana T. (nd, 2000). Television programs and advertising: Measuring the effectiveness of product placement within *Seinfeld*. Student project, Pennsylvania State University. Available online at: *http://www.psu.edu/dept/medialab/research/ prodplace.html*. See also Weaver, D. T., and Oliver, M. B. (2000, June). Television programs and advertising: Measuring the effectiveness of product placement within *Seinfeld*. Paper presented to the Mass Communication Division at the 50th annual conference of the International Communication Association (ICA), Acapulco, Mexico.

BOOKS

NOTE: Many of the best books on the subject are in German, reflecting the great European interest in the topic.

Asche, Florian (1996). *Das Product Placement im Kinospielfilm*. Frankfurt, a. M.: Peter Lang Publishing, ISBN/ASIN: 3631302541.

Bente, Klaus (1990). *Product Placement: Entscheidungsrelevante Aspekte in der Werbepolitik*. Wiesbaden: Deutscher Universitèats-Verlag, ISBN/ASIN: 382440043X.

Dörfler, Gabriele (1993). Product Placement im Fernsehen–Unlautere Werbung oder denkbare Finanzierungsquelle im dualen Rundfunksystem?: Eine Beurteilung aus dem Blickwinkel des Wettbewerbsrechts unter Berücksichtigung der Mediengesetze. Frankfurt, a. M.: Peter Lang Publishing, ISBN/ASIN: 3631455720.

EPM Entertainment Marketing Sourcebook, 2004 edition (2003). New York: EPM Communications, Inc. Issued annually and also available on CD ROM. The only directory that delivers instant access to more than 5,000 sponsors, entertainment and media companies, retail chains and service providers committed to entertainment marketing, including product placement firms. Listings are indexed by company, by individual and by geographic location.

Laermer, Richard, and Prichinello, Michael (2003). *Full Frontal PR: Getting People Talking About You, Your Business, or Your Product.* Princeton, NJ: Bloomberg Press, 256 pages, ISBN: 1576600998. The publisher states: "With entertaining case studies, *Full Frontal PR* breaks down the publicity process and demonstrates how you can use the press productively. You'll learn how to identify your unique news-making hook, build relationships with the mainstream and industry press, and gain strategic placements that will build your business and get people talking. These tactics are based on proven methods that are easy to implement and, most importantly, cost-effective."

Müller, Olaf (1997). *Product-Placement im öffentlich-rechtlichen Fernsehen: In der Grauzone zwischen unlauterem Wettbewerb und wichtiger Finanzierungsquelle.* Frankfurt, a. M.: Peter Lang Publishing, ISBN/ASIN: 3631320868.

Scherer, Beate (1990). *"Product Placement" im Fernsehprogramm: Die werbewirksame Einblendung von Markenartikeln als wettbewerbswidriges Handeln der Rundfunkanstalten.* Baden-Baden: Nomos Verlagsgesellschaft, ISBN/ASIN: 378901883X.

Solomon, Michael R. (2003). *Conquering Consumerspace: Marketing Strategies for a Branded World.* New York: AMACOM, 304 pages, ISBN: 0814407412. The publisher states: "Once upon a time, marketers barraged customers with hard-sell tactics. Today, consumers use products to define themselves and others. People are swayed not by corporate-generated hype, but by consumer-generated buzz. That means companies must shift their focus away from marketing to people and toward marketing with them. In 'consumerspace,' firms partner with customers to develop brand personalities and create interactive fantasies. The winners understand that we buy products not just because of what they do, but because of what they mean. Market share is out; share of mind is in. *Conquering Consumerspace* reveals the accelerating blurring of traditional boundaries between branded commodities and everyday life. Solomon's timely book presents a new way of looking at customers: recognizing them as partners in an ongoing marketing transaction rather than as passive pawns at the receiving end of a sales pitch. *Conquering Consumerspace* also defines the place of customer feedback in product conception, design, and production, and why customizability is no longer a luxury option but a requirement. From online 'buzz communities' to theme stores and product placement to guerrilla marketing, what we consume is inextricably woven into our daily life experience, creating both challenges and opportunities for companies to accelerate and deepen their customers' relationships with their products, services, and brands."

Weng, Hsiao-Ling (1999). *Rechtsprobleme der Indirekten Werbung durch Sponsoring und Product Placement im Kinospielfilm: Eine Untersuchung zur Bedeutung der Kunstfreiheitsgarantie fuer die Anwendung des 1 UWG.* Frankfurt, a. M.: Peter Lang Publishing, ISBN/ASIN: 3631348282.

Index

T - #0072 - 230425 - C6 - 212/152/15 - PB - 9780789025357 - Gloss Lamination